Critical Criminological Perspectives

The Palgrave Critical Criminological Perspectives book series aims to showcase the importance of critical criminological thinking when examining problems of crime, social harm and criminal and social justice. Critical perspectives have been instrumental in creating new research agendas and areas of criminological interest. By challenging state defined concepts of crime and rejecting positive analyses of criminality, critical criminological approaches continually push the boundaries and scope of criminology, creating new areas of focus and developing new ways of thinking about, and responding to, issues of social concern at local, national and global levels. Recent years have witnessed a flourishing of critical criminological narratives and this series seeks to capture the original and innovative ways that these discourses are engaging with contemporary issues of crime and justice.

More information about this series at
http://www.palgrave.com/gp/series/14932

Úna Barr

Desisting Sisters

Gender, Power and Desistance in the Criminal (In)Justice System

palgrave
macmillan

Úna Barr
School of Humanities and Social Science
Liverpool John Moores University
Liverpool, UK

Critical Criminological Perspectives
ISBN 978-3-030-14275-9 ISBN 978-3-030-14276-6 (eBook)
https://doi.org/10.1007/978-3-030-14276-6

Library of Congress Control Number: 2019934467

Cover illustration: Alamy FG9H5G

This Palgrave Macmillan imprint is published by the registered company Springer Nature Switzerland AG.
The registered company address is: Gewerbestrasse 11, 6330 Cham, Switzerland

*This thesis is dedicated to the memory of two women who left us too soon—
the woman known as 'Sue' in this book, and my beautiful cousin and friend
Fiona Kelly, who is so missed.*

Acknowledgements

There are many people and organisations to thank for the opportunity to write the original thesis, allowing me to think that I could have the audacity to publish it as a book, and supporting me to get there in the end. Firstly, of course, huge thanks go to Seán and Paula Barr. Thank you for always encouraging me to do what I want to do and to try to make a difference while doing it. Special thanks to my da for letting me barrow 'medicalising the marginalised'. To my brother, Dermot. Thanks for always being available to chat through any issues I had and offering great insights. To Éimear, my real-life sister and hero, Seánna, Eilís and Rossa O'Cóinn. To Janet Raven-Martin and Ian Martin and, of course, and always, to Tom. You are the best. Thank you also to a person who we have yet to meet, but who has encouraged me to get the book finished before their arrival. We love you so much already.

To everyone who supported me in my PhD at the University of Central Lancashire (UCLan) and onwards, particularly my good friend Laura Kelly and my supervision team: Maria Sapouna, Megan Todd and, in particular, Martin O'Brien. To Helen Codd and Fergus McNeill for examining my thesis and offering insightful guidance.

Colleagues at Liverpool John Moores University (LJMU) have been overwhelmingly kind and supportive, in particular the 'Shut Up and Write' crew and Lindsey Metcalf for all her organisational skills and encouragement, former LJMU colleague Adam Westall, and my ever-supportive boss, Janet Jamieson. Particular and special thanks go to Joe Sim, without whom this book would never have been either submitted to publishers or finished. Thank you for all your guidance and encouragement on my draft chapters. It is such a privileged position to work with people you see as your academic heroes, and I am so lucky to work with so many of mine. Kym Atkinson, Katie Tucker, Helen Monk and the Centre for Crime Criminalisation and Social Exclusion deserve special thanks. Thanks to all the students in LJMU who continue to teach me. In particular, conversations with Natalie Christian have been invaluable. Thanks to John Moore for asking a question which I thought about for a year after in Lesbos, and to all at the European Group for the Study of Deviance and Social Control.

To the services known in this book as the Northshire Women Centres and the Housing for Northshire project. Special thanks to the women referred to as Rebecca, Christine, Mary and Jenny.

Thank you to everyone at Palgrave Macmillan, especially Liam Inscoe-Jones and Josie Taylor. Thanks to Critical Criminological Perspectives and Deborah Drake in particular for the encouragement.

Most of all, I'd like to thank all the women who gave up their time to speak to me about their lives, something which was not always easy. I can only hope I have done justice to your stories. The resilience you have shown in the face of injustice will be a constant source of inspiration.

Contents

1

Defining Desistance

Desisting Sisters is the culmination of my doctoral research. The studentship through which the fees for my thesis were funded originally bore the title: *Young Offenders on the Road to Desistance*. It was not, initially, intended as an exploration of the gendered desistance journey. However, upon exploring the desistance literature, it quickly became apparent that women's experiences were largely side-lined, marginalised and incorporated within the male-focused explorations of desistance. For example, one of the first texts I considered was Farrall and Calverley's 2006 *Understanding Desistance from Crime: Theoretical directions in resettlement and rehabilitation*. This book dedicates 3 pages of 209 to women. Two of these are dedicated to the limitations of the study. A book published in 2013 by Sam King, *Desistance Transitions and the Impact of Probation*, contains only a single short paragraph about women. As of late, there have been moves to consider female desistance experiences (Rodermond et al. 2016; Gomm 2016; Hart 2017). Yet women's voices within desistance literature are still marginalised, particularly in England. Therefore, this book examines the desistance experiences of a small group of Northshire-based women. Through a re-analysis of traditional desistance perspectives, the book contends that a 'critical desistance' (Hart 2017)

Ú. Barr, *Desisting Sisters*, Critical Criminological Perspectives,
https://doi.org/10.1007/978-3-030-14276-6_1

must ground desistance research and practice within the structural conditions in which it does or does not occur. It must have at its base an abolitionist outlook and an awareness of the intersectionality of both criminalisation and desistance, as well as the harmful impact of the Criminal Justice System (CJS). This chapter provides an introduction to the book by setting out definitional issues and plotting the emergence of desistance as a separate theoretical concern within criminology. An explanation will be offered for the apparent gender blindness (Gelsthorpe and Morris 1988) of desistance research. It will be argued that this blindness is a consequence of a wider insidious gender blindness of patriarchal criminological research. An outline of the book's chapters, including some limitations of this research, follows.

Defining Desistance

Crime and deviance involve normative behaviours, and most criminalised individuals do eventually stop offending, arguably undergoing desistance (Barry 2006). Establishing a definition of desistance is necessary before any consideration of how desistance 'works' can be established. However, the exact meaning of desistance, has been much contested. Weaver and McNeill (2010) note that 'most criminologists have associated desistance with both ceasing and refraining from offending' (p. 37).

It is not assumed that desistance is a simple process which follows a straight and definite line. A consistent, but not unchallenged (e.g., see Sampson and Laub 1993 or Giordano et al. 2002), finding in the desistance literature is that there is no specific 'turning point' in time where former law breakers become 'desisters' (Maruna 2001; Bottoms and Shapland 2011). On the contrary, desistance has been likened to a zigzag path (Glaser 1964). Healy (2012) describes desistance as the area 'betwixt and between' crime. Leibrich (1993) meanwhile refers to the 'curved' pathway of desistance. Matza's (1964) theory of 'drift' suggests that people tend to move between conventional and delinquent behaviour throughout the life course and especially in their younger years. Most desistance authors now recognise desistance as a process or a path rather than a specific event. These definitions suggest that a person may go through many periods of desistance throughout the life course, making it difficult to categorise individuals in terms of 'desisters' and 'persisters'.

Maruna and Farrall (2004) have differentiated between 'primary' and 'secondary' desistance. 'Primary' desistance can be taken to mean any lull or crime-free period in the course of a criminal career. The Stockholm Life Course Project findings (Carlsson 2012) have suggested that there are two forms of 'intermittency' in criminal careers, or two forms of primary desistance. The first is when an offender experiences breaks or pauses in offending for various reasons but which are not related to any long-term commitment to change, whilst the second can be understood as attempts to desist where attempts to change are present but for various reasons are not realised (Carlsson 2012). These may be people who stop deviant or addictive behaviour but for various reasons return to it at a later date. As the author notes, 'Intermittent offending is the criminal career, because the great majority of offenders, if not all, tend to follow a zigzag path between onset and desistance' (2012: 931). 'Secondary' desistance, on the other hand, can be described as 'measureable changes at the level of personal identity or the "me" of the individual' (Maruna et al. 2009: 34). Essentially, secondary desistance involves the casting off of the former 'offender' identity and a move towards generative concerns consistent with a new identity. It can also be known as 'true' or 'complete' desistance. It is worth noting that both these forms of desistance can apply to criminalised people previously considered as persistent or serious offenders at different points in the life cycle.

More recently, the dual nature of desistance has been called into question. Healy and O'Donnell, in their 2006 study of Irish male probationers found little evidence of agency or generative concerns consistent with notions of secondary desistance in the narratives they collected. Vaughan (2007) has introduced a tertiary and final stage of desistance which suggests a commitment to a new identity so powerful that it is incompatible with any former criminal identity. Rumgay (2004) has meanwhile asserted that desistance is better described as a process of maintenance which tends not to emanate from a single event or decision 'but as a process in which skills and advantages accumulate over time, mutually reinforcing each other and progressively the offender's capacity to avoid recidivism' (p. 413). This process of maintenance is pertinent for the current research. As the following chapters will show, desistance for the research participants involved constant maintenance. Kelly-Marie's narrative, for example, highlighted this process of accumulation of skills and advantages over time. Desistance can also mean the collection of bricolage as a method of survival. As will be seen in the following chapters, desistance for the women studied herein often meant survival and resistance to the structural conditions of their criminalisation. In contrast, traditional desistance theories have linked the cessation of crime with factors such as maturity, adult social bonds, agency, identity and hope (Bottoms et al. 2004). The structural conditions of both criminalisation and desistance are notable for their absence amongst traditional (male-focused) desistance theories. This book aims to address this fissure and re-examine these traditional perspectives through the lens of criminalised women's experiences.

The study of desistance has evolved from its beginnings as an afterthought of developmental, life-course and criminal career research into a substantial body of literature in its own right. Life-course studies can be traced back to 1937 in the form of Sheldon and Eleanor Glueck's pioneering, in-depth work which was eventually published as *Unravelling Juvenile Delinquency* (1950), which involved the study of 500 juvenile delinquents in an effort to untangle the causes of delinquent behaviour. The Gluecks linked desistance with the ageing process. During this time however, criminology tended to be concerned with the onset rather than the diminishment of criminal behaviour. For example, Gove (1985: 118), in his study of six of the most influential theories of deviance: labelling theory, conflict theory, differential association theory, control theory, anomie theory and functional theory, concluded that 'all of these theoretical perspectives either explicitly or implicitly suggest that deviant behaviour is an amplifying process that leads to further and more serious deviance' (p. 118).

A more formal interest in desistance appeared in the 1970s and 80s, influenced by the influx of longitudinal studies which appeared in the 1960s and the emergence in these groups of cohorts of those whose offending patterns began to slow down (see, e.g., Meisenhelder 1977). Yet at the same time the 'Nothing Works' discourse was promoting a mood of despondency over probation and offending patterns in general.

The 1980s saw a more positive mood with the move to the 'What Works' period of community interventions. However, this period reflected few advancements in opening the 'black box' of 'why' and 'how' (re)integration (following prison) and (re)settlement worked (Maruna and Farrall 2004). The 1990s saw the re-emergence of sociological and developmental interests in both the causes and continuation (or otherwise) of offending behaviour including explanations for the age-crime curve (Moffitt 1993; Sampson and Laub 1993). Sampson and Laub have been particularly influential in their linking of desistance with turning points such as employment and marriage. Developmental theorists such as Terrie Moffitt (1993) suggested that a dual taxonomy can explain the sharp escalation of the age-crime curve during adolescence. Moffitt proposed that there are two types of offenders: life-course persistent offenders who begin their antisocial behaviour at a young age and continue to offend over their lives and adolescence-limited offenders (the vast majority of offenders) who are involved in criminal behaviour only during their adolescent years. This, developmental theorists have argued, can explain the shape of the age-crime curve which tends to peak significantly during adolescence. However, as Bottoms and Shapland (2011) note, even for the recidivist, offending behaviours tend to decline sharply between the ages of 20 and 30.

Up until the end of the twentieth century, criminal career studies had tended to focus on persistence. At the time, Neal Shover remarked, '[F]or the most part, the desistance literature has been approached inferentially' (1996: 124). More recently, desistance theories have begun to emerge as a topic in their own right rather than an adjunct to life-course studies. This has been coupled with a move towards a focus on the subjective experiences of the offender themselves, with an emphasis on the individual as an actor and narrative, life-course interviews as the research tool through which desistance is studied (Leibrich 1993; Maruna 2001; Farrall and Bowling 1999). From here, we have seen a development of cessation of offending studies to include studies on desistance and diversity, for example in terms of gender or ethnicity (Rumgay 2004; Calverley 2013; Rodermond et al. 2016) and how these identities can affect the desistance process. Chapter 2 concentrates on these various explanations for the process of desistance. First however, we must consider *why* desistance theories and practice have neglected the 'woman question'.

Desistance and the (Absence of) the 'Woman Question'

Feminist criminologists (Smart 1977; Heidensohn 1985; Chadwick and Little 1987; Gelsthorpe and Morris 1988; Stanko 1998; Heidensohn 2004 amongst many others) would argue that the absence of the woman question in this relatively new criminological theory is simply a continuation of women's absence in criminological research more generally. Scraton (1990, 18) noted that young women tend to have 'occasional walk on parts' in these kinds of studies and this skimming over of gendered realities should be addressed. Certainly women occupy a marginal position within the CJS in the UK. In 2015, women represented 5% of the total prison population and 17% of the 125,934 offenders under supervision in the community as a result of community and suspended sentence orders (Ministry of Justice 2016). By locating women's desistance as parallel to men's, criminology replicates the substantive inequalities which often result in women entering the CJS in the first place, in addition to the substantive inequalities which they then face in a patriarchal system. The structural conditions of female criminalisation; patriarchy and neoliberalism, as well as racism and heteronormativity, are conditions which contextualise women's criminalisation and desistance. Whilst desistance theory has largely been a progressive light within criminology by turning the central criminological question (why do some people 'commit' 'crime'?) on its' head, it has mostly (with a few exceptions) neglected its sisters. Crucially, even those studies which consider female desistance fail to contest the inequalities evident in the criminalisation and therefore desistance experiences of these women. *Desisting Sisters* argues that the male desistance paradigm is unfit for women. The experience of desistance can mean challenging gender norms, just as women's deviance often does. Desistance contests neoliberal ideals. Desistance theories which do not account for difference nor for structural inequalities reinforce the inequalities and repressions which difference, including gendered difference, creates.

Aims of *Desisting Sisters*

As has been seen, desistance theory has attempted to explain the process by which individuals come to live life free from criminality and may mean any crime-free gap in a criminal career. Yet as has also been noted, desistance theories are broadly constructed from the hegemonic white, heterosexual, male experience; female voices tend to get side-lined or not discussed at all (Rumgay 2004). Indeed this suppression of female voice is nothing new in criminological research. Whilst some studies have included the view of desistance from the female point of view (Jamieson et al. 1999; Giordano et al. 2002; Rumgay 2004; Barry 2006) the fact that most of the studies are over a decade old is concerning. Recent moves to address this gap have been largely considered outside England (Rodermond et al. 2016). Other than Rumgay's (2004) study, Hart's (2017) work regarding women leaving prison, and Österman (2018) comparative study, modern research on female desistance has taken place outside the England and Wales CJS—for example, both Barry's (2006) and Jamieson et al.'s (1999) studies were based in Scotland. The current changes in probation provision, including the recent part-privatisation of probation under the Transforming Rehabilitation agenda (see Chap. 6), suggest that now is a critical time for desistance research.

Desisting Sisters contests the male-dominated narrative by placing females in conflict with the law as protagonists in the desistance paradigm. The choice to revisit traditional desistance perspectives, problematic though they often are, through the eyes of criminalised women, is intentional. In her revisit of *Women, Crime and Criminology* (1977), Carol Smart refers to Paul Rock's (1977) critique of the book's analysis of what he sees as redundant criminological theory through a feminist perspective, 'poring over that which does not deserve detailed scholarly attention' (p. 394, quoted in Smart 2016: 62). Smart (2016) contends that this was a necessary element in developing a feminist criminology. Forty years on, this continues to be the case for feminist theorists; there is a need to revisit problematic, masculinist theories and concepts through intersectional feminist lenses. Yet this is useful for two reasons. First, these problematic arguments (around maturation, social bonds and cognitive changes, for example) continue to be influential in both (desistance) theory and practice. The problems with these theoretical perspectives must therefore be located and critiqued. Yet it is not enough to simply critique problematic theory by viewing it through female eyes. Secondly, therefore, revisiting these theories through the eyes of criminalised women helps shed light on what is missing in desistance theory, namely, a structural paradigm which supports a 'woman-wise penology' (Carlen 1990: 109). The imposition of patriarchal and neoliberal conceptions of desistance in the lives of criminalised women will become clear in the following chapters. Often their narratives act as rejection of these conceptions. This book aims to enable a discussion around alternative desistance theory and praxis.

Desistance Contexts

> Why do I wake up every morning to it all? You can't shake it off can you? (Anna, age 36)

The following sections set out the context of *Desisting Sisters*. The place names in *Desisting Sisters* have been (relatively unimaginatively) anonymised. Firstly, the overall setting of Northshire will be examined through brief overviews of the social and economic environment of the areas where the observation research and interviews took place, during the time of the research. A brief synopsis of the contexts of Southton, Easton, Weston,[1] Central Town and Northton between February 2014 and August 2015 will be provided. These are the Northshire areas where the women were living, working, raising children, attending probation appointments and generally living their lives. The link between place, community, citizenship and desistance has been well explored in the literature (Farrall et al. 2011; Calverley 2013) and it is important to locate the sites of the women's daily joys and struggles. Subsequently, the two community justice projects, *Northshire Women's Centres (WCs)* and the *Housing for Northshire (HfN) Project*, which formed the backdrop for this research will be discussed. In order to consider the desistance narratives of these particular women, within this particular area, I conducted a year's observation at the Northshire WCs and carried out life-course interviews with women affected by the CJS who were undertaking specified activity requirements in the WCs, as well as women who were living in the HfN Project following a prison sentence (see the Appendix). An overview is provided here, whilst Chap. 6 provides analysis of these projects and their link with desistance-promotion (see also Barr 2018).

Northshire

In 2015, the usual resident figure for broader Northshire was just under 1.5 million, an increase of 0.2% on 2014 (Northshire.gov.uk).[2] Economically, the rate of growth of the Northshire economy lagged behind the national rate of change. Median income in 2014/15 varied in local authority areas between £17,500 (the lowest median income in the UK) to £22,200 (below the UK average at the time of £22,400). As a whole, Northshire is an economically deprived area. Average (median) gross weekly earnings were noticeably below the average in Britain. Life expectancy for both men and women were lower than the England average (Public Health England 2014). In some of the Northshire local authorities, male and female life expectancy at birth rates were amongst the worst in England and Wales. In 2015, one in five children in Northshire were living in poverty. In 2016, 7 of the 14 local authority areas within Northshire ranked in the top 50 most deprived areas in England. Yet Northshire is also an area of gross economic inequality. Whilst the county is home to a number of universities, the overall educational outturn suggested that Northshire needs to increase the proportion of its residents qualified to National Vocational Qualification (NVQ) level 4 in order to be on a par with the national average. There were pockets of severe deprivation including a high proportion of 'hidden' and long-term unemployed with low levels of basic skills (Northshire.gov.uk). Northshire's population is largely white (90%); the black and minority ethnic group make up 10% of the population, the majority of which were Asian/Asian British (2011 Census).

Southton

Southton, where the Tulip Centre was based, experienced population growth of almost 7% between the 2001 and 2011 census, a percentage point under the national average. Its central population is approximately 35,000 with approximately 113,000 in the greater Southton area (Mid 2015 Estimate, ONS). Overall, deprivation was lower than the England average in Southton; about 14% of children lived in poverty, according to Public Health England (2014). In the case of the five Northshire areas studied for this project, Southton could be described as the least economically disadvantaged as measured by the 2015 English Indices of Multiple Deprivation (ONS 2015). At the time of research, there were lower levels of unemployment and working age benefit claimants than the rest of England. Nonetheless, gender inequality was evident, with life expectancy for women a year lower than the English average at 82 years, whilst for men the life expectancy was consistent with the English average at 79 years (Public Health England 2014). In the 2011 census, 97% of those living in Southton identified as white, with 2% identifying as Asian/ Asian British and 1% mixed/multiple ethnic groups.

Easton

Easton was home to the Rose Centre and also the home of the *Housing for Northshire Project*. The mid-year ONS population estimate for 2015 was approximately 87,000 usual residents. Easton was the 17th most deprived local authority area in England in 2015 according to the Office of National Statistics (2015). Easton had some of the lowest property prices in England (Northshire.gov.uk). A former mining town, Easton was hit badly by the pit closure of 1981. However, it has since been the site of multiple high-profile regeneration schemes which have resulted in high end manufacturing remaining strong in the town. Nonetheless, according to Public Health England (2014), the health of people in Easton was generally worse than the England average. Deprivation was higher than average and about 27% of children in Easton were living in poverty in 2011. Unemployment rates and claimant count of Jobseekers

Allowance were higher than average in England.[3] Life expectancy for both men and women were also lower than the England average at 76 and 81, respectively. Drug misuse, alcohol-related hospital stays and teenage pregnancy rates were amongst the highest levels in England, and levels of General Certificate of Secondary Education (GCSE) attainment and breastfeeding rates were lower than the English average according to the 2014 Public Health England report. In the 2011 census, 87% of Easton's population identified as white, with 11% identifying as Asian/Asian British and 1% as mixed/multiple ethnic groups.

Central Town

Central Town, where the Daisy Centre was based, was one of the only Northshire areas to see an increase in population between the 2001 and 2011 Census (along with Southton). In this period, there had been an increase of over 10,000 people and the 2011 population numbered approximately 147,000 in the Greater Central Town area. Central Town faced a number of social and economic challenges both historically and more recently. Much like Southton, Central Town was an area of contrasts with inequality evident, whilst the suburbs contain some of the wealthiest areas in Northshire. Deprivation nonetheless was higher than average and about 25% of children lived in poverty at the time of research. In the 2015 indices of multiple deprivation, Central Town was ranked as the 24th most deprived area in England and Wales. Total unemployment rates and the number of working age people were well above the national average. Like Easton, the health of people in Central Town was generally worse than the England average. Life expectancy for both men and women was lower than the England average at 77 and 81, respectively. Drug misuse and alcohol-related hospital stays were higher than the English average according to Public Health England (2014). There was also a high rate of suicide within the area. Compared with other areas in this project, Central Town had a relatively lower number of respondents to the 2011 Census identifying as white (69%); 28% of respondents identified as Asian/Asian British and 1% identified as multiple/mixed ethnic groups.

Northton

Northton, where the Daffodil Centre was based, was one of the smallest areas studied with a 2011 population of 35,000. Northton is a former centre of the cotton and textile machinery industries. Northton is part of a larger district, Hilldale, where there has been a deteriorating economic profile over the years. Hilldale had an approximate population of 80,000 in the 2015 mid-year population estimate. The total proportion of Jobseekers Allowance claimants at the time of research was above both the England and Northshire averages. There was distinction in Hilldale as a place to work and a place to live; average earnings were low in 2015 when measured by place of residence, but local employment strength meant that earnings were comparatively high when measured by place of work, indicating that there was a draw to Northton and surrounding areas by those living outside the area. Hilldale had a similar ethnic profile to Easton with 88% of Hilldale's population identifying as white, 11% as Asian/Asian British and 1% as mixed/multiple ethnic groups in the 2011 census.

Weston

In Weston, where the Iris Centre was based, the 2015 mid-year population estimate was approximately 140,000. The population was biased towards people of retirement age. Weston had the fourth largest population density outside Greater London in England and Wales. In 2015, the English indices of multiple deprivation named Weston as the most deprived local authority in the county, and the 4th most deprived in the country. Around one in three children lived in poverty in Weston at the time. The seasonal nature of tourism in Weston had meant that there were high unemployment rates in the winter months. Even at the height of the tourism season the unemployment rate in Weston was usually well above the county and national averages. Income level was the lowest in Northshire in 2014. The percentage of pupils achieving five or more A*–C grades at GCSE or equivalent including English and Maths in 2012/13 was 46% in Weston, below the Northshire average of 60%. The health of people in Weston was generally worse than the England average, with life expectancy for men and women at 74 and 80 respectively. The rate of alcohol-related hospital stays was much higher than the England average as was the rate of self-harm hospital stays, smoking-related deaths, excess weight and smoking rates according to Public Health England (2014). In 2011, 97% of Weston's population identified as white, 2% as Asian/Asian British and 1% as mixed/multiple ethnic groups.

Overall, Northshire was, and continues to be, a place of deprivation relative to the rest of England and Wales. Within Northshire however there were pockets of affluence and extreme deprivation, both within the county generally and within the smaller areas researched. Inequality has been linked with both high rates of crime and punitive justice policies (Pickett and Wilkinson 2009; Dorling 2015). It is argued that these high rates of inequality created by neoliberal economic policy do not provide a fertile desistance backdrop. To explore the contexts of the Northshire women's desistance experiences, it is necessary to consider the formal sites of desistance-promotion, which the next section does by providing a descriptive account of the provision within the WCs and HfN Projects.

Formal Desistance Settings

The Women's Centres

During the time of my observations at the Women's Centres (WCs) from 2014 to 2015, the WCs provided a 'one-stop shop' for women entering the CJS as part of the Northshire Women's Specified Activity requirement (NWSAR). They provided these services by way of a contract won through Northshire Community Rehabilitation Company (CRC). Mary, a staff member at the Women's Centre, provided a useful overview of the services available for these women:

> We don't say we're specialists in everything, we're not specialists in domestic abuse, drug services etc. But we do provide counselling and one to one support and assist with them [criminalised women] accessing that. So under that umbrella where you say 'one stop shop' kind of thing, you might get a woman who has an alcohol problem but doesn't quite feel ready… it's like,

> what do you address first? And it might be that you address some of the issues, and then if they're ready to go into alcohol treatment and then for that afterwards. (Mary, Criminal Justice Project Manager, Women's Centres)

Women were referred from the police, courts, probation and other parts of the CJS. All the women interviewed in this research were referred by the courts as part of their sentences under the NWSAR. The women spent ten weeks attending weekly two-hour sessions at the various centres, with the first two weeks taken up by a one-on-one induction, followed by eight weeks of group work sessions and a final conclusion session on the last week. At the time of my observations, the topics offered in the group work sessions were substance misuse awareness, health and well-being, housing and money management, community and citizenship, employment training and education, thinking and behaviour, victim awareness, and family and relationships. As can be seen, these follow many of the similar themes found within the desistance literature. For example, the themes covered by McIvor et al. (2004) in their study of youth offending and desistance in Scotland were education, employment, use of leisure and lifestyle, drug and alcohol use, offending, relationships with family, friends and partners, neighbourhood, community and society, values and beliefs, victimisation, identity, and aspirations for the future. It must be noted however that, in 2015, the NWSAR was undergoing change, including condensing the eight sessions into six and giving more sway to using the sessions as introductions to the 'add on support' that women may need. In the introductory one-on-one sessions, women were given information about the 'one stop shop' project and asked to sign a contract relating to their behaviour at group sessions including discussing their offences, taking part in sessions and respecting others. In reality, the women were not forced to reveal their offences at any time during the groups I attended. Groups were as big as ten people (including staff) or as small as a one-on-one session.

The Housing for Northshire Project

Rebecca Brown's Housing for Northshire Project was opened in September 2014. Rebecca described the project as a 'supportive, abstinence-based housing project', divided into services for women and services for men. Rebecca started the project as a service for women but, with help from her partner Paul, developed a parallel service for men:

> So we offer a shared accommodation within community housing so that could be 2, 3, 4-bedroomed units. And for people of no fixed abode. So it is primarily people from prison ... We're coming from a community standpoint, and we're about community regeneration, rather than it being a project for people from prison, which is why the CJS is not mentioned in any of the project vitals. So whilst primarily it is women from the CJS, and men from the CJS, it's not something that is effectively designed towards that. (Rebecca, Project Manager, Housing for Northshire)

Rebecca described the project as having a 'peer-led, co-operative structure'. Women and men from the CJS were referred to the project from police, prison and various probation services, whilst non-criminal justice referrals were often self-referrals. Whilst the focus was on housing, Rebecca and Paul also referred women and men into counselling, domestic violence services, health services, employment and training and so on. Rebecca's office had an open door policy and she herself was available to be contacted at any time. The houses were not set up as permanent accommodation for the women and men but as a 'stop gap', with a view to enabling people to become 'responsible functioning members of society, with a view to getting back to work' (Rebecca). Interestingly, in the early days of the project, Rebecca was approached by Christine Smith, CEO of the WCs, who asked her to provide the project under the Women's Centre premises. Whilst initially positive about the idea, Rebecca decided she did not want to be employed by the Centres, preferring to offer support under her own service and focus on housing.

Participant Profiles

Neither offending, nor desistance, are carried out in a vacuum. To understand the desistance process it is important to understand the context-specific circumstances in which offending and change in offending take place. The research for *Desisting Sisters* brought me into contact with 16 criminalised women, who undertook at least one self-narrative life-course interview between summer 2014 and spring 2015. All the women had served or were serving a sentence for an offence. Although other women's narratives are included in the book, including staff members of both the WCs and the HfN Project, as well as additional criminalised women who attended WC group meetings, much of the analysis is based around these 16 women. The women's narratives include everyday stories of everyday lives and backgrounds as well as stories of horror and victimisation, but also of resilience and hope, often against all odds. The words used to describe the offences committed by the women are from their own narratives, which, although often replete with criminal justice discourse, tended to use the terms below to describe the women's contact with the CJS (Table 1.1).

As can be seen, the women were interviewed at a variety of ages. As will become clear from their narratives, the criminalisation of women is situated in contexts of abuse, relationship problems (including separation from children), material deprivation, poverty, mental health issues, and drug and alcohol dependency (Prison Reform Trust 2017). The women's offences differed in consistency, frequency and severity. Largely, the women's offences were relatively low level; only one of the most recent offences could be described as violent and most could be described as acquisitive crimes. Yet these findings are typical. In 2007 Baroness Corston argued that women are likely to be criminalised when facing certain conditions:

> [First] … domestic circumstances and problems such as domestic violence, child-care issues, being a single-parent; second, personal circumstances such as mental illness, low self-esteem, eating disorders, substance misuse; and third, socio-economic factors such as poverty, isolation and unemployment. When women are experiencing a combination of factors from each of these three types of vulnerabilities, it is likely to lead to a crisis point that ultimately results in prison. (The Corston Report 2007: 2)

The lives of criminalised in the CJS, whether serving community sentences or serving time in prison, have changed little since Baroness Corston's 2007 report. Whilst these 'vulnerabilities' are often the factors which lead to offending, they often still remain, or indeed are deepened

Table 1.1 Sixteen criminalised women interviewed for this research

Name	Age at first interview	Most recent offence[a]	Originally contacted through	Based (living, working. Attending WCs/ probation)
Sue	40	Drink driving	Women's Centres	Southton
Paula	36	Theft	Women's Centres	Easton
Katie	60	Benefit fraud	Women's Centres	Northton
Grace	31	Growing cannabis	Women's Centres	Northton
Heather	24	Benefit fraud	Women's Centres	Northton
Bridget	27	Drug dealing	Women's Centres	Northton
Ruth	31	Non-payment of housing benefit overpayment	Women's Centres	Southton
Karen	36	Burglary (joint enterprise)	Women's Centres	Southton
Anna	36	Burglary (joint enterprise)	Women's Centres	Central town
Marie	40	Handling stolen goods	Women's Centres	Easton
Holly	23	Shoplifting	Women's Centres	Easton
Julie	59	Tax fraud	Women's Centres	Easton
Shelly	53	Assault on a police officer	Housing for Northshire Project	Easton
Michaela	34	Shoplifting	Housing for Northshire Project	Easton
Kelly-Marie	48	Violating terms of probation after a shoplifting offence	Housing for Northshire Project	Easton
Rebecca	46	Credit card fraud	Housing for Northshire Project	Easton

[a]For which the women were most recently criminalised

(as a result of the harms of CJS contact) during desistance attempts. Yet Corston (2007: 15) argued that the way to address these issues was 'by helping women develop resilience, life skills and emotional literacy'. As will become clear, the Corston Report did not go far enough. Although women's narratives contained many examples of resilience, and indeed were great sources of resilience themselves, the patriarchal capitalism which was the source of the victimisation of the women I spoke with (through their experiences of domestic violence, abject poverty and cuts to sources of support, for example) which, as well as their criminalisation, made desistance an arduous and often unsuccessful task. Individualising women's experiences of both criminalisation and desistance is harmful both in stark desistance terms linked to offending and criminalisation, and more holistically in terms of women's life circumstances.

Although noted above, the offence(s) carried out were rarely the pivot around which the woman's life has turned. As posited by Corston (2007), offending can be a normative consequence of the personal, social and structural inequalities faced by women. The strength and resilience of women as highlighted in so many of their narratives can be celebrated and practitioners can work to build upon this resilience where it is present. Yet responsibilisation cannot be the only desistance response. Contesting and resisting structural inequalities can be central to any desistance intervention.

Chapter Outline

Desisting Sisters is set out in eight chapters. Chapter 2 explores the three traditional desistance theories; maturational (ontogenetic), social bonds (sociological) and narrative (subjective) theories and the development of the study of desistance and difference, to include what is currently 'known' about female desistance journeys. The subsequent chapters offer a feminist perspective on the three current explanatory themes for desistance. Chapter 3 briefly examines the ontogenetic perspective, concluding that it offers an incomplete and gender-blind approach to explaining contemporary female desistance journeys. Chapter 4 moves on to examine sociological explanations, particularly focusing on Sampson and Laub's (1993) and Laub and Sampson's (2003) theoretical paradigm. The conclusion here is that 'social bonds' theories which do not take account of the gendered inequalities faced by women within and outwith criminal justice contexts are woefully incomplete and often dangerous. Myths perpetuated about the central importance of marriage and employment to desistance, in a context where women facing CJS sanctions are experiencing abuse as well as the structural inequalities of austerity, can be destructive. Alternative and modified social bonds are considered. Subjective theories are examined from a feminist perspective in Chap. 5. It will be argued that subjective experiences are crucial in the desistance narratives of women travelling or attempting to travel desistance journeys. Yet subjective processes cannot be divorced from their contexts; hope and self-efficacy are not one and the same. Problematic ideas around stigma and shame as well as identity change (particularly surrounding women's relational identities) will be explored in this chapter, concluding that the double deviance which surrounds women's criminalisation is entrenched when women 'exit' the CJS. This can mar desistance attempts and create psychological harm. Having examined these three thematic explanations for desistance, the book moves on to consider interventions of the CJS (Chap. 6) which to a greater or lesser extent are justified for their desistance-promoting qualities. In particular, the book examines the new CJS paradigm, 'Transforming Rehabilitation' (TR), as linked with 'Payment by Results' (PbR), focusing on their problematic nature, particularly in the context of women's desistance and the neoliberal agenda pursued. Chapter 7 draws the key themes of *Desisting Sisters* together, with a focus on the structural contexts of desistance. It considers what an anti-carceral feminist approach, grounded in the elimination of social harms can offer and locates the invisible analytic structures ever present in desistance discourse. Finally, Chap. 8 critiques ongoing liberal reform of the CJS, and, linking with arguments made by Pat Carlen some 30 years ago (1990), sets out recommendations for a woman-wise, community-based penology.

Conclusion

It is important to note the context of women's offending and desistance pathways. Desistance does not happen in the absence of other factors and this chapter has attempted to highlight the importance of space and place in desistance experiences. Additionally, this chapter has briefly highlighted the social and structural 'vulnerabilities' or harms which so often provide the backdrop to both criminalisation and desistance. As the following chapters will argue, without addressing these harms, desistance may yet be forthcoming but will be a much more arduous experience for women.

A cross-European meta-analysis of 44 studies on female desistance (Rodermond et al. 2016) found that having children and pro-social, supportive relationships as well as economic independence, agency and an absence of drugs, were important for women attempting desistance, much as the literature suggests these factors are for men. Nonetheless, the authors found gender differences in the influence of children (children were more important to women), supportive relationships (relationship dynamics were arguably more complicated for women), employment (studies comparing genders found that employment had a greater effect on males) and the absence of criminal peers (males were more likely to be influenced by deviant friends). As will be highlighted in the chapters which follow, this research has reached *some* similar conclusions.

However *Desisting Sisters* will trouble this patriarchal idea of women as relational beings. It will examine whether motherhood has inherent desistance-inducing features or whether women feel compelled to relate their desistance journeys to their children, as a result of the social construction of what it is to be female. The research highlights the position of criminalised women as victims of a patriarchal, neoliberal condition; as victims of rape, domestic violence and childhood abuse, as voluntary, part-time or unpaid care workers within a system which does not reward them as well as their male counterparts, yet cuts their services in increasing increments. Yet the research also highlights female desisters as bricoleurs of their own fate, working against the notion of victimhood. Much like Emma Perry (2013), the current research will question whether within the CJS, the (re-)habilitation of female 'offenders' continues to be one of conformity to traditional 'feminine' gender norms within both theory and practice. The research highlights the intrinsic harmful nature of the CJS. By offering an anti-carceral feminist analysis of desistance, this book aims to shed new light on previous analyses of why women desist from offending. In order to create such a paradigm, an understanding of what is already 'known' about the desistance process must be garnered. It is to this overview that the book now turns.

Notes

1. No interviews were carried out in Weston, although observation research took place here.
2. Northshire.gov.uk (last accessed on 28 November 2017). In order to preserve anonymity, the website address has been altered.
3. Universal Credit had not been rolled out in Northshire at the time of the research. Although at the time of writing, full-service roll-out of Universal Credit was underway despite great opposition in the area.

Bibliography

Barr, U. (2018). Gendered Assisted Desistance: A Decade from Corston. *Safer Communities, 17*(2), 81–93.

Barry, M. (2006). *Youth Offending in Transition: The Search for Social Recognition*. London: Routledge.

Bottoms, A., & Shapland, J. (2011). Steps Toward Desistance Among Male Young Adult Recidivists. In S. Farrall, M. Hough, S. Maruna, & R. Sparks (Eds.), *Escape Routes: Contemporary Perspectives on Life After Punishment*. London: Routledge.

Bottoms, A., Shapland, J., Costello, A., Holmes, D., & Muir, G. (2004). Towards Desistance: Theoretical Underpinnings for an Empirical Study. *The Howard Journal, 43*(4), 368–389.

Calverley, A. (2013). *Cultures of Desistance: Rehabilitation, Reintegration and Ethnic Minorities*. London: Routledge.

Carlen, P. (1990). *Alternatives to Women's Imprisonment*. Milton Keynes: Open University Press.

Carlsson, C. (2012). Processes of Intermittency in Criminal Careers: Notes from a Swedish Study on Life Courses and Crime. *International Journal of Offender Therapy and Comparative Criminology, 57*(8), 913–938.

Chadwick, K., & Little, C. (1987). The Criminalisation of Women. In P. Scraton (Ed.), *Law, Order and the Authoritarian State*. Milton Keynes: Open University Press.

Corston, J. (2007). *The Corston Report: A Report by Baroness Jean Corston of a Review of Women with Particular Vulnerabilities in the Criminal Justice System*. London: Home Office.
Dorling, D. (2015). *Inequality and the 1%*. London: Verso.
Farrall, S., & Bowling, B. (1999). Structuration, Human Development and Desistance from Crime. *British Journal of Criminology, 39*(2), 253–268.
Farrall, S., & Calverley, A. (2006). *Understanding Desistance from Crime* (Crime and Justice Series). London: Open University Press.
Farrall, S., Sharpe, G., Hunter, B., & Calverley, C. (2011). Theorising Structural and Individual-Level Processes in Desistance and Persistence: Outlining an Integrated Perspective. *Australian and New Zealand Journal of Criminology, 44*(2), 218–234.
Gelsthorpe, L., & Morris, A. (1988). Feminism and Criminology in Britain. *British Journal of Criminology, 28*(2), 93–110.
Giordano, P. C., Cernokovich, S. A., & Rudolph, J. L. (2002). Gender, Crime and Desistance: Toward a Theory of Cognitive Transformation. *American Journal of Sociology, 107*, 990–1064.
Glaser, D. (1964). *Effectiveness of a Prison and Parole System*. Indianapolis: Bobbs-Merrill.
Gomm, R. (2016). *Women Making Meaning of Their Desistance from Offending: An Interpretative Phenomenological Analysis*. Doctoral Thesis, Durham University, Durham.
Gove, W. (1985). The Effect of Age and Gender on Deviant Behaviour: A Biopsychosocial Perspective. In A. Rossi (Ed.), *Gender and the Life Course*. New York: Aldine.
Hart, E. L. (2017). Prisoners Post-Release, The Need for a Critical Desistance. In E. L. Hart & F. J. C. Van Ginneken (Eds.), *New Perspectives on Desistance*. London: Palgrave Macmillan.
Healy, D. (2012). *The Dynamics of Desistance* (2nd ed.). New York: Routledge.
Heidensohn, F. (1985). *Women and Crime: The Life of a Female Offender*. New York: New York University Press.
Heidensohn, F. (2004). Gender and Crime. In M. Maguire, R. Morgan, & R. Reiner (Eds.), *The Oxford Handbook of Criminology*. Oxford: Oxford University Press.
Jamieson, J., McIvor, G., & Murray, C. (1999). *Understanding Offending Amongst Young People*. Edinburgh: The Scottish Executive.
Laub, J., & Sampson, R. (2003). *Shared Beginnings, Divergent Lives*. Harvard: Harvard University Press.
Leibrich, J. (1993). *Straight to the Point: Angles on Giving Up Crime*. Otago: University of Otago Press.

Maruna, S. (2001). *Making Good – How Ex-Convicts Reform and Rebuild Their Lives*. Washington, DC: American Psychological Association Books.

Maruna, S., & Farrall, S. (2004). Desistance from Crime: A Theoretical Reformulation. *Kölner Zeitschrift für Soziologie und Sozialpsychologie, 43*, 171–194.

Maruna, S., LeBel, T. S., Naples, M., & Mitchell, N. (2009). Looking-glass Identity Transformation: Pygmalion and Golem in the Rehabilitation Process. In B. Veysey, J. Christian, & D. J. Martinez (Eds.), *How Offenders Transform Their Lives*. Willan: Devon.

Matza, D. (1964). *Delinquency and Drift*. New York: Wiley.

McIvor, C., Murray, C., & Jamieson, J. (2004). Is Desistance from Crime Different for Women and Girls? In R. Immarigeon & S. Maruna (Eds.), *After Crime and Punishment: Ex-offender Reintegration and Desistance from Crime*. Willan: Cullompton.

Meisenhelder, T. (1977). An Exploratory Study of Exiting from Criminal Careers. *Criminology, 15*(3), 319–334.

Ministry of Justice. (2016). *Statistics on Women and the Criminal Justice System 2015*. London: Ministry of Justice.

Moffitt, T. (1993). Adolescent-Limited and Life-Course-Persistent Antisocial Behaviour: A Developmental Taxonomy. *Psychological Review, 100*, 674–701.

Office for National Statistics. (2015). *English Indices of Deprivation 2015*. London: Office for National Statistics.

Österman, L. (2018). *Penal Cultures and Female Desistance*. London: Routledge.

Perry, E. (2013). 'She's Alpha Male': Transgressive Gender Performances in the Probation 'Classroom'. *Gender and Education, 25*(4), 396–412.

Pickett, K., & Wilkinson, R. (2009). *The Spirit Level: Why Equality Is Better for Everyone*. London: Penguin.

Prison Reform Trust. (2017). *Why Focus on Reducing Women's Imprisonment?* London: Prison Reform Trust.

Public Health England. (2014). *Northshire Prospectus*. London: Public Health England.

Rodermond, E., Kruttschnitt, C., Slotboom, A. M., & Bijieveld, C. C. J. H. (2016). Female Desistance: A Review of the Literature. *European Journal of Criminology, 13*(1), 3–28.

Rumgay, J. (2004). Scripts for Safer Survival: Pathways Out of Female Crime. *The Howard Journal, 43*(4), 405–419.

Sampson, R. J., & Laub, J. H. (1993). *Crime in the Making: Pathways and Turning Points Through Life*. London: Harvard University Press.

Scraton, P. (1990). Scientific Knowledge or Masculine Discourses? Challenging Patriarchy in Criminology. In L. Gelsthorpe & A. Morris (Eds.), *Feminist Perspectives in Criminology*. Milton Keynes: Open University Press.
Shover, N. (1996). *Great Pretenders: Pursuits and Careers of Persistent Thieves*. Boulder: Westview.
Smart, C. (1977). *Women, Crime and Criminology: A Feminist Critique*. London: Routledge.
Smart, C. (2016). In J. Sim & H. Monk (Eds.), *Women, Crime and Criminology: A Celebration*. Bristol: EG Press.
Stanko, E. A. (1998). Making the Invisible Visible in Criminology: A Personal Journey. In S. Holdaway & P. Rock (Eds.), *Thinking About Criminology*. London: UCL Press.
Vaughan, B. (2007). The Internal Narrative of Desistance. *The British Journal of Criminology, 47*(3), 390–404.
Weaver, B., & McNeill, F. (2010). *Changing Lives? Desistance Research and Offender Management* (3rd ed.). Glasgow: The Scottish Centre for Crime and Research.

2

Explaining Desistance: Traditional Perspectives

In July 1997, at the British Society of Criminology Conference, Shadd Maruna remarked, 'few phenomena in criminology are as widely acknowledged and as poorly understood as desistance from crime.' This statement, made over two decades ago, can no longer be said to be true. Certainly in the past 20 years, the concept of desistance from crime has been critically analysed and researched. In July 2017, at the British Society of Criminology Conference, for example, there were at least 4 dedicated panels and 16 presentations, as well as keynote speeches on desistance. These incorporated national and international perspectives and case studies, quantitative and qualitative approaches to studying desistance and research located in various criminal justice institutions, including prison, probation and community alternatives. At the 1997 conference, Maruna observed that desistance theories tend to fall into the

---

Throughout this chapter the words 'offender' and 'former offender' have been used, as these are words used in the wider literature. In the following chapters I will argue a move away from this discourse to describe criminalised women who have been affected by the CJS as such (for more see Chap. 5).

Ú. Barr, *Desisting Sisters*, Critical Criminological Perspectives,
https://doi.org/10.1007/978-3-030-14276-6_2

dichotomy of ontogenetic (maturational) and sociogenic (social bonds) explanations. To these positivist explanations, Maruna et al.'s analysis can now be added, which have been formed through the study of the subjective narratives of the offenders/former offenders themselves.

Whilst desistance theories have developed over this time, the unique experience of criminalised women has only begun to be examined. Referring to the obstacles that individuals must overcome on the path towards desistance, Weaver and McNeill argued, 'to focus solely on overcoming these obstacles at the individual level runs the risk of accepting the world as it is, thus colluding with the social structures and attitudes that diminish the resources for desistance available to marginalised groups' (2010: 71). Nonetheless, since Rumgay's (2004) assertion about the absence of the female voice in desistance literature, there have been some movements in the area (Barry 2006; McIvor et al. 2011; Sapouna et al. 2011; Carr and Stovall Hanks 2012; Matthews et al. 2014; Leverentz 2014; Rodermond et al. 2016; Hart 2017; Barr 2018; Österman 2018 amongst others). This chapter considers what ontogenetic, social bonds and cognitive theories have offered the study of desistance, with an exploration, in particular, of what can be gleaned from the minimal desistance literature which does consider women's experiences. Whilst this book does not have the scope to examine all of the nuances of the central theoretical perspectives, a recapitulation of the key theories will be presented with an analysis, in particular, of theories which have included women's experiences. This is done to set the context for the feminist analysis which will be developed in the following chapters.

Ontogenetic Explanations

The first explanation, surrounding how and why offending stops is also the longest-held theory, emerging from the Gluecks' (1950) study of juvenile delinquency in America. It was here that the apparent link was made between ageing and the decline of criminal or delinquent behaviour. The study concluded that 'ageing is the only factor which emerges as significant in the reform process' (1950: 105). The Gluecks suggested that desistance was a natural process which happened spontaneously and without the influence of other factors.

Although the ontogenetic explanation has largely fallen out of favour with researchers (Steffensmeier et al. 2017), it is important to note that the behaviour which the modern penal state criminalises is largely that which is associated with the transgressions of youth, particularly working-class, black and male youth. When age-crime curves are plotted using this data, therefore, it is perhaps no wonder that this offending declines with age. As Bottoms and Shapland conceded, the 'criminality of even recidivist offenders declines sharply in the age range 20–30' (2011: 44). The authors argue that this is true of both recorded and self-reported offending patterns, which provides an interesting insight into how definitions of crime become hegemonic.[1] McIvor et al. (2011), in their study of young people in Scotland, have agreed that offending is usually a transitory phenomenon. Ontogenetic explanations suggest that the age-crime curve can be easily explained by ageing in itself. Desistance in this paradigm therefore is linked to individual biological processes and the passage of time whilst deviance can be explained as something that (most) offenders will eventually 'grow out of'. As Gottfredson and Hirschi maintain, 'spontaneous desistance is just that, change in behaviour … that occurs regardless of what else happens' (1990: 136). Crime, according to this argument, is linked to processes of self-control that are related to biological change brought about, for the most part, by the ageing process.

Gove similarly concluded that ageing is 'the most powerful predictor' (1985: 1) of the cessation of crime and deviance which involves significant risk and/ or physically demanding behaviour, and argued that this is true across genders, although more pronounced amongst males. Therefore, the argument posed, a purely sociological explanation for desistance from crime is incomplete and must incorporate biological and physiological maturation explanations. Gove (1985) explained the rapid rise and decline of deviant behaviour in young adulthood by the corresponding peaks and troughs of physical strength, energy and psychological drive that come with age and the reinforcement effect of an adrenaline high. Desistance, in his view, is a natural 'stage' in the process of human development.

Critiquing Maturational Theory

As noted, explanations based on an 'ageing-out process' explanation of offending trajectories has been criticised in more contemporary desistance studies. Bushway et al. (2001) suggested that this explanation 'offers no insight into the causal mechanisms that generate these changes' (pp. 492–493). As Rumgay (2004) elaborated, if we are to believe that desistance is a natural process, we suggest that external factors are unnecessary to promote desistance. If so, this virtually eradicates the need for any form of intervention, whether this is practical or psychological. Maruna (2001) argued that a consequence of viewing desistance in this way may be the suppression of public support for rehabilitative programmes and re-integrative services. He critiqued Gove's (1985) view that biological factors can explain the sharp decline by suggesting that testosterone levels actually drop slower than the sharp peak evident in the age-crime curve, whatever way the curve is plotted.[2] Age not only accounts for changes in biology or physiology but also in subjective beliefs, attitudes, life experiences and social contexts, including experiences of social or institutional processes not limited to the CJS (Weaver and McNeill 2010). Monica Barry (2006) argued that desistance is not just a natural consequence of the ageing process, but something which is more likely because of the increased opportunities for social recognition through both the desire to care for others in a generative fashion and the responsibility that ageing offers. As Moffitt (1993) recognised, society does not treat a young person in the same manner as their elders. Criminalisation of normative youth behaviour is certainly a factor to consider, and viewing desistance as a natural process tends to ignore this systemic discrimination. As Sampson and Laub (1992) maintained, maturational reform theorists fail to 'unpack' the meaning of age.

Maturational Theory and Gender

Some of the literature which considers maturation and gender has nonetheless found commonalities within the experiences of men and women. McIvor et al. (2011) noted that for both young men and women offending is essentially an age-related behaviour. Asquith and Samuel (1994) argued that there is a similar relationship between age and incidence of offending for men and women, even though women's convictions are lower. Although there are variations evident in the male and female offending trajectories, when plotted in an age-crime graph, it can be fairly reasoned that across-gender offending is predominantly reserved for young adulthood.[3]

Nuances in the age-crime curve nonetheless have been examined by Rex (1999), who found the peak of male offending in England and Wales to be 18; whilst the female age-crime curve was different, with even less embarking in 'offending careers' but also flattening to something approaching a plateau at 16 before slowly declining. The well-known maxim that girls mature faster than boys has been replicated in terms of criminological trajectories according to this argument. Graham and Bowling (1995), for example, noted that young women appear to desist earlier than their male counterparts and link this to early maturation amongst females. Women and girls, they proposed, are more likely to take advantage of life transitions with a particular view to ending offending. McIvor et al. (2011) similarly noted that females 'grow out of crime at an earlier age than males' (p. 10). On the whole, whilst contemporary examinations of desistance have critiqued ontological theory on both a methodological and theoretical basis, they have been successful in shaping much criminological research. When women's experiences are examined through this maturational lens, the most popular conclusion is that there appears to be an argument that women mature faster than men and their offending therefore is represented by a sharper decline in the age-crime curve.

Sociogenic Explanations

In their 1993 quantitative extension and re-evaluation of the Gluecks' (1950) longitudinal study, Sampson and Laub developed an age-graded theory of informal social control. The authors latterly followed up on the study in their seminal work entitled *Shared Beginnings, Divergent Lives* (2003), which traced local and national death records and criminal history searches for all 500 men in the Glueck's original delinquent sample until age 70. Importantly, this work also included a qualitative element where the authors carried out 52 detailed life-story interviews with men from the original delinquent sample. Essentially, Sampson and Laub concluded that focusing on desistance as a natural process of ageing overlooked the various 'social bonds' which ageing accounts for. What was important to the authors was the 'bond' between the individual and society. In their proposal of an organic, relational process of desistance, Sampson and Laub (1993) and Laub and Sampson (2003) emphasised the importance of both informal and formal 'turning points' related to social institutions—such as education, leaving home, getting married, becoming a parent and finding employment—that all exert social control on an individual and are inversely related to changes in adult crime.

The authors stressed the importance of social ties at all ages across the life course and concluded that factors such as job stability and marriage attachment were significantly related to changes in adult crime. In the retrospective follow up of these original subjects of the Massachusetts study, Laub and Sampson (2003) argued that the men who desisted from crime were embedded in structured routines, socially bonded and virtually supervised and monitored as a result of these social ties. According to Carlsson (2011) social bonds such as a good relationship and/ or stable employment can help an individual (a) 'knife off' the past, (b) invest in new relationships that foster support and growth, (c) be under direct control or supervision, (d) engage in routine, conventional life activities and/ or (e) perform an identity transformation (adapted from Carlsson 2011).

Marriage

Two specific 'turning points'—getting married and finding employment—have been particularly positively related to desistance and have been the subject of much criminological research. Marriage especially has been described as a robust indication of a reduction in offending (Bersani et al. 2009). Sampson et al. (2006), in their study of 'high-risk' boys up to the age of 32, found that marriage correlated with a 35% reduction in crime, and have linked this with the opportunity for emotional and practical support, a move away from deviant peers, and the routine structure which a marriage can provide. Other academics have positively linked marriage with desistance, particularly amongst male former offenders (Farrington and West 1995; Horney et al. 1995; Healy and O'Donnell 2006). An early study by Knight et al. (1977) found that whilst marriage in itself did not reduce criminal behaviour, it had links with reduced anti-social behaviour such as drug and alcohol use. Warr (1998) also found an indirect relationship between marriage and desistance, finding that marriage was likely to indicate a move away from prior anti-social relationships and friendship circles.

The hypothesis that marriage is positively related to desistance has been criticised for tending to apply only to heterosexual males—same sex relationships are virtually invisible in the social bonds literature (Leverentz 2006; Codd 2013)—and for not being applicable to contemporary relationships where couples tend to get married later in life, if at all. Conversely, co-habitation, has been found to be negatively related to desistance (Horney et al. 1995). The assumption that marriage is a desistance-related phenomenon only for men, and dependent on both time and place was examined by Bersani et al. (2009) in a study using data from the Criminal Career and Life-course Study (CCLS), which tracked the criminal conviction histories of almost 5000 men and women convicted in the Netherlands in 1977. The authors found that the effect of marriage was significantly lower for women than for men, yet was still associated with a decrease in the odds of being convicted. The authors also found that the 'good marriage effect'—that is, the finding that marriage would lead to desistance—was most salient in the most contemporary context, suggesting, they argued, that the quality and stability of a marriage is likely to be better in the modern day, with fewer instances of separation evident in the Netherlands at the time. Furthermore, as co-habitation and children before marriage are now more likely, these may reinforce the social bonding and control effects of marriage. The authors also pointed to economic explanations, suggesting that the increasing strength of marriage is influenced by the strength of the economy in contemporary contexts. It was concluded that there were no significant differences in the effect of marriage across either gender or socio-historic context.

Employment

Much like marriage, employment has been linked with processes of informal social control, providing incentives to comply with non-offending behaviour and a decreased opportunity and will to be involved in crime (where a legal source of income is available) and non-engagement with delinquent groups. Employment has been positively linked to desistance by numerous authors (Farrall 2002; Horney et al. 1995; Carlsson 2012; Verbruggen et al. 2012). A UK Ministry of Justice document (2013) also linked employment and desistance.[4] Both Healy (2012) and Farrall (2002) have appealed to probation services in Ireland and the UK respectively to provide practical assistance to former offenders in finding employment. Warr (2002) has linked unemployment and subsequent continued association with deviant peers to sustained deviance, while Aresti et al. (2010) found that meaningful employment tended to satisfy the need to belong, in particular where there was a strong moral element attached. Employment helped maintain a positive sense of self for the former prisoners involved in this study, and promoted community belonging and acceptance by others. However, the universality of employment effects on desistance has been disputed; for example, Uggen (2000) found that employment effects depend on age; as the individual ages, consequently employment becomes a more significant factor in promoting desistance.

Other Social Bonds

Further 'turning points' such as completing education, leaving home, becoming a parent or even joining the army have also been associated with a decline in offending (see Maruna 1999 for a full list). These 'turning points', Sampson and Laub maintain, can often be chance events, arguing that sometimes 'good things happen to bad people' (Laub et al. 1998: 237). It is not, therefore, necessary to have a great desire to cease offending in order for offending to be controlled by social bonds nor vice versa. Conversely, advancements on sociogenic theories, including Sampson and Laub's own work (2005), have suggested that the effect of 'social bonds' on offenders is subjective: it is not simply the bonds themselves but what the bonds mean to the offenders, and their effect in supporting informal social control which reduce opportunities and motivations to offend. The authors noted: 'the men we studied in *Shared Beginnings, Divergent Lives* were not blank slates any more than they were rational actors in an unconstrained market of life chances' (Sampson and Laub 2005: 42).

It should be noted that most sociogenic explanations of desistance tend to see these life events or 'turning points' as contributing to the dynamic process of desistance but as not necessarily directly causing a move away from a deviant lifestyle. As Laub and Sampson (2003: 149) have argued, 'offenders desist in response to structurally induced 'turning points' that serve as the catalyst for sustaining long-term behavioural change.' Carlsson (2012) argued that 'turning points' are gradual processes which are difficult to capture quantitatively, yet 'turning points' are useful in bringing clarity in the complex, dynamic life course of any individual and help identify which processes are more or less important in changing offending behaviour.

Critiquing Social Bonds Theory

Nonetheless, social bonds explanations have been criticised for numerous reasons. Carlsson (2012), whilst recognising the usefulness of the concept of 'turning points', criticised the methodology of Laub and Sampson's (2003) seminal work. In their interviews with the Glueck men, the authors asked about 'any significant turning points' in their lives. Carlsson contended that such an interview style tends to 'get what you ask for' (2012: 2). The author found that when questions do not explicitly ask about 'turning points', desistance appears as a much more gradual process that can include many so-called turning points as well as within-individual stores of human agency that sociogenic theorists tend to ignore.

As Giordano et al. (2002) noted, the original Glueck sample upon which much of the sociogenic literature has been based, consisted entirely of white, male offenders who matured into adulthood in the 1950s. Adam Calverley (2013) argued that social bonds theorists tend to overlook the experiences of minority ethnic groups. Calverley claimed that access to social capital through the social bonding effects of finding employment, family formation and engagement in social institutions like religion and marriage differs according to ethnicity. He found that for Indian and Bangladeshi desisters in the UK, the route from crime and the CJS was described as a collective experience involving their families actively intervening in their lives. Contrastingly, black and dual heritage former offenders' desistance was a much more individualistic endeavour. Furthermore, Calverley argued that sociogenic theorists tend to promote an uncritical, conformist perception of socially constructed institutions such as marriage, employment, parenthood and schooling as essentially 'good' and conversely social resistance as negative. This point is noted by Berger and Quinney (2005) who argue that as individuals experience social structures and institutions differently, their ability to transition is highly dependent on their past and present, 'location in social structures of inequality, based on class, race, gender and other social statuses' (quoted in Carlsson 2012: 13).

Social Bonds Theory and Gender

However, there has also been some concordance evident in the purported social bonds factors influencing desistance for women. Bersani et al. (2009), for example, highlight that studies which have examined the link between gender and desistance have found more similarities than differences in the social control factors that promote desistance. This was also reinforced by Rodermond et al.'s (2016) meta-analysis. Bersani et al. (2009) argued that the social institution of marriage in particular reduces the odds of offending, regardless of gender, and this was particularly true in the most contemporary contexts. Positive relationship experiences, and particularly marriage, therefore tended to represent 'turning points' in the lives of both male and female former offenders. Similarly, parenthood has also been noted to be a factor in male and female desistance (Graham and Bowling 1995). Another factor which has had cross-gender salience in the sociogenic literature is the effect of employment. Whist it is well noted that criminalised individuals are marginalised as a result of economic and social constraints, particularly following a period in prison, this is true for both criminalised men and women. Although women are more likely to be employed on a part-time, temporary or precarious basis than men, nonetheless employment, according to some, can pave the way to an offending-free lifestyle regardless of gender (Giordano et al. 2002). McIvor et al. (2011) found that the move away from delinquent peers as a result of marriage, parenthood or employment can be a desistance-promoting factor for men and women.

Conversely, Graham and Bowling (1995) found that the transition to adulthood was more important for women. They found that whilst transitions such as leaving home and forming a new family were highly correlated with desistance from crime for females; for young males, these social transitions seemed to have little effect on patterns of offending. Uggen and Kruttschnitt (1998) noted that women are likely to attach greater importance to intimate relationships than men, which they argued often results in female law breakers being introduced to offending by a delinquent partner. In a number of studies, marriage did not result in desistance for women (Sampson et al. 2006; King et al. 2007). These authors have suggested that men tend to 'marry up', whilst women with an offending background are more likely to 'marry down' and therefore the 'good marriage effect' cannot be replicated amongst criminalised women. In other studies where marriage has been found to have a positive effect for female offenders (e.g., Bersani et al. 2009), there is a significantly lower effect for women, and marriage has been found to be more beneficial for men. Even here, the authors note that the positive effect of marriage on offending patterns may be spurious. There is a suggestion that married women are likely to be treated differently and more leniently by the CJS (especially if the woman has children) and so this supposed 'good marriage effect' for women may actually be representing the effect of gendered criminal justice processes.

Leverentz (2014) noted that whilst relationships with men were central to women's offending, heterosexual relationships, and in particular marriage, were less important defining factors for African American women in supporting desistance. McIvor et al. (2011) also found that the end of a heterosexual relationship was more likely to be associated with a move towards desistance for women rather than the beginning of one. Bersani et al. (2009) noted that, for women, parenthood seems to be the determining relationship-related desistance factor, a conclusion which has been supported in other research (Giordano et al. 2002; Graham and Bowling 1995; Uggen and Kruttschnitt 1998; McIvor et al. 2011;

Sapouna et al. 2011). Rutter et al. (1998), for example, found that teenage motherhood, in particular, may facilitate desistance. These studies have indicated that motherhood, like fatherhood, is associated with less opportunity for criminal offending. Graham and Bowling (1995) contended that if parenthood is accompanied by leaving home for women, it is particularly predictive of desistance. They also found that the consequences of criminal behaviour are more salient for mothers (Graham and Bowling 1995). Giordano et al. (2002) noted that women are more likely to assign prominence to both parenthood and the socialising effect of religious transformation in their desistance narratives, whilst men were more likely to focus on prison or treatment or family in a general sense.

Rodermond et al. (2016) have found that both quantitative and qualitative studies of women's desistance highlight that employment is more important for men than women on the road to desistance. Yet, employment did impact on cessation of offending. Österman (2018) has contended that there is a lack of research into women's desistance and employment in particular. Katz (2000) is also careful to note that women's desistance may be culturally determined; she found that becoming a parent was most likely to be associated with desistance amongst white women, whilst minority ethnic women were more likely to define themselves in relation to kinship networks, neighbourhood and work. Leverentz (2014) noted that stable, well-paying jobs were not readily available for the formerly imprisoned, African American women involved in her study. Expectations around caring roles of mother and daughter, whilst at the same time, a lack of support from family members, were common experiences. Analysis of social bonds explanations into female desistance has, therefore, highlighted the gendered (and other) nuances which can be applied to the theory.

Subjective Explanations

As noted in the introduction to this chapter, more recently, a third theory has emerged from considerations of desistance. Gottfredson and Hirschi (1990) argued, 'jobs do not just "attach themselves to individuals" and "subjects are not randomly assigned to marital statuses"' (p. 188, quoted in Maruna 1999: 5). Although this was something which Laub and Sampson (2003) did recognise, generally the role of human agency in the promotion of desistance tended to be left behind or included as an afterthought in the social bonds literature. Advances on social bonds theories have, therefore, noted the importance of social bonds in life transformations but have also linked them to subjective changes in agency and identity. For example, Giordano et al. (2002) noted the importance of within-individual change in their subjective-social model of desistance. The authors proposed that pathways to desistance began with a shift in an individual actor's openness to change, this was followed by the presentation of a 'hook' for change (e.g., marriage or employment) which acted in interaction with the individual's outlook, especially the extent to which it was compatible or otherwise with continued deviance; the subsequent cognitive transformation was particularly focused on internal changes and their relation to delinquency. Similarly, Aresti et al. (2010) described the 'defining moments' of desistance as points in time which may lead to a decision to change, often linked to feelings of loss and struggle and being cut-off from pre-existing social networks and structures of meaning. This may be followed, the authors suggested, by a moment of clarity and self-change, promoting the taking of control and, subsequently, the emergence of new goals and aspirations. The importance of subjective changes underlying external deviations which were often beyond the control of the individual is evident in both of these accounts. There was an emphasis on individuals actively thinking for themselves, both in the reaction to these events (marriage, employment, parenthood, etc.) and as influencing factors in the path taken towards them. As Gartner and Piliavin argued, within-individual changes 'do not simply accompany changes in the objective sphere of life, but trigger them as well, and determine how external events and physiological states will be interpreted and acted upon' (1988: 299).

LeBel et al. (2008) attempted to untangle the subjective and objective processes involved in desistance by looking at data collected as part of the Oxford Recidivism Study. The study involved interviews with 130 male repeat 'persistent' offenders, both prior to their release from prison and 4–6 months following release. The authors found evidence to support a subjective-social model of desistance. It was found that social problems after release have a significant impact on the probability of both re-conviction and re-imprisonment. The authors concluded that subjective states have an effect on exterior circumstances and vice versa:

> Positive 'mind-over-matter' helps the individual to triumph over problems and make the best of situations while a negative frame of mind leads to drift and defeatism in response to the same events. (LeBel et al. 2008: 155)

Maruna (2001) has reiterated this point by drawing upon a well-known probation slogan, 'You rehabilitate yourself.' He argued that agency is an important factor in social bonding and both elements should be considered as complimentary to each other in a dialectic manner. This point has significantly influenced the life-course analysis approach to explaining desistance. Healy (2012: 186) argued:

> Significant life events constitute opportunities for change that can be exploited. But desistance does not automatically follow … in addition to social support, successful change also requires strong reserves of personal agency.

As contended by Maruna (1999: 5):

> Essentially, what appears to be missing from both ontogenetic and socio-genic approaches is 'the person'—the wholeness and agentic subjectivity of the individual … we need a literally intelligible sequence or a coherent 'story' of the individual if we want to understand changes in behaviour such as desistance.

Narrative theorists support the demand for, and analysis of, the lived-in experiences of offenders (and former offenders) to understand criminal trajectories (Carlsson 2011). Within desistance research, narrative theorists have focused on subjective cognitive shifts (Giordano et al. 2002) in self-identity for the offender. Leibrich (1993) proposed that the cognitive processes involved in how offenders interpret their lives can affect the specifics of their life course. Maruna's (2001) seminal study of former offenders 'making good' suggests that desisters must recognise themselves as good and conventional. He found a difference in the 'scripts' of persistent and desisting/ desisted offenders. Desisters' life-course narratives promoted a view of the former offender as a victim trapped in a cycle of deviance. The author found that these narratives included a crucial intervention from someone who always believed in the offender leading them to accomplish what they were 'always meant to do' (ibid) and suggested that desistance, for these people, included a desire to give something back to society in a generative action. What was central for desistance therefore was the discovery of agency. Persisting offenders on the other hand were likely to be linked to scripts which promoted a feeling of being 'doomed to deviance', with individuals regarding themselves as victims of life circumstances.

Monica Barry (2006) argued that offending is an ephemeral profession, dependent not only on objective structural factors but also on individual self-determination. Whilst she recognised that individuals differ in their ability to structure and be structured by their surroundings, those who were involved in offending behaviours were more than passive reactors to social events, instead they 'take an active role in bringing about change in their lives' (Healy 2012: 176). LeBel et al. (2008) identified four interrelated subjective-level themes which they contended emerged as most buoyant in the desistance literature: Hope and Self-efficacy; Shame and Remorse; Internalising Stigma and Alternative Identities. These themes have had salience in the literature and will now be discussed in turn.

Hope and Self-Efficacy

Hope and self-efficacy are factors which LeBel et al. argue require both 'the will and the ways' (2008: 136) to initiate self-change. This means that both the perception of the ability to succeed in achieving one's goals and also the belief that there are successful pathways available to achieve these goals are necessary. The role of hope has also been noted by Burnett and Maruna (2004) and Farrall and Calverley (2006) amongst others. Self-efficacy is something which is one step further towards this feeling of hope, suggesting a belief that a goal is achievable, and takes into account 'the ways' in addition to 'the will' to change. Self-efficacy is related to agency which can determine how individuals respond to these 'hooks for change' (Shover 1996). Bottoms and Shapland (2010) proposed that self-efficacy was central to views about future offending. Furthermore Aresti et al. (2010) noted the centrality of feelings of hope and self-efficacy in their accounts of formerly imprisoned men's experiences of self-change particularly during defining moments where there is a moment of clarity, leading to taking control, following a period of loss and struggle, and being cut-off from existing social networks. Burnett (1992) highlighted that offenders' post-custodial intention to 'go straight' was not enough to bring about desistance following release, but those who were most confident and optimistic about their ability to be law abiding had most success in doing so. For these authors, hope and, more importantly, self-efficacy, were built upon by positive experiences and the social bonds which Laub and Sampson (2003) espoused (meaningful employment, a family, etc.). Yet feelings about the possibility of achievable goals can be destroyed by the negative experiences which are all too common following criminal justice contact, bringing to mind the feelings and experiences of 'doing time after time' which Aresti et al. (2010) describe. Maruna (2001), for example, maintained that former prisoners tended to lack such agentic feelings due to negative experiences and therefore the resultant narrative is one which appears 'doomed to deviance'. An individual's sense of hope can be trampled by the CJS and, where this has not occurred, the experiences former offenders have in the outside world (e.g., following release from prison) can effectively destroy any chance of hope for a different life (Hart 2017). LeBel et al. (2008) concluded that hope (or lack thereof) can have an impact on social problems which can in turn have an effect on re-conviction. On the other hand, promotion of human achievements and positive mental well-being require 'an optimistic sense of personal efficacy' (Bandura 1989: 1176). LeBel et al. (2008) found this to be the most important subjective factor in the process of desistance.

Shame, Remorse and Stigma

Shame and remorse are the next factors which LeBel et al. (2008) linked to processes of desistance. Feelings of regret for previous behaviour and a revised perspective of youthful activities were an important cognitive factor in any move towards desistance. This finding is evidenced by Shover (1996) and Giordano et al. (2002). Furthermore, Julie Leibrich (1993) reported that shame was the 'primary reason' her participants reported for giving up crime. Conversely, Healy and O'Donnell (2006) found that a tendency to externalise blame for past behaviours was linked to a continuation of these behaviours. The centrality of shame and remorse is linked to a theme which Aresti et al. (2010) found in the scripts of the former prisoners whom they interviewed; the authors found that the desisting men expressed a preference for their new non-offending life whilst describing their previous (offending) lifestyles as meaningless. Shame does not necessarily, LeBel et al. (2008) were quick to note, have a direct, inverse relationship with recidivism. In fact, feelings of shame may be linked to feelings of depression and powerlessness and the 'doomed to deviance' persistence scripts which Maruna (2001) proposed. Linked to feelings of shame and remorse, the internalisation of this stigma is the third subjective factor which LeBel et al. (2008) recognised. Considering the work of John Braithwaite (1989), the authors made a distinction here between re-integrative shame, where the criminal act is regretted but the internal self-worth of the individual is preserved, and stigmatising shame, where both the act and the actor is degraded. Whilst the authors maintained that re-integrative shame can have positive effects in the move towards desistance, stigmatising shame can lead to defiance and further recidivism. Uggen et al. (2004), for example, suggested that the stigma of a criminal conviction, and especially of a prison sentence, can be extremely severe and is likely to have an effect on employment and therefore negatively impact desistance.

Identity

The final subjective-level theme which LeBel et al. (2008) recognised was alternative identities. The authors noted that amongst the male former prisoners they studied, who successfully desisted from crime, the development of a new pro-social identity was part of the process. These men were able to deflect the stigma of the past through taking on new roles such as that of a 'good parent', 'provider' or 'family man'. According to these authors, new identities can help maintain and reinforce the attraction of non-offending lifestyles, whether for men or women. As these identities are reinforced, the pall cast by the past tends to contract (Healy 2012) enabling the individuals to move on with their lives. Maruna (2001) found that these kinds of identity changes were reflected in a reconstruction of one's internalised self-narrative.

Matsueda and Heimer (1997) also linked desistance with a change in the reformed offender's sense of self through taking on conventional roles and positive social bonds (Aresti et al. 2010; Maruna 2001). Vaughan (2007) proposed that desistance is a moral and cognitive process where the desister must realise that their former self is morally incompatible with who they want to be. As noted by Aresti et al., 'in definitional terms, by its nature criminal desistance or the long-term abstinence from crime involves self-change' (2010: 170). However the concept of identity change is not as simple as it at first may seem and may involve holding on to some part of the previous self.

Aresti et al. (2010) support Maruna's (2001) findings of generative concern amongst desisters; however, for some, the 'ex-offender' label could be instrumental in maintaining a positive sense of self, for others, the label had negative connotations, both personally and in terms of societal reaction, and tended to be rejected for these reasons. The authors set their findings in a social identity theory framework. They found a fear of prejudice and discrimination amongst these individuals which tended to remind them of earlier experiences of social exclusions, leading to a desire to be accepted and belong—either by rejecting the 'former offender' label or by encapsulating the new identity within the old, through maintaining a positive sense of self. This is similar to Maruna's (2001) notion of the 'professional ex' who develops according to different social contexts. Through this analysis, Aresti et al. (2010) bring to light the multi-layered, dynamic and relative nature of identity.

Others have further questioned the extent to which this identity change process is a conscious conversion. Whilst Maruna and Farrall (2004) maintained that identity change involved agency and a will to alter oneself, Bottoms et al. (2004), alongside Healy and O' Donnell (2006), questioned the extent to which the individual is aware of the process of change. As conceded by the latter, however, this difference in the role of agency may have much to do with the point at which the process of desistance is viewed. When studied prospectively, Burnett (1992) has suggested that desistance appears as a process that is full of uncertainty, relapse and hesitancy. The opposite may be said to be true for accounts that are studied retrospectively. As Weaver and McNeill suggested, these accounts 'may be susceptible to cognitive rationalizations that place undue or unrealistic emphasis on the role of agency' (2010: 61). The effects of 'role strain' (Carlsson 2012) suggest that even when agency and a strong will to change are present, a person may experience difficulties in conforming to a conventional life associated with desistance. Nonetheless, there is a general agreement amongst desistance academics that, by its very definition, the process of desistance from crime involves an identity change, whether influenced by a conscious decision or not.

Narrative Theory and Gender

It is perhaps surprising given the focus on identity change within narrative studies of desistance that academics, especially within the UK, have been relatively quiet on linking gendered identity and the process of desistance. However, Rumgay (2004) has argued that due to women's unequal role in society, female desistance scripts not only involve the opportunity for reform, self-efficacy and identity transformation that are found in male scripts, but also involve a strong sense of resilience. This finding has been backed by Rebecca Gomm (2016) who noted the centrality of resilience in women's desistance narratives. Identity change, she argued, involved a challenge to female stereotypes. Matthews et al. (2014) found that for female sex workers, part of the desistance process involved a disassociation from the previous self, contrary to Maruna's (2001) findings. Matthews and colleagues have suggested therefore that female desistance is likely to be different from male desistance as female narratives of offending are not consistent with gendered expectations, and therefore their move to desistance may involve a denial or disassociation with this offending past (see also Leverentz 2014).

As Maruna et al. note, structured self-images are 'not created in a vacuum, they are socially shaped and individually constructed' (2004: 274). McIvor et al. (2011) highlighted the significance of gendered assumptions in the reasons young people attribute for their 'decisions' to desist; young women tended to attribute their decisions to desist to the assumption of parental responsibility whilst young men focused on personal choice and agency. Giordano et al. (2002) found that whilst men were more likely to explain desistance in utilitarian terms, women often mentioned the moral dimensions of the offending or non-offending behaviour. Sommers and Baskin (1994) similarly found that 'shame' was a more significant experience for women as compared to men, again highlighting societal gendered expectations. Stigma and shame have been consistently found to be related to gendered expectations. Jamieson et al. (1999) suggested that the fact that young women were more keen to be viewed as desisting than young men further supports the role of gender expectations in offending trajectories. The social construction of female offending is central. McIvor et al. quote a Scottish Office document that reiterates this point, 'Whilst offending may be a socially inclusive experience for many men and they may gain prestige amongst their friends for their criminal behaviour, this is rarely the case for women and this may be a partial explanation of why so few women offend' (Scottish Office 1998: 6 taken from McIvor et al. 2011: 195).

Graham and Bowling (1995) argued that, for many, gendered expectations and stigma surrounding female offending have led to a denial of the offending behaviour of women. However, as the identity literature has noted, in order for desistance to occur, the offending behaviour must first be recognised (Maruna 2001; Graham and Bowling 1995). For men (especially younger men), the beginning of offending can be a socially inclusive and relational experience, whilst the opposite may be the case for women. Paradoxically, desistance for men is an individual experience which draws on reserves of personal agency; whilst for many women, desistance tends to have a relational dimension (Gilligan 1982; Barr 2018) where the individual is either 'shamed' into desistance (as a result of breaking the gender code) (Sommers and Baskin 1994) or is welcomed back into society as a result of the acquisition of a socially desired and approved identity (McIvor et al. 2011; Rumgay 2004; Maruna 2001; Sapouna et al. 2011; Leverentz 2014).

Rumgay (2004) has argued that female offenders' processes of desistance are rooted in recognising an opportunity to claim an alternative, desired and socially approved personal identity. For example, the identity of a mother may provide a 'script' by which to enact a conventional, pro-social role to enhance the individual's confidence in their ability to enact it successfully, which in turn assisted in perpetuating the newly acquired identity. Therefore, coping strategies were of particular importance to female offenders who were likely to experience material deprivation, social exclusion and psychological vulnerability. She suggests, therefore, that the 'scripts' should be accessible so that the individual is able to fulfil the requirements of the new identity and avoid being set back on the offending pathway. Social reaction is therefore essential and wider societal recognition that these scripts may take time to have an effect may form an essential desistance element. These scripts can build up self-efficacy and social control through increasing participation in conventional roles and relationships. Positive reinforcement of the script can reinforce resilience and survival. Much like Carlsson (2011 and 2012), she notes that deviation from desistance can be an important part of the desistance process. As a society, she therefore argues, we must be patient with female offenders in particular as they become masters of this new 'script'. Again, studies which have examined cognitive theories of desistance through women's experiences have highlighted that there may be a gendered element to the theory.

Combining Explanations

Whilst it can be seen that the study of life-course narratives tends to provide an effective method through which to study desistance, more recent studies have suggested that desistance cannot be explained without reference to subjective-level thought-processes explanations, sociogenic explanations and ontogenetic explanations combined. In their attempt to unravel 'The Chicken and the Egg' of subjective and social forces on the process of desistance, LeBel et al. conceded, 'it might be reasonably argued that a quest to identify the sequencing of cognitive and external influences is both impossible and pointless because these operate through dynamic, interactive processes' (2008: 153).

The authors pointed to the inseparability of cognitive and social forces; their differential impacts are equally required for desistance to occur. As Christopher Carlsson (2012: 925) argued, agency and social control 'should be thought of as dialectic, where both elements can inform one another'. Carlsson points to the dynamic nature of agency as desires and wishes tend to change with the passing of time, requiring the reinforcement of social bonds to conventional society. Giordano et al. (2002: 992) contended that social control theory is 'important but incomplete', arguing that 'hooks for change [...] will serve well as catalysts for lasting change when they energise fundamental shifts in identity and changes in the meaning and desirability of deviant/criminal behaviour itself.' They proposed that combining social control and symbolic interactionist perspectives provides researchers, practitioners and offenders with a 'more complete conceptual toolkit than either perspective on its own' (ibid). Uggen et al. (2004) likewise presented their symbolic interactionist perspective which recognised both the role of age-graded social bonds and the social-psychological processes underpinning these related role transitions. However, they found that, even where there is a desire to assume pro-social roles, there can be societal obstacles in terms of lack of resources, (including a lack of political will to expend social resources) and/or a lack of social relationships, which are central to supporting these new identities. The authors therefore reinforce the importance of societal reaction in supporting desistance. Roger Matthews and colleagues reiterate this sentiment in their 2014 study of women exiting prostitution; desistance, they argued, would be achieved not only by the provision of drug or housing services but also by emphasising the importance of emotions and identity formation.

The importance of the combination of the positivist ontogenetic and social bonds theories and life history narratives in explaining pathways to desistance has been articulated by Fergus McNeill in his attempt to reconcile probation practice with what was 'known' about desistance:

> Desistance lies somewhere in the interfaces between developing personal maturity, forming new or stronger social bonds associated with certain life transitions, and individual subjective narrative constructions which offenders build around these key events and changes. (2003: 151)

Conclusion

This chapter has highlighted the triumvirate of theories which exist to explain the complex process of desistance from crime. It has shown that the desistance literature has offered insights into the how and why of the end of offending, particularly through three separate but interlinked theoretical perspectives. Ontogenetic and social bonds literature initially offered positivist explanations of the process of desistance. Maturational theory argued that desistance involved a 'natural' process of getting older. Sociogenic theorists felt this was incomplete and argued that 'social bonds' to conventional life, particularly gained through the processes of finding employment and getting married, indicated moves towards desistance. Using narrative methods, subjective themes such as hope, self-efficacy, shame, stigma, remorse and identity change were examined by the final group of desistance theorists. Yet most desistance theorists now argue that these theories are connected.

However, desistance theory has been examined mainly through a white, male perspective. Recently, there have been some forays into exploring possible gendered desistance experiences, as has been seen in this chapter. Nonetheless, as will be discussed in the next chapter, these have often been limited by their absence of a structural analysis. Where commonalities are found with the male experience, these are sometimes uncritically presented as proof of the salience of maturational, social bonds and cognitive theories. Where differences are found, these have often not been situated within feminist understandings of gender and the structural forces of patriarchy and neoliberalism in particular. Desistance literature has begun to have a tangible effect on the operations of the Criminal Justice System (CJS) (Ministry of Justice 2013; HMIP Probation 2016). It is clear to see how the theories linked above have given credence to a liberal reformist agenda within the CJS, whether intentionally or not, which has enabled expansionist moves and a focus on individual personal responsibility without critically interrogating the structural forces which surround experiences prior to, during and following criminal justice contact.

As noted in the introduction, Chaps. 3, 4, 5 and 6 will explore whether desistance theory as examined here can help to explain the journeys of Northshire women convicted of diverse offences, particularly following the pathways of 16 women interviewed throughout the course of 2014 and 2015. To do this, an analysis of maturational, sociological and subjective theories in the context of these women's narratives will be put forward. The role of the CJS, particularly the community contexts of the aforementioned journeys, will also be examined. The analysis will note the particular importance of approaches which are intersectional in nature. In addition, the chapters will consider the importance of the concepts of social harm (as opposed to crime) as well as critically interrogating the concepts of patriarchy and neoliberalism which provide the lens through which the desistance experiences of the female narratives studied in this book can be viewed.

Notes

1. For example, the harm caused by war, austerity, pollution or corruption is unlikely to be represented in these graphs (Hillyard et al. 2004).
2. For more on this point, see Bottoms and Shapland (2011).
3. Again, this finding places a lot of faith in hegemonic understandings of crime and the CJS. Also, for an alternative view, see Carr and Stovall Hanks (2012), who use life-course perspectives to explain the pathways of late-onset criminalised women.
4. Although it is ironic that in their study of a 2008 cohort of released prisoners, only 28% had been employed in the two-year period following release, indicating that much more work needs to be done to get former offenders into meaningful employment if it is truly the aim of the Ministry of Justice to reduce offending.

Bibliography

Aresti, A., Eatough, V., & Brooks-Gordan, B. (2010). Doing Time After Time: An Interpretative Phenomenological Analysis of Reformed Ex-Prisoners' Experiences of Self-change, Identity and Career Opportunities. *Psychology Crime and Law, 16*(3), 169–190.

Asquith, S., & Samuel, E. (1994). *Criminal Justice and Related Services for Young Adult Offenders: A Review*. Edinburgh: HMSO.

Bandura, A. (1989). Human Agency in Social Cognitive Theory. *American Psychologist, 44*, 1175–1184.

Barr, U. (2018). Gendered Assisted Desistance: A Decade from Corston. *Safer Communities, 17*(2), 81–93.

Barry, M. (2006). *Youth Offending in Transition: The Search for Social Recognition*. London: Routledge.

Bersani, B. E., Laub, J. H., & Nieuwbeerta, P. (2009). Marriage and Desistance from Crime in the Netherlands: Do Gender and Socio-Historical Context Matter? *Journal of Quantitative Criminology, 25*, 3–24.

Bottoms, A., & Shapland, J. (2010). Steps Towards Desistance Among Young Adult Recidivists. In S. Farrall, R. Sparks, S. Maruna, & M. Hough (Eds.), *Escape Routes*. London: Routledge.

Bottoms, A., & Shapland, J. (2011). Steps Toward Desistance Among Male Young Adult Recidivists. In S. Farrall, M. Hough, S. Maruna, & R. Sparks (Eds.), *Escape Routes: Contemporary Perspectives on Life After Punishment*. London: Routledge.

Bottoms, A., Shapland, J., Costello, A., Holmes, D., & Muir, G. (2004). Towards Desistance: Theoretical Underpinnings for an Empirical Study. *The Howard Journal, 43*(4), 368–389.

Braithwaite, J. (1989). *Crime, Shame and Reintegration*. Cambridge, UK: Cambridge University Press.

Burnett, R. (1992). *The Dynamics of Recidivism*. Oxford: Centre for Criminological Research, University of Oxford, Research Report for the Home Office.

Burnett, R., & Maruna, S. (2004). So Prison Works, Does It? The Criminal Careers of 130 Men Released from Prison under Home Secretary, Michael Howard. *Howard Journal of Criminal Justice, 43*, 390–404.

Bushway, S. D., Piquero, A. R., Broidy, L. M., Cauffman, E. E., & Mazerolle, P. (2001). An Empirical Framework for Studying Desistance as a Process. *Criminology, 39*(2), 491–516.

Calverley, A. (2013). *Cultures of Desistance: Rehabilitation, Reintegration and Ethnic Minorities*. London: Routledge.
Carlsson, C. (2011). Using "Turning Points" to Understand Processes of Change in Offending. *British Journal of Criminology, 52*, 1–16.
Carlsson, C. (2012). Processes of Intermittency in Criminal Careers: Notes from a Swedish Study on Life Courses and Crime. *International Journal of Offender Therapy and Comparative Criminology, 57*(8), 913–938.
Carr, N. T., & Stovall Hanks, R. (2012). If "60 Is the New 40," Is 35 the New 15? Late Onset Crime and Delinquency. *Deviant Behaviour, 33*, 393–411.
Codd, H. (2013). *In the Shadow of Prison: Families, Imprisonment and Criminal Justice*. Cullompton: Willan.
Farrall, S. (2002). *Rethinking What Works with Offenders*. Cullompton: Willan.
Farrall, S., & Calverley, A. (2006). *Understanding Desistance from Crime* (Crime and Justice Series). London: Open University Press.
Farrington, D. P., & West, D. J. (1995). Effects of Marriage, Separation, and Children on Offending by Adult Males. In Z. Blau Smith & J. Hagan (Eds.), *Current Perspectives on Aging and the Life Cycle* (4th ed.). Greenwich: JAI Press.
Gartner, R., & Piliavin, I. (1988). The Aging Offender and the Aged Offender. In P. B. Baltes, D. L. Featherman, & R. M. Lerner (Eds.), *Life-Span Development and Behaviour* (9th ed.). Hillsdale: Lawrence Erlbaum Associates.
Gilligan. (1982). *In a Different Voice: Psychological Theory and Women's Development*. Harvard: Harvard University Press.
Giordano, P. C., Cernokovich, S. A., & Rudolph, J. L. (2002). Gender, Crime and Desistance: Toward a Theory of Cognitive Transformation. *American Journal of Sociology, 107*, 990–1064.
Glueck, S., & Glueck, E. (1950). *Unravelling Juvenile Delinquency*. New York: Harvard University Press.
Gomm, R. (2016). *Women Making Meaning of Their Desistance from Offending: An Interpretative Phenomenological Analysis*. Doctoral Thesis, Durham University, Durham.
Gottfredson, M., & Hirschi, T. (1990). *A General Theory of Crime*. Stanford: Stanford University Press.
Gove, W. (1985). The Effect of Age and Gender on Deviant Behaviour: A Biopsychosocial Perspective. In A. Rossi (Ed.), *Gender and the Life Course*. New York: Aldine.
Graham, J., & Bowling, B. (1995). *Young People and Crime* (Research Study No. 145). London: HMRSO.

Hart, E. L. (2017). Prisoners Post-Release, The Need for a Critical Desistance. In E. L. Hart & F. J. C. Van Ginneken (Eds.), *New Perspectives on Desistance*. London: Palgrave Macmillan.
Healy, D. (2012). *The Dynamics of Desistance* (2nd ed.). New York: Routledge.
Healy, D., & O'Donnell, I. (2006). Criminal Thinking on Probation: A Perspective from Ireland. *Criminal Justice and Behaviour, 33*, 782–802.
Hillyard, P., Pantazis, C., Tombs, S., & Gordon, D. (2004). *Beyond Criminology: Taking Harm Seriously*. London: Pluto Press.
HMIP. (2016). *Desistance and Young People*. Manchester: Her Majesty's Inspectorate of Probation.
Horney, J., Osgood, D. W., & Marshall, I. H. (1995). Criminal Careers in the Short Term: Intra Individual Variability in Crime and its Relation to Local Life Circumstances. *American Sociological Review, 60*(5), 655–673.
Jamieson, J., McIvor, G., & Murray, C. (1999). *Understanding Offending Amongst Young People*. Edinburgh: The Scottish Executive.
Katz, R. (2000). Explaining Girl's and Women's Crime and Desistance in the Context of their Victimization Experiences. *Violence Against Women, 6*, 633–660.
King, R. D., Massoglia, M., & Macmillan, R. (2007). The Context of Marriage and Crime: Gender, the Propensity to Marry, and Offending in Early Adulthood. *Criminology, 45*(1), 33–65.
Knight, B. J., Osborn, S. G., & West, D. J. (1977). Early Marriage and Criminal Tendency in Males British Journal of Criminology. *British Journal of Criminology, 17*, 348–360.
Laub, J., & Sampson, R. (2003). *Shared Beginnings, Divergent Lives*. Harvard: Harvard University Press.
Laub, J. H., Nagin, D. S., & Sampson, R. J. (1998). Trajectories of Change in Criminal Offending: Good Marriages and the Desistance Process. *American Sociological Review, 63*, 225–238.
LeBel, T. P., Burnett, R., Maruna, S., & Bushway, S. (2008). The "Chicken and Egg" of Subjective and Social Factors in Desistance from Crime. *European Journal of Criminology, 5*(11), 131–159.
Leibrich, J. (1993). *Straight to the Point: Angles on Giving Up Crime*. Otago: University of Otago Press.
Leverentz, A. (2006). The Love of a Good Man? Romantic Relationships as a Source of Support or Hindrance for Female Ex-Offenders. *Journal of Research in Crime and Delinquency, 43*(4), 459–488.
Leverentz, A. (2014). *The Ex-Prisoner's Dilemma: How Women Negotiate Competing Narratives of Re-entry and Desistance*. New Brunswick: Rutgers University Press.

Maruna, S. (1999). Desistance and Development: The Psychosocial Process of "Going Straight". *The British Criminology Conferences: Selected Proceedings, 2*, 1–19.
Maruna, S. (2001). *Making Good – How Ex-Convicts Reform and Rebuild Their Lives*. Washington, DC: American Psychological Association Books.
Maruna, S., & Farrall, S. (2004). Desistance from Crime: A Theoretical Reformulation. *Kölner Zeitschrift für Soziologie und Sozialpsychologie, 43*, 171–194.
Maruna, S., LeBel, T. P., Mitchell, N., & Naples, M. (2004). Pygmalion in the Reintegration Process: Desistance from Crime through the Looking Glass. *Psychology Crime and Law, 10*(3), 271–281.
Matsueda, R. L., & Heimer, K. (1997). 'A Symbolic Interactionist Theory of Role Transitions', Role Commitments. In T. P. Thonberry (Ed.), *Advances in Criminological Theory, Vol. 7, Developmental Theories of Crime and Delinquency*. New Brunswick: Transaction.
Matthews, R., Easton, H., Reynolds, L., Bindel, J., & Young, L. (2014). *Exiting Prostitution*. New York: Palgrave Macmillan.
McIvor, G., Murray, C., & Jamieson, J. (2011). Desistance from Crime: Is It Different for Women and Girls? In S. Maruna & R. Immarigeon (Eds.), *After Crime and Punishment: Pathways to Offender Reintegration*. Willan: Cullompton.
McNeill, F. (2003). Desistance-Focused Probation Practice. In W.-H. Chui & M. Nellis (Eds.), *Moving Probation Forward: Evidence, Arguments and Practice* (pp. 146–162). Harlow: Pearson Longman.
Ministry of Justice. (2013). *Analysis of the Impact of Employment on Re-offending following Release from Custody, Using Propensity Score Matching*. London: Ministry of Justice.
Moffitt, T. (1993). Adolescent-Limited and Life-Course-Persistent Antisocial Behaviour: A Developmental Taxonomy. *Psychological Review, 100*, 674–701.
Österman, L. (2018). *Penal Cultures and Female Desistance*. London: Routledge.
Rex, S. (1999). Desistance from Offending: Experiences of Probation. *The Howard Journal, 38*(4), 366–383.
Rodermond, E., Kruttschnitt, C., Slotboom, A. M., & Bijieveld, C. C. J. H. (2016). Female Desistance: A Review of the Literature. *European Journal of Criminology, 13*(1), 3–28.
Rumgay, J. (2004). Scripts for Safer Survival: Pathways Out of Female Crime. *The Howard Journal, 43*(4), 405–419.
Rutter, M., Giller, H., & Hagell, A. (1998). *Antisocial Behaviour by Young People*. New York: Cambridge University Press.
Sampson, R. J., & Laub, J. H. (1992). Crime and Deviance in the Life Course. *Annual Review of Sociology, 18*, 63–84.

Sampson, R. J., & Laub, J. H. (1993). *Crime in the Making: Pathways and Turning Points Through Life*. London: Harvard University Press.
Sampson, R. J., & Laub, J. H. (2005). A Life-Course View of the Development of Crime. *Annals of the American Academy of Political and Social Science, 602*, 12–45.
Sampson, R. J., Laub, J. H., & Wimer, C. (2006). Does Marriage Reduce Crime? A Counterfactual Approach to Within-Individual Causal Effects. *Criminology, 44*(3), 465–508.
Sapouna, M., Bisset, C., & Conlong, A. (2011). *What Works to Reduce Reoffending: A Summary of the Evidence*. Justice Analytical Services. Edinburgh: Scottish Government.
Shover, N. (1996). *Great Pretenders: Pursuits and Careers of Persistent Thieves*. Boulder: Westview.
Sommers, I., & Baskin, D. R. (1994). Factors Related to Female Adolescent Initiation into Violent Street Crime. *Youth Society, 25*, 468–489.
Steffensmeier, D., Zhong, H., & Liu, Y. (2017). Age and Its Relation to Crime in Taiwan and United States: Invariant, or Does Cultural Context Matter? *Criminology, 55*, 377–404.
Uggen, C. (2000). Work as a Turning Point in the Life Course of Criminals: A Duration Model of Age, Employment, and Recidivism. *American Sociological Review, 67*, 529–546.
Uggen, C., & Kruttschnitt, C. (1998). Crime in the Breaking: Gender Differences in Desistance. *Law and Society Review, 32*, 339–366.
Uggen, C., Manza, J., & Behrens, A. (2004). Less Than the Average Citizen: Stigma, Role Transition and the Civic Reintegration of Convicted Felons. In S. Maruna & R. Immarigeon (Eds.), *After Crime and Punishment: Pathways to Offender Reintegration* (pp. 261–294). Cullompton: Willan Publishing.
Vaughan, B. (2007). The Internal Narrative of Desistance. *The British Journal of Criminology, 47*(3), 390–404.
Verbruggen, J., Blokland, A. A. J., & Van Der Geest, V. R. (2012). Effects of Employment and Unemployment on Serious Offending in a High-Risk Sample of Men and Women from Ages 18 to 32 in the Netherlands. *British Journal of Criminology, 52*(5), 845–869.
Warr, M. (1998). Life–Course Transitions and Desistance from Crime. *Criminology, 36*, 183–216.
Warr, M. (2002). *Companions in Crime*. Cambridge, UK: Cambridge University Press.
Weaver, B., & McNeill, F. (2010). *Changing Lives? Desistance Research and Offender Management* (3rd ed.). Glasgow: The Scottish Centre for Crime and Research.

3

A Case of Growing Up? A Feminist Critique of Maturational Theory

'I've just got to grow up really, more than anything.'
—Marie

This chapter critically explores the ontogenetic theory of desistance from offending as put forward by authors such as Glueck and Glueck (1950) and Gottfredson and Hirschi (1990). These authors suggest that offending is a behaviour that most individuals will 'naturally' desist from. As a starting point, it is worth noting that the average age of the women interviewed was 39 at the time of first interview and the vast majority of these women were convicted of a crime in the two-year period prior to interview. The average age of last offence was therefore approximately 37. Whilst sampling issues for this study are explored in the methodology (see Appendix), it can nonetheless be immediately surmised that for the women involved in this study, offending was not a behaviour limited to adolescence. Certainly, for these women, age was not the most powerful predictor of the end of offending (Gove 1985). It may reasonably be suggested therefore that these women form part of Terrie Moffitt's (1993) 'life-course persistent' offending group. Yet, as will be seen, the women in this study highlight a variety of offending trajectories. For example,

Ú. Barr, *Desisting Sisters*, Critical Criminological Perspectives,
https://doi.org/10.1007/978-3-030-14276-6_3

I interviewed women who had only ever committed one offence, women who confined their offending to later in life and there is some qualitative support nonetheless in some of the women's narratives for the power of ageing and the passage of time.

Support for the Ontogenetic Theory

Some of the women interviewed followed a 'typical' offending trajectory of offending during their late teens and early twenties followed by a decline into adulthood. In particular, the narratives of Holly, Anna and Grace who were 23, 36 and 31 respectively at the time of interview reflected this pattern. For Holly, what she saw as 'deviant' behaviours began in high school:

Una: And what were you like when you were at school?
Holly: I got kicked out in year 10
Una: What happened?
Holly: I got excluded for fighting with some girls, me and my best friend. So we both got excluded at the same time
Una: And did you go back after that?
Holly: No we got kicked out permanently; I didn't go to another school after that
Una: What were your first experiences of offending?
Holly: Skiving
Una: When did that start?
Holly: Year 9
Una: And why was that?
Holly: It were 'cause everyone else were doing it so I followed into their footsteps. And most of my friends from where I live had been excluded so I think it were just the normal thing. (Holly, Age 23)

Holly noted that, at the time, being excluded was not something she worried about; indeed she noted that she felt '[h]appy at the time 'cause all my friends were excluded … but I regret it now'. From here there was a period where Holly remembers being regularly cautioned by the police for 'just bits and bats, and stuff like criminal damage and drunk and disorderly, just little bits like that'. Holly related offending during this time to her friends and the area in which she lived, where the behaviour was routine and normalised. However, whilst for Holly's best friend Ciara, becoming a mother signalled a turning point, Holly carried on offending once her friend had desisted and when she became a mother to her own four-year-old daughter:

> She got pregnant and that, settled down and stuff, she stopped doing everything and I still carried on. (Holly, age 23)

During the interview, however, Holly had expressed a desire to stop offending and 'settle down' herself. This process began with giving up smoking weed when her partner, Nick, was released from prison:

> 'Cause like everyone around me were, my cousins and my friends and that. Everyone were smoking it so I was just doing what everyone else around me were doing. But then he'd stopped when he were inside, so I stopped smoking 'cause he weren't and we were on two different levels, so I've cut everything out now. I just smoke tobacco. (Holly, age 23)

Whilst stopping smoking weed, just like becoming a mother, did not automatically lead to stopping shoplifting for Holly, she moved in with Nick. They hoped to regain custody of their daughter from Holly's grandmother and looked forward to a 'stable' future. At the time of interview, Holly had not shoplifted nor otherwise offended for 'five or six months'. Holly noted that amongst her peers, 'everyone is growing up a bit now.' In particular, Holly makes reference to her older brother who had followed a very maturational (Gottfredson and Hirschi 1990) desistance pathway with elements of the social bonds thesis (Sampson and Laub 1993) clearly evident in Holly's retelling:

> He were getting into crime at one point. He got sent down... he got sent down for like three and a half year... it was like for fighting and stuff, he were always lashing out at people. And then he met a really nice girl, and she works at the chemist round there near Rivertown, and he's got a job now.

> He works doing boiler installations and he's got a kid on the way so it's right good. She's only seven weeks [pregnant] so they're right happy. He's settled down now. He hasn't been in trouble for a few year now. (Holly, age 23)

Bringing together social bonds theory with Gottfredson and Hirschi's theory of developmental self-control, Laub and Sampson (2001) argued that, 'traits like self-control can change over time as a consequence of changes in the quality or strength of social ties' (p. 7). Holly's brother certainly appears to follow this trajectory in Holly's subjective narrative. As a woman with a history of domestic abuse, mental health issues and self-harm, as well as being a mother, Holly's own desistance journey was situated in structures which would require more support. Her desistance would not only involve looking to the future but also recovering from past victimisations (these themes will be developed in the following chapters.) Yet it is clear that for Holly 'growing up' naturally involved a move away from offending. Just as the beginnings of offending were a natural process for Holly, once her peers began offending, attempts towards desistance were now also normalised as part of the process of 'growing up'.

For Anna, offending also began at an early age. Spurred on by the encouragement of her older brother and sister and what she saw as the naivety of her parents, Anna misbehaved in school, taking drugs and alcohol:

> Anna: I were really good, really really goody two shoes until about 11, 12… And then I remember going to high school, and starting to be a bitch. And learning the ways, as you do, to manipulate the system, and all that. Yeah, and come second year at high school I'd become a real pain in the bum; I was taking trips, I was smoking, drinking. I always got home on time 'cause my dad, he were pretty ruthless with them rules. He seemed to think everybody dropped their knickers after the age of 10 (laughs). Honest! So yeah, we still followed the rules and managed to get away with it because my mum and dad didn't drink or know about drugs so it was quite a while before they knew about it. So, yeah… the teachers went mad because I could have done really well, I had the brains. I just didn't want to do it. I was working nights part time during my exams and to be honest with you, my dad went to

prison around the time of my exams, so it kind of like blew me into a world of criminality, to be honest with you, because he'd went down for guns. They'd made him out to be some big gangster as well, the papers. Aw yeah, it spiralled, my life, out of control 'cause then you get all the naughty ones coming forward then it's like, 'oh guns!' It's like a big thing.

Una: So that …

Anna: … attracted the wrong kind of people, yeah. And obviously I was at an age where I was attracted to the wrong kind of people. So yeah, life were rough. (Anna, age 36)

For Anna, early offending was amplified by her father's criminal background related to gun ownership and production which in turn attracted 'the wrong kind' of peers. Anna's offending continued into her late teens and mid-twenties:

> If you'd have caught me ten years ago, I would have deserved everything. I were a proper bitch; drugs, fraud, insurance fraud. I used to do all the insurance documents in court when they got caught, I used to write them up, but it were the family that got me doing it. Then my daughter's dad, he was a severe alcoholic, so they were all stealing from shops blatantly, fighting, robbing flats. Not me personally, I was always outside going, 'what the fuck are you doing?' (Laughs). But yeah… I've partied most of my life to be honest with you. At 22 I had my first kid, Stacey, and when I finished with her dad … I finished with an alky and started drinking. So I had a few years where I was pretty… a mess to be honest with you. And then, I pulled back out of it and realised, right, 'You can't do this shit, you've got a kid.' So I sorted myself out, and like did the perfect mum shit. (Anna, age 36)

The role of a mother provided the 'alternative pro-social identity' (Rumgay 2004: 405) required to desist in Anna's later years. Whilst certainly the role of mother provided the social bonds (Laub and Sampson 2003) and the identity change (Maruna 2001) required to desist, desistance was also related to ageing and the passage of time.

For Grace, typical youth deviance also began in secondary school:

Una: And… what were you like at school? You said you were quiet?
Grace: Yeah, as I say I was very good, I liked going to school, the teachers liked me, I was always you know, top marks for everything… Got to high school, and it just went downhill from there basically. I think, I just, you know, got in with the wrong people and you know, other circumstances along the way. I started smoking weed quite young, I was 12, maybe 13, em … drinking at weekends, to the point of passing out, you know having to be carried home and that… Basically just buying cannabis, I have no other offences other than that one [growing cannabis] … Apart from when I was 16 I was caught shoplifting. (Grace, age 31)

Whilst Anna and Grace (both single mothers) felt that they had moved towards more conventional non-offending since the days of their youth, both were charged with offences in the years and months prior to my interview with them. Anna remained in the same area where she had grown up and remained close to family and friends from her younger years who were involved in criminal behaviour. It was these relational ties which provided the context for Anna's most recent joint-enterprise burglary offence. This was therefore something unexpected for her, out of the ordinary from her pro-social identity:

> Witnesses will say what I say, even the guy… there was a lad in the house, a 19 year old, but we didn't know, he said I didn't move out the car, I didn't do nothing. So I'm like, 'well why have I got charged?' (Anna, age 36)

For Anna, therefore, this offence was associated with bad luck and did not reflect a deviation from her pro-social identity.[1] Contrastingly, for Grace, she viewed her most recent offence as a product of choice and indeed careful consideration, yet this also did not indicate a move away from her pro-social identity which was also grounded in motherhood. When viewed through the lenses of capitalism, Grace's choice can be seen as entrepreneurial. When patriarchy is considered, however, the element of 'choice' can be troubled:

> I was growing cannabis, um… I will say it was the wrong thing but for all the right reasons. There was reasons why I did it. I had a young daughter

> and the house, the house that I'm still in, it's, you know in winter, it's very cold, it's draughty, and somebody offered. I didn't go out looking for it, somebody offered... If I were to set up some plants, you know, whatever they made of it, they would give me half, and, you know it's like two and a half grand, it's a lot of money when you haven't got and I were thinking about it and I basically worked out I could do it twice a year, all I had to do was water them, that's all I have to do with them. And then, April, round about my daughter's birthday, I would get a big lump sum then, and then like in the winter, just before Christmas, I'd get another lump, so it was sorta like it would see me through Christmas, make sure I could buy presents, make sure I could keep the house warm, because it was very cold. That was it basically. (Grace, age 31)

For Holly, Anna and Grace the 'natural process' of growing up did occasionally mean deviations into offending. Importantly, this did not always mean deviations from the pro-social identity which they had been individually cultivating as they matured. Matza's (1964) theory of 'drift' has salience here with the sporadic nature of offending seen in these women's narratives which appear chaotic at times. As Carlsson noted, '"drifts" or "lulls" in offending are likely to occur due to the nature of the social world, full as it is with its complexity, coincidences and contingencies' (2012: 915). The structural conditions of neoliberal patriarchy are clearly evident in these routes into offending.

For these three women, offending in earlier years was associated with a carefree attitude and a normalised behaviour related to what 'everyone else' was doing. Offending in youth also tended to involve drugs or alcohol. Whilst a relational experience in youth, drug use tended to be an isolating experience in older age for the women. We can note the links here to cultural criminology, for example, Jack Katz's 1988 work on emotions and crime where offending is related to a buzz, where at the time there are no regrets and offending is exciting. In later years however this type of offending lost its appeal for the women and they began to consider alternative 'settled' lifestyles much like the desisting young people in Barry's (2006) study.

As these examples show, offending was not solely a process which Holly, Anna and Grace inevitably 'grew out of'. Social reaction theory

(Becker 1963) can explain the onset of offending, particularly for Holly and Anna. Overall, offending was generally a transitory phenomenon (Jamieson et al. 1999) for the three women. Yet desistance was not a process which happened (or was happening) 'naturally'. Desistance, on the contrary, required both the 'will and the ways' to stop. For Anna, this was an ongoing process which meant moving out of the area where she grew up, severing ties with friends and family. For Holly, desistance meant 'settling down' with her partner and regaining custody of their daughter. Grace's desistance narrative meanwhile focused on her relationship with her best friend and gaining education and employment. Whilst self-control gained through the ageing process had a role here, it was not the sole desistance-promoting factor. The structural constraints felt by the women were key to both offending and non-offending.

Late-Onset Offending

The beginnings of offending occurred at different points for the women studied. Whilst Marie's quote introduces us to this chapter, it must be noted that Marie was 40 at the time of our interview, certainly out of the peak of the age-crime curve found within traditional criminology. Marie herself recognised that her offending trajectory was the opposite to what a researcher might usually expect:

> Una: We're going to talk about your background, community, family and school and so on. So what were you like as a child?
> Marie: Um… Better behaved than I am now (laughs). I were basically, I were quite a good child really…
> Una: And do you remember what you were like at school?
> Maire: I were a bit of a bugger but I weren't really bad. I wasn't as bad then as I was now, I seem to have gotten worse as I've got older. (Marie, age 40)

Although Marie mentioned a shoplifting incident when she was 10 or 11, she described the incident as a one-off and a 'giggle thing', not something she was regularly involved with. Marie spoke in great detail about her background and employment history to highlight that the change in her behaviour did not actually mean a change in her identity as an essentially good and caring person:

> I mean I were a nurse, I were in St John Ambulance when I were a kid. Ten year I used to teach first aid, I've got a qualification, A B.Tech national diploma in science, I've got all qualifications in things. And then I got pregnant. I had Jo, I couldn't go back to nursing. And I'll tell you how I started offending. I lived on a building site, this building site and they were building round me. And this lad said to me, 'oh that's that Kingspan there' you know, insulation? It were like insulation for like walls. He said, 'if you get me some of that I'll give you like fifteen quid a pack.' So I started half inching it didn't I? Right. So I were making a fortune off it (laughs). And I started going all over, started going on other work sites and that. Anyway, I didn't really get caught doing any of that. And then I started hiring tools, it just got… it grew should I say. It's just… not greed, I'm not a greedy person. I've had money and then lost it. And that's even… I think it's worse than going from not having money to not having *any* money (laughs). But I used to have money… I used to make £1000 a week cash and that were legit money, I had my own pub and hotel so… But I went from that, then everything went tits up, and then I just started basically doing it 'cause I were skint… It's been like possibly, over the last ten years really that I've been in bother … I'm not a naughty, naughty girl, I wouldn't go and burgle someone or owt like that, I've got an heart do you know what I mean? One of them, it's [that] I'm stubborn and I'd rather go out and dig some flags up from an old farm that's disused than ask me mum for money, do you know what I mean? And this is why my mum gets upset. I feel like I should work for my family, if I can't put food on the table there's something wrong. So I go out to an old farm, but I usually get caught on the way back, put in the slammer for a flag! (Marie, age 40)

Marie is quick to note that she is not a 'greedy person' or a 'naughty girl' but that offending in later life was related to both poverty and subsequent entrepreneurialism which came with her post-pregnancy unemployment. Marie's partner, Claire, claimed that Marie has 'ODD' or Oppositional Defiance Disorder, which explained Marie's late-onset offending. In my field notes, I noted that Marie was probably in the 'primary desistance' (Maruna and Farrall 2004) phase of her offending trajectory. As part of her sentence Marie was banned from driving and she was proud when relating that she has not driven 'yet', the 'yet' here suggestive of her possible actions in the future. She related stealing stone flags to a 'buzz' as well as a needed income stream, much like the early offending of Holly, Grace and Anna. Marie spoke about her offending in the present tense. Marie's trajectory did not follow a maturational course as desistance had not happened naturally nor without the influence of other factors (Glueck and Glueck 1950). Whilst Marie recognised she must 'grow up', without the will and the ways to do so, desistance had not been forthcoming.

Similarly, Rebecca noted that her offending had been confined to later life. Although Rebecca remembered being expelled from school, after a difficult childhood caring for her schizophrenic mother and dealing with her parent's divorce, she quickly turned her life around whilst in a privileged school in Europe which she was able to attend thanks to her grandfather's connections:

> I went into secondary school; while I did all my school work, I was an A+ student, I still became a bully, that's what I became, I became a bully. So I was quite manipulative … I knew exactly what … I still remember it now, so I'd get other girls… to actually, I'd primed them to deliver what I wanted to say so that I would not get in trouble … And then eventually that resulted in me being excluded, or, as it was called then, expelled from school … So as soon as I'd been expelled from school, I then was on a boat to Belgium and I was packed off to boarding school … And that was it; I went to boarding school … And they were all diplomats, very … you know quite wealthy children … I felt totally isolated for the first six months. But again the headmaster and the dormitory parent was the one who dragged me through basically. So it took me about 6 months and then from then on, in it was essentially the main kick up the bum … well I say that it put me on the right track until I was 42. So you know, and I did manage to get my head down. (Rebecca, age 46)

Rebecca lived a fairly privileged life, working for international companies and travelling the world with her husband and two young children. However, on the family's return to England, at the age of 32, Rebecca began to develop an alcohol dependency which essentially led to her offences:

> So while I still got up for work, what it was doing was draining my finances, it was affecting my marriage, it was clearly affecting my children, and it began to affect my life… it began to affect my work. You know, the tired, the not wanting to get up in the morning. So, and that was the decline then. So from being 33 up until I was 42 was the real decline with alcohol. And you know, my marriage broke down, my ex-husband then took the children, didn't bring them back, took them out of the country. I then went through probably as many courts as I could, hired solicitors, racked up huge legal fees, and ran away from it all. Moved to Austria, thought I'd go back to Europe, worked there, tried to get my life on track. But the booze was, you know, it had now got a complete grip of me. So rather than it being a total dependency, it was a mental dependency. So I just blew every penny I had, I was getting in a mess … And I then rang my father and sort of said, 'Come and help'… I was just in a total mess. So he said, 'Yeah.' Came back to Easton, so I was 42. Came back to Easton, sort of, you know, quite broken. Moved in with my father and my step-mother who I'd had quite a difficult history with. Found out, you know, so much more about my own mother who was living then on the streets in Easton. Then what happened was my own bills caught up with me, because they always do… I ended up committing credit card fraud in my step-mother's name. And she reported that to the police. I knew what I was doing; I knew it was wrong… I paid it off for a while so until my money ran out and then it all caught up with me. And you know I got found out, she reported me to the police and then obviously I went through the CJS. (Rebecca, age 46)

Following this conviction Rebecca signed a cheque for rent which bounced, and was once again convicted of fraud and eventually became homeless. Unlike Marie, however, Rebecca was certainly in the secondary desistance phase (Maruna and Farrall 2004). Her generative work and cognitive identity shifts have led to desistance, something which could clearly be seen with her work with her HfN Project:

> So I then went back to my mother's and began researching, saved up enough to get my deposit, and moved into my own house … I spent a while thinking. Well actually, looking around for other women who had written their own narratives, I couldn't really find very much. And I thought, 'Well there's a lot of men's stuff out there, there's not a lot of women's stuff.' So … and then it sort of grew, I never really expected it to

> grow like it did…And I thought… 'I've got to do something for women in the CJS. I am going to do something.' (Rebecca, age 46)

For both Marie and Rebecca, acquisitive offending was partly a product of the conditions they found themselves in in later life. Carr and Stovall Hanks (2012) found that women with late-onset offending shared characteristics including frequent mention of loss, caretaking (both social and economic) and addiction as turning points or periods that contributed to their involvement in crime. For Marie, caretaking, and for Rebecca, addiction and loss were also factors that contributed to the onset of offending. The authors also noted that social bonds (Sampson and Laub 1993; Laub and Sampson 2003) such as entering a new job or relationship were factors in the desistance of women who were criminalised in later life. The same can be said for Rebecca and Marie here. Desistance for both the women had not been something which happened naturally over time as they aged, but was linked to active and difficult processes requiring relational support as well as agency.

One-off Offending

A final trajectory was recognised in the narratives of the women who had experienced criminalisation for the first and only time, and can be seen in the narratives of Heather and Katie who both were charged with benefit fraud offences. Both of these women had little to no contact with the Criminal Justice System (CJS) prior to their fraud offences. Offending here was not a behaviour but a one-off action[2]:

> It [the police and courts] were all new (Heather, age 24)

> I had quite a sheltered life really and didn't go out much. Mum and dad were quite strict, very strict. So I didn't go out much… here [in school] was some people that did offend. And there was lots of stealing going on from cloakroom pockets and things, because you used to leave your bags and coats in the cloakroom. So there were things like that but, no I didn't, I kept away, I kept away from people like that, otherwise my parents wouldn't

have liked it. If they didn't like somebody I couldn't speak to them so... (Katie, age 60)

Particularly for Katie, the entry into the CJS was something which was wholly unexpected and out of the ordinary. She did not see herself as an offender but maintained her pro-social identity which was connected to her childhood and proud working-class upbringing:

> If somebody had have sent me a letter, I wouldn't have ignored it, I've never been like that. I've always been brought up to, you know, know right from wrong. My father, he would never claim benefit or anything. My mother wouldn't, they didn't believe in it you know, so I weren't brought up that way. (Katie, age 60)

Nonetheless both Katie and Heather had lives which are typical of women and girls entering the CJS. Both suffered from myriad mental health issues including self-harm and suicide attempts, Heather had a history of childhood abuse from her father and her alcoholic mother, whilst Katie had physical health problems and relationship problems with her husband and daughters. For both women, their problems were exacerbated and multiplied with their entry into the CJS. Minor offences by women are resulting in harsher responses across the western world (Sheehan et al. 2007; Barry and McIvor 2008; Prison Reform Trust 2017). Whilst neither Katie nor Heather can be considered persistent offenders, their lives share many of the conditions and disadvantages of criminalised women in general, and their desistance narratives are therefore important. Neither Katie nor Heather's desistance occurred as part of a natural process, but much like the other women previously mentioned, required both support and agency.

Women who may be viewed as 'one-off' offenders or even offenders without intent, cannot be eliminated from any consideration of desistance. Like the women who follow a traditional trajectory of offending, or those who come to offending in later life, 'one-off' and non-intentional offenders travel the same criminal justice pathway; they are arrested, put on trial, 'punished' or 'treated' accordingly. This pathway has an effect on their lives and identities. It is likely that, as Katie and Heather's experiences show, their lives have been blighted by gendered structural inequalities. Furthermore, they travel the same journeys of resilience and survival which often mirror their fellow 'offenders' desistance attempts.

Conclusion

Whilst many of the women studied decreased the concentration and level of their offending as they aged, others did not offend until later in life, and for yet others criminalisation was comparable to a blip in an otherwise law-abiding narrative which was nonetheless marred by disadvantage. Whilst the maturational theory, which considers offending to be a behaviour that (most) individuals will 'grow out of' does have some salience in the experiences of the criminalised women who were part of this study, it is far from the only factor in explaining their desistance pathways. Attempts to 'go straight' such as those noted by Grace, Anna and Holly were challenged when the structural inequalities they faced were insurmountable. For Marie, who was arguably most aware of the expectations placed on her to change, self-control had not been enough to prevent her from offending in later life. Neither was Rebecca prevented from offending by her maturity. For Katie and Heather, at either ends of the age spectrum of the women studied, maturity and self-control had nothing to do with their convictions. These were women criminalised because of the very inequalities which blighted their life experiences. The social circumstances in which they live their lives, faced as they are with abuse, mental health issues, poor relationships and poverty, are the common circumstances of women entering the CJS. Desistance for these women was not only therefore related to criminalisation but also resilience in the face of neoliberalism and heteropatriarchy.

The notion that desistance is a 'natural process' effectively silences the narratives of criminalised women. Although many of the women interviewed as part of this study appeared at first glance to follow the ontogenetic perspective that offending is something which individuals essentially 'grow out of', this viewpoint ignores the conditions in which the criminalisation and desistance journeys of women take place. To suggest that desistance is a natural process for women is to ignore the poverty, domestic abuse, drug and mental health issues that invade both their offending and desistance. The next chapter examines the social conditions which can encourage and stifle desistance and will examine the issues mentioned above, particularly in light of the social bonds theory of desistance.

Notes

1. Of course we may question Anna's 'vocabulary of motive' (Wright Mills 1940) speaking to myself as a researcher here or to justice practitioners in the past. Nonetheless her subjective interpretation is important despite 'techniques of neutralisation' (Matza and Sykes 1957) employed.
2. See Chap. 6 for more on Heather and Katie.

Bibliography

Barry, M. (2006). *Youth Offending in Transition: The Search for Social Recognition*. London: Routledge.

Barry, M., & McIvor, G. (2008). *Chaotic Lives: A Profile of Women Offenders in the CJS in Lothian and Borders*. Peebles: Lothian and Borders Justice Authority.

Becker, H. (1963). *Outsiders*. New York: Free Press.

Carlsson, C. (2012). Processes of Intermittency in Criminal Careers: Notes from a Swedish Study on Life Courses and Crime. *International Journal of Offender Therapy and Comparative Criminology, 57*(8), 913–938.

Carr, N. T., & Stovall Hanks, R. (2012). If "60 Is the New 40," Is 35 the New 15? Late Onset Crime and Delinquency. *Deviant Behaviour, 33*, 393–411.

Glueck, S., & Glueck, E. (1950). *Unravelling Juvenile Delinquency*. New York: Harvard University Press.

Gottfredson, M., & Hirschi, T. (1990). *A General Theory of Crime*. Stanford: Stanford University Press.

Gove, W. (1985). The Effect of Age and Gender on Deviant Behaviour: A Biopsychosocial Perspective. In A. Rossi (Ed.), *Gender and the Life Course*. New York: Aldine.

Jamieson, J., McIvor, G., & Murray, C. (1999). *Understanding Offending Amongst Young People*. Edinburgh: The Scottish Executive.

Katz, J. (1988). *Seductions of Crime: Moral and Sensual Attractions in Doing Evil.* New York: Basic Books.
Laub, J. H., & Sampson, R. J. (2001). Understanding Desistance from Crime. *Crime and Justice, 28*, 1–69.
Laub, J., & Sampson, R. (2003). *Shared Beginnings, Divergent Lives.* Harvard: Harvard University Press.
Maruna, S. (2001). *Making Good – How Ex-Convicts Reform and Rebuild Their Lives.* Washington, DC: American Psychological Association Books.
Maruna, S., & Farrall, S. (2004). Desistance from Crime: A Theoretical Reformulation. *Kölner Zeitschrift für Soziologie und Sozialpsychologie, 43*, 171–194.
Matza, D. (1964). *Delinquency and Drift.* New York: Wiley.
Matza, D., & Sykes, G. M. (1957). Techniques of Neutralization: A Theory of Delinquency. *American Sociological Review, 22*(6), 664–670.
Moffitt, T. (1993). Adolescent-Limited and Life-Course-Persistent Antisocial Behaviour: A Developmental Taxonomy. *Psychological Review, 100*, 674–701.
Prison Reform Trust. (2017). *Why Focus on Reducing Women's Imprisonment?* London: Prison Reform Trust.
Rumgay, J. (2004). Scripts for Safer Survival: Pathways Out of Female Crime. *The Howard Journal, 43*(4), 405–419.
Sampson, R. J., & Laub, J. H. (1993). *Crime in the Making: Pathways and Turning Points Through Life.* London: Harvard University Press.
Sheehan, R., McIvor, G., & Trotter, C. (2007). *What Works with Women Offenders.* Cullomtpon: Willan.
Wright Mills, C. (1940). Situated Actions and Vocabularies of Motive. *American Sociological Review, V*, 904–913.

4

'A Good Job and the Love of a Good Woman': A Feminist Critique of Social Bonds Theory

> *If we are to rehabilitate female offenders, we must take proper account of the* realities of their lives *and ensure that resources are best targeted to help more women turn their lives around.*
> —*The* Rt Hon. Chris Grayling *MP, Former Secretary of State for Justice, 2014 (emphasis added)*

The previous chapter considered the possibility that desistance may be a natural process which relates to ageing and the passing of time. For many years, criminology considered this the key theoretical underpinning of the process of ending offending behaviour. However, as has been seen, this is problematic. Not only does the maturational theory inadequately explain the various offending trajectories of criminalised individuals, and particularly those of criminalised women who may be described as 'late onset' or minimal transgressors of the law, the theory also neglects to explain the social/structural processes and events which may coincide with change or stagnancy in offending behaviour or actions.

It is to these social/structural influences that this chapter turns. The events and processes which have influenced (whether positively or not) the desistance journeys of the women who were part of this research will

Ú. Barr, *Desisting Sisters*, Critical Criminological Perspectives,
https://doi.org/10.1007/978-3-030-14276-6_4

be considered. The 'social bonds' which connect criminalised women to society will be examined. Throughout, the chapter will compare findings with what has been found to be useful in the (overwhelmingly male) desistance experiences considered by the desistance literature.

Adult Social Bonds

The 'respectability package' (Giordano et al. 2002: 1052) which Sampson and Laub (1993) and Laub and Sampson (2003) have argued can produce a positive change in offending behaviour for desisting men, is largely based around finding employment and entering marriage or a stable relationship. According to the sociogenic thesis, changes in adult life circumstances such as these can have a direct effect on the ability of an individual to (a) 'knife off' the past, (b) invest in new relationships that foster support and growth, (c) be under direct, informal control or supervision, (d) engage in routine, conventional life activities and/or (e) perform an identity transformation (adapted from Carlsson 2011). Other social bonds or institutions which proponents of the sociogenic thesis have found to be positively related to changes in offending for both men and women include becoming a parent (Katz 2000; McIvor et al. 2011), joining the army, moving away from home (Sampson and Laub 1993; Laub and Sampson 2003), finding religion (Giordano et al. 2008), changing groups of friends or developing friendships (Weaver and McNeill 2014) and gaining stable accommodation (Farrall 2002). Jamieson et al. (1999) found that the 'respectability package' gained by these 'turning points' was more important for women than men. Whether this caveat can be said to be true for the women involved in this study will be explored in this chapter. The effect of social bonds such as meaningful employment or education and a stable, romantic relationship will be examined alongside changes such as becoming a mother, the effect of friendship groups, moving from a specific area and stable accommodation, which, in particular, emerged in the women's narratives as the most significant influencers in the desistance process.

It is imperative to note the social and structural contexts in which both offending and desistance occur if we are to promote change in women's offending. The '*Transforming Lives*' 2014 Report produced by Soroptimist

International and the Prison Reform Trust noted that for women in prison in England, 53% report having experienced emotional, physical or sexual abuse as a child, and 46% of women in prison have attempted suicide at some point in their lifetime. In 2013 women represented 26% of all incidents of self-harm in prison despite accounting for less than 5% of the total prison population; 52% of women in prison self-reported that they had used heroin, crack or cocaine in the four weeks prior to custody. Around one-third of women prisoners lose their homes, and often their possessions, whilst in prison. In 2011–2012 just 8% of women leaving prison had a positive employment outcome. For men the proportion was 27%. In 2016, the number of women who took their lives in prison reached an unprecedented high (INQUEST 2018). The findings from this study, although small scale and qualitative in comparison, paint a similar picture, not only of women who had spent time in prison, but of women serving community sentences. Of the 16 criminalised women interviewed as part of this study, 8 freely told stories of domestic abuse or childhood abuse without being asked a direct question about this,[1] all discussed mental health issues ranging from anxiety and depression to self-harm and suicide attempts, 13 related offences to issues surrounding drugs and alcohol, 1 was homeless whilst 4 were living in temporary accommodation and 13 out of 16 were unemployed at the time of interview. Neither offending nor desistance occur in a vacuum. When considering social bonds theory as a lens through which to view women's desistance, it is crucial to consider the social circumstances and patriarchal and neoliberal environments through which women attempt desistance.

Employment

Contexts of Employment

The first 'social bond' which emerged from the observation and interview research as important was employment. Although women suffer generally from what has been termed the feminisation of poverty (Carlen 1988) and are more likely to be part-time, temporary or voluntary workers or full-time carers,[2] the women in this study came from a variety of employment backgrounds. Eight of the 16 criminalised Northshire women interviewed had never been employed in the conventional sense, indicating that material deprivation of women is a contemporary experience, particularly amongst criminalised women. As noted above, at the time of the first interview, 13 of the 16 women were unemployed,[3] 2 were employed and 1 worked full time in a voluntary capacity. Other than the two women who were unable to work for health reasons, all the remaining unemployed women expressed a desire to gain a paid or voluntary job and/or additional training or education. The employment histories of the women were varied. For example, Julie, the daughter of a policeman, worked in the legal profession all her life until her most recent offence. Grace was a former labourer, working as a roofer until she became pregnant. Sue was a travel agent before the death of her father resulted in a move to voluntary work. And Rebecca worked in the private sector in London before losing contact with her children in a divorce settlement and developing an alcohol problem which led to her leaving the UK. Many of the women had exited employment recently. To understand employment as an element in the desistance process, it is important to consider the historical relationship with employment in the women's narratives. Many of the women who had not worked or had given up work or education did so for mental health reasons. For example, Heather's mental health formed the context of her ending her voluntary employment:

Heather: I'm not employed. I did do voluntary work before I got ill. I went … I'd say about 3 years ago, before things just went out of control

Una: When you say things went out of control what do you mean?

Heather: I started self-harming. I had OCD really bad, I was frightened to go out of the house and frightened for my partner to go out of the house. This is before I got any help so it were just terrible. I didn't know what was going wrong. I didn't know what was wrong with me either until someone said to me, 'You need to see the doctor.' And I did and I got the help I needed. (Heather, age 24)

Anna ended her job working in a fast food van to become her mother's carer when her mother became sick. When her mother died, the grief that

Anna experienced resulted in her not returning to employment. Ruth was working as a bartender and cleaner when she became homeless and gave up the work as a result of the strain it was having on her mental health:

> Ruth: I'm currently not working; I'm currently on the sick. I was working 55 hours up until the end of February this year. I just ... they couldn't help me find anywhere. I was going to work, leaving, and having nowhere to go. I carried it on as long as I could and they still wouldn't help me. So I eventually, 12 week ago, went on the sick.
> Una: And where were you working before?
> Ruth: Well I've got my bar licence so I've done bar work. I was cleaning in a school 40 hours a week and then working on the bar 15 hours as well. And then coming out with nowhere to live ... I couldn't physically do it anymore, I was just so tired. (Ruth, age 31)

This relationship between mental health and employment is particularly poignant considering the current political landscape in the UK where full-time, paid employment is considered the desired position, certainly by the main political parties. Whilst there is a tendency to link unemployment with the continuation of offending (Warr 2002), a 2006 government directed meta-analysis by Waddell and Burton nonetheless found that for a minority of people unemployment could be related to improved health and wellbeing including mental health. Certainly the historic and ongoing relationship with employment and mental health for criminalised women is something which is analytically absent from desistance research.

It was perhaps unsurprising that the women expressed a desire not just to enter into employment, but to enter into employment that was meaningful to them. For example, Kate, one of the group members in the Southton centre, when asked about her future employment hopes by Jenny, the group leader, noted:

> I've done care,[4] I've done pub work and retail. I quite liked retail. My friend does that mad scientist thing, you know where you go into schools and do science experiments with the kids. I'd love to do something like that, something that gets me thinking. (Kate, Tulip Centre)

It was often the woman's most recent offence and subsequent sentencing which caused her to express a desire for meaningful employment. When asked about how her sentence has affected her life, Julie, a former town council clerk, replied:

> I would like to try and make sure I can do something useful, purposeful, whether it's paid or unpaid. (Julie, age 60, second interview)

The importance of employment's desistance-promoting factors was clear to many of the women. Yet for Kelly-Marie, the failure of past desistance attempts was linked to the superficial qualities of former job roles which she saw as playing a role in her return to prison:

> So I've gone to jail and I thought, 'Right, better sort me shit out now.' And I've got there, I've got meself clean, I got meself into education. I've come out after two and a half years a qualified beautician and hair stylist. I was interlinked with recovering addicts, I was a recovery mentor. I got meself a full time job wi' Timpson's.[5] But I took meself off all me medication. And I thought I were fine. I thought I'd got it made now, everything's fine. Anyhow, I've got home and everything were fine for about 3 weeks. I started to think, 'I don't want to be out here; I can't cope out here. I'm not ready to be out here.' … I didn't want this job at Timpson's, I didn't get this hair and beauty [qualification] to go and cut keys at Timpson's. And I'd stopped taking me mental health medication. I'd took meself off me methadone. And within 7 months of being home, I'd started using… But I felt I wanted to go back to prison and I needed to go back to prison. So I went out and I were reoffending and I didn't go to appointments so I got a 28-day recall. (Kelly-Marie, age 48)

Clearly for the women in this study, employment on its own could not produce meaningful change. Whilst a source of income may provide temporary relief from acquisitive offences, employment needed to have a meaningful position in their lives other than to make money. Whether through providing mental enrichment, or being something that the women enjoy and are good at, employment needed to be significant to women's lives to be desistance-enabling. This finding is not without backing in the wider desistance literature (Laub and Sampson 2003; Aresti et al. 2010).

Again, similar to the literature, an element which emerged as significant time and again in the women's narratives was the potential for generative employment to encourage desistance (Maruna 2001). For Kelly-Marie, for example, practising hair and beauty would not be enough to sustain change. She stated that when the time was right for her to go back to employment, the generative route was the most desirable:

> I would probably use it with a project; a project within a project, yeah? To give other women self-worth and to let them know that you can do something with yourself and there is hope. (Kelly-Marie, age 48)

Kelly-Marie was very focused on her own desistance journey, she showed agency over this course. It is what she learned along this journey that she wanted to share with other women through her work. It was evident throughout Kelly-Marie's narrative that she had been influenced not only by the change in her practical circumstances provided by her situation within the HfN Project, but also by Rebecca's influence. Rebecca's desistance pathway included the most obvious generative employment change. Rebecca moved from working in a commercial, international business to developing a grassroots level, community organisation designed to offer support to women in need. It is clear that this generative (Maruna 2001) and meaningful move helped to sustain Rebecca's desistance:

> I wrote an article on the mental health of female prisoners. And yeah that's where I ... I spent a while thinking ... And I thought, 'Well there's a lot of men's stuff out there, there's not a lot of women's stuff.' ... And then it sort of grew, I never really expected it to grow like it did. So then it started growing and growing and growing... And then other publications started saying, 'Will you do this? Will you do that?' And I thought, 'Well I could do my research... I've got to do something for women in the CJS. I am going to do something.' So I started thinking, 'Well I'm going to set up, I don't know, a women's refuge for women from prison?' I looked at the different housing models, I studied it up. I studied a lot, a lot, a lot... And that's when I approached a construction company... and I sent them a couple of emails and I said, 'Do you know what? I know you've got some properties in Easton, would you be willing to work with me on the

> Northshire Housing Project' … So they were like, 'OK' and I met with them and they gave me four houses to work with, and that's how it started. (Rebecca, age 46)

However, many of the other women also spoke, unprompted, about generative desires, sometimes following on from a community service placement which they enjoyed, but also in a desire to share their experiences and life lessons in various ways:

> The lady who I'm counselling with said, 'Why don't you get some voluntary … look at a charity shop or something?' And I thought, 'Right, yeah.'… So I went in and I just said, 'Do you need any volunteers?' And they just took my name and number and rang me out of the blue. And so it's been really good. (Katie, age 60, second interview)

> There's a voluntary service I go to once a week… and there's like a charity that I go to there. Now they're saying that if I work with them I can basically start doing voluntary work there. (Karen, age 36)

> I want to qualify as a drugs counsellor, an alcohol counsellor, I want to do that. I want to do the mental health side of things as well. So hopefully I want to be running drug awareness groups and helping other people. (Paula, age 36)

This generative desire was also reflected in the staff narratives of those who worked both at the Women's Centres (WCs) and the Housing for Northshire (HfN) Project and was related often to staff members' narratives of victimisation and survival which were common to all the women. (Further links between staff and service user narratives will be explored in Chap. 6.) The moral element provided by these roles offered the women the chance to 'belong' to their respective communities (Aresti et al. 2010). This generative desire nonetheless was not only related to the position of these women as ex-offenders with a desire to 'make amends' by 'giving back' to their communities, but also as women with stories to tell, experiences to share and lessons to be taught about drug and alcohol addiction, domestic abuse and violence as well as mental health issues or the loss of loved ones.

Another clear theme to emerge from the narratives of generativity was that this generativity did not solely exist within the confines of employment, whether paid or voluntary. From Karen's role as a carer for her sick friend in prison, to Shelly adopting a mother role to her partner's son, to Anna's offering of advice and support to friends and neighbours, generativity was a common theme within the vast majority of the women's narratives:

> If anything it's just an experience isn't it? And I suppose one day I'd like to put it back into others because I know exactly what I'm dealing with in a lot of situations, way too many. The knowledge is there. That's what I do, basically, when I go up there, [to her friend's estate] I've got lines of people waiting to ask me questions, 'What would you do if this happened? How would you get the kid back?'... I don't know, I just seem to pick things up, bullshit things from the social and things like that. And they all need advice. But I've tried to stop doing it all and helping people 'cause they end up relying on me and then I'm like, I'm stuck with someone again. And if they go down the wrong path, it makes me look like I've done it meself. And I don't want that, I don't want the kids to be like on to the social. (Anna, age 36)

As Anna noted, the desire to be generative is not without complications. In order to be desistance-promoting, work must first and foremost be meaningful to the women. Generative desires were also recognised as occurring outside the confines of employment. Generative opportunities can be promoted as part of community provision where they are welcomed by individuals.

Educating Northshire

Almost as prominent in the women's narratives was the desire for further education and skills training to support their desistance journeys. Many of the women had negative educational experiences as young people, either being removed from school for various reasons, being bullied or 'acting up' in class. This finding mirrors the research of Gillian Richards (2018) who found that working-class girls are not valued nor supported in schools. In addition, gendered expectations around motherhood and local employment affected their sense of choice. In the current research, there was a prominent sense amongst many of the women of not having achieved their full potential, something they wanted to correct. Education was also seen as a stepping stone towards employment and the 'respectability package' which it can provide:

> I didn't really get educated to be honest with you. I came out with Cs, Ds and Es and all the teachers were waiting for me at the gate, telling me how disappointed they all are. I remember saying the same thing as everybody else, 'like I care.' It were only then about ten years later, 'oh you fucking bastards, I'm not going back to tell you: you were right.' But I can admit my faults; I can admit anything like that. (Anna, age 36)

> I've had no work ever so I'm starting a college course in January with what's her name downstairs? [in the Women's Centre], Claire I think she is. (Holly, age 23)

For Grace, despite having the desire to better her prospects through education, this was not straightforward nor without difficulty, including financial difficulty. We can see here the harmful nature of neoliberal education structures:

> I'm hoping to go to college but I'm struggling with finding funding because the only thing I could claim if I was going to college would be jobseekers allowance, but I wouldn't be actively seeking work because I would be at college. So I'm trying to find a part time course which I have to pay for… I've just found out there is actually funding for it, you can get a loan. I've only recently heard this, the other day from Easton College. And I don't know how much it's for, I've not looked into it but apparently it would cover the courses I want to do but I'm not sure about living expenses. I don't know how much the loan would be for but… If it's only funding for the courses I'm going to have to do part time because I'm still going to have to be actively seeking work part time as well… But if this funding does cover costs, no matter how long the course lasts I will hopefully do it full time, get it done. Because I've no GCSEs and I know I am very clever, you know I was predicted straight As at the end of primary school but left at the end of year 9. (Grace, age 31)

The above quotes from Anna, Grace and Holly further highlight the increasing importance of education and employment with age as noted by Uggen (2000). The desire for further education is conspicuous amongst criminalised women, particularly if they have had a negative relationship with it in the past. If the aspiration of state agencies includes supporting desistance, investment in education and training at all stages so that women and girls are supported must be a priority.

The Paradox of Volunteering

For the majority of women interviewed and indeed observed, the offences for which they were convicted could be considered acquisitive. Paradoxically, many of the women had been encouraged to become involved in volunteering work since their sentencing. During the Conservative/Liberal-Democrat coalition government which was in power when the interviews took place, the 'Big Society' rhetoric of voluntarism as linked to social solidarity was pervasive. On the other end of the scale, so too was the idea of working for free as encouraged by the government's 'Help to Work' programme. The benefits of volunteering for mental health, increasing the individual's pro-social networks and helping the individual to overcome any gaps in their CV are well known in the literature (Edgar et al. 2011) and were advocated by both the WCs and HfN Projects. Additionally, volunteering can provide the 'restoration to society' element which can be part of identity change (Maruna 2001: 8). Indeed many of the women extolled the virtues of volunteering from their own personal experience:

> And mentally I'm not bad, I'm not bad at all mentally … I help out at a charity shop when I'm needed, I'm going to have been there for like 9 weeks now … So I just do Saturday to help out and that gets me out meeting people again, I'm not as nervous going out and contacting people. And everybody's lovely down there, they're really helpful. Nobody knows about … what's happened [Katie's convictions]. If they happened to say, mention it, I'd tell them, I wouldn't be frightened of telling them. But nobody's asked and you know so … I've thought, 'Well you know if they ask, I will tell them, but otherwise you know it's alright.' They're all lovely, I think I'm

> the youngest there they're all like a lot older than me, retired, but it's nice. (Katie, age 60, second interview)

Nonetheless, volunteering, by its definition, does not provide the economic benefits of paid employment. Sue, for example, noted her own 'luck' in inheriting from her father, creating the conditions for her volunteering which has provided not only mental health benefits but enabled her to attend the courses and training which have been part of her desistance journey (it must also be noted that Sue was one of only two women involved in the project [observed or interviewed] who had never been convicted of an acquisitive offence). Julie meanwhile lamented the lack of paid opportunities for women in the CJS:

> I basically inherited quite well. I mean obviously it would be difficult to get a job now because of my criminal record. But I'm quite happy doing the volunteer work. Ok, I'm 40 and I've still got time, but I don't … It just works for me. I've got the flexibility because I'm doing these courses[6] and I need to be doing the courses because a lot of them are during the day. I don't want to start working for somebody and then say 'Oh can I have time off?' that kind of thing. (Sue, age 40)

> I've volunteered to do whatever might be appropriate, just to give me something to do because it would be nice to be able to earn something, it really would. But for the time being to get into things again, I'm happy to do voluntary work. So I'm hoping that some of those, I keep putting the feelers out here and there and I'm hoping that somewhere along the line, something will come. (Julie, age 60)

It appears that women with convictions are often encouraged into hyper-moral roles (Matthews et al. 2014), perhaps as both an individual and societal reaction to their supposed 'double deviance'. In doing so, these women become 'the ideal neoliberal agent' (Mirowwski cited in Sim 2018/Cederstrom and Spicer 2015: 104). Additionally, there is a concern that promoting volunteering specifically for women will reinforce gender specific roles, further entrenching the feminisation of poverty (Carlen 1988) and limiting the pro-social scripts (Rumgay 2004) available to criminalised women attempting desistance.

Employment, Education and the Justice System

Both the WCs and the HfN Project offered opportunities for women to enrol on training courses, education courses, employability workshops and volunteering. Many of the women, including Grace and Karen, who were sentenced to unpaid work also kept this work up when their sentences finished. A particularly positive example of the work done by criminal justice agencies to encourage women to enter employment was noted in the 'Succeed' course run by the WC, parallel to their group work specified activity courses, to encourage criminalised women and others to improve their CV, apply for vacancies, provide interview tips and help with money for interview outfits, and so on. During my observational research I witnessed first-hand the effect of this course when one of the Weston-based women, Fiona, gained employment whilst enrolled on the course. Paula also enrolled on the course and noted that she found the course helpful and useful in providing information about how to achieve her goal of becoming a drugs and alcohol counsellor. Heather also noted how the WC had been useful in providing her with help to get back into education, whilst Shelly, Michaela and Kelly-Marie all made reference to the encouragement of employment within the HfN Project.

However, the links between criminal justice agencies and employment were not always positive. When asked about the effects of their sentences on their lives, the interviewees almost unanimously noted that their sentence would negatively affect their employment prospects, even if this was something they did not experience first-hand:

> I still don't know why I pleaded guilty.[7] Looking back now, I wouldn't have done, because like I can't go out and get another job with a criminal record. It's not as bad as if I've been given a suspended sentence or anything but I don't know how long it's there for. I got a sheet from the women's centre that said because it was only supervision that I can write it off. But I've heard it's up to seven years, so I don't know. (Katie, age 60, first interview)

A WC staff member based in Easton, Claudia, also had clear opinions on offences remaining on women's employment records as a result of her own experiences:

> I'll tell you this. When I lived in Germany, I was 18 and my friends were 17 coming up to 18, they shoplifted, I didn't even take anything. But I was convicted because I was the 18-year-old and I found out that came up on my record when I applied for a job [at the WC] … My opinion is there are offences that should stay on people's records like sex offences, but all the rest of this silly rubbish needs to be deleted. (Claudia, group leader, Easton Women's Centre)

Even where the women had not directly experienced the negative employment effects of a criminal record, it was clear that their records restricted their employment goals. In Marie's case, receiving a driving licence ban resulted in her dog-walking business being negatively affected:

> But he [the magistrate] said to me, he said 'I'm going to give you a chance, so you can start up your business and carry on with your mum and stuff.' And then I thought, 'Eh? Without a license? I'd be better off doing a month in prison.' (Marie, age 40)

As noted by Farrall (2002), if interventions are to work, they need to take into consideration the contexts of offending and desistance. Indeed this was a sentiment reiterated by Chris Grayling, former justice secretary, in the introduction to this chapter. It has been proven time and again that there is a positive link between employment and desistance (Horney et al. 1995; Carlsson 2012; Verbruggen et al. 2012). Yet paradoxically, it is often the CJS which stands in the way of true desistance by blocking access to education and employment. Whilst 'on the ground' services such as the WC and HfN Project appear to be providing positive steps to helping women into work, the legal formalities and stigma surrounding the employment of people with convictions stands in the way of desistance-promotion. Much like the (subsequently u-turned) ban on books in prison, the CJS seems to be shooting itself in the foot by not providing easier access to employment and education.

Overall, education and employment provided the women in this study with the 'stability package' required to effectively promote desistance. Education, paid and voluntary employment have been shown in these women's narratives to sometimes reduce the likelihood of reconviction, improve mental health and produce social bonds. Particularly where the employment was meaningful and, where appropriate, generative, it was capable of producing change. These findings reflect what is already known about men and desistance. Yet the CJS further stigmatises criminalised women by only offering hyper-moral or unpaid roles which entrench their already disadvantaged gendered inequalities. Recently, the level of in-work poverty has reached unprecedented levels in the UK (Joseph Rowntree Foundation 2018). Women are suffering disproportionately by austerity measures (Women's Budget Group 2016). It is crucial to examine the historical context of employment, education and voluntary work in women's lives, noting where its promotion may be inappropriate and adopting, therefore, a holistic approach.

Romantic Relationships

Within the desistance literature, there is a wealth of data to connect desistance with marriage (Farrington and West 1995; Sampson and Laub 1993; Laub and Sampson 2003; Sampson et al. 2006; Bersani et al. 2009). This link, however, has largely been explored through male, heterosexual experiences. Even amongst the strongest supporters of the 'marriage factor' there has been some acknowledgement that criminalised women may be less likely to marry a pro-social partner than their heterosexual male counterparts (Sampson et al. 2006). Another criticism of the marriage factor thesis is that marriage is a somewhat outdated measurement device in contemporary society where couples are more likely to marry later in life, if at all. For this reason, this study does not use marriage as the measuring stick of a good relationship, instead the qualitative relationship experience as a whole will be considered to include both hetero and same sex romantic relationships. The findings from this study suggest that for criminalised women in contemporary England, romantic relationships are not the turning point around which desistance pivots. Whilst relationships were important as context for the beginning of offending for many of the women, they largely were not as important in the cessation of offending. Jamieson et al.'s (1999) finding that the end of relationships can be important in desistance for females, however, is replicated in the narratives of many of the women, yet other trajectories also were evident.

Holly's Story

The link between offending and romantic relationships for women is narrated well by Holly's experience. The month before our interview, Holly's partner, and father of her daughter, Nick, had been released from prison. He had served a second sentence of two years and three months for burglary. However, Holly did not link the beginning of her own offending with Nick's offending; instead she linked her own offending first with normal youth behaviour and gradually with poverty and smoking weed. She did, however, link her desistance with her partner's. For example, Holly had quit smoking weed since Nick's release as he no longer smoked. Generally, Holly also linked getting back together with Nick following his release with 'settling down' and regaining care of their daughter:

> I just want to get my child back, and hopefully start another family up with my child's dad and just be happy with my grandma. Let my grandma have a happy life, let her be happy and free. She shouldn't be babysitting for my child now. (Holly, age 23)

Whilst Holly was concerned with her own desistance, she was also consumed with being a positive example to Nick and directing his desistance journey by settling down together. In this sense, Holly was the invisible, usually female, pro-social partner we so often hear about in the male desistance literature. Holly's narrative therefore provides an insight to the lives of these non-protagonist women, who may also be struggling with their own (although perhaps not as prolific) desistance attempts and other difficulties. Holly, for example, highlighted the struggles herself and Nick continued to have with money:

> I only get £81 a fortnight so it's really hard, it is. I think it's because like I had fines and that in the past and they take money out so I'm only getting £81 but I manage because my boyfriend's on jobseekers as well so he gets like £140 a fortnight so we manage 'cause like when he were in prison and

I were on my own I were only getting like £81 that were making me go out offending and that so it's mainly only the money situation innit? But we're managing. (Holly, age 23)

Clearly this financial issue[8] could have resulted in continued offending for Holly or Nick, but Holly's desire for the 'respectability package' which included a life together, prevented her from offending in the months prior to our interview. When considering Holly's desistance, it is also necessary to consider her relationship history, which, like the majority of the women interviewed for this research (criminalised women and staff), contained domestic abuse by a former partner:

I met a guy while he [Nick] were inside and he were violent, that's why she [Holly and Nick's daughter] ended up going to my grandma, 'cause he were violent. He took amphetamines and he always bullied me and stuff and that's why my grandma had to take the child because he were beating me up and stuff. So I split up with him and then I started getting back together with her dad. So it were really hard, it were ... I went through a lot of depression and stuff and started like slicing myself a little bit. I went through a rough time 'cause I couldn't see my child and everything. But I went to the doctors, and I'm on tablets now, antidepressants and stuff, so everything's looking a lot brighter now. I'm feeling better in myself. I'm right happy at home with my kid's dad, so everything's happy now. The last year I just went through a really bad phase in my life, meeting that guy and stuff. I only were with him for eight month, but then he followed me round for a year and a half, putting my windows through 'cause I wouldn't get back with him. (Holly, age 23)

For Holly, desistance was linked with a move away from a violent relationship, regaining custody of her daughter and improvements in her mental health which have coincided with her partner's release from prison. The tone with which Holly described her mental health and domestic violence, 'and stuff', 'a little bit', and so on, perhaps suggests their normative presence in Holly's experience. Alternatively, this could be a coping mechanism. For Holly, a stable relationship represented hope for change. So, whilst a positive relationship experience was central to Holly's desistance, the link was complicated both by Holly's past relationship experiences, and her desire to be the pro-social partner in the future. This narrative highlights the complicated link between romantic relationships and desistance for the women in this study.

Supportive Relationships, Domestic Abuse and Desistance: Similar Desistance Outcomes for Vastly Different Experiences

Some of the women, however, reported positive relationship experiences which, whilst not always directly resulting in desistance, certainly provided the foundations for it. For Shelly and Michaela, meeting each other whilst in prison proved to be a turning point in both their narratives:

> Michaela: I've not offended since July this year and normally I'd be nicked by now and back in prison.
> Una: What do you think is the main reason for that?
> Michaela: I've got into a new relationship, I've been clean 16 month now so I don't need to shoplift any more to feed an addiction, I'm no longer in that domestic violence relationship where he was an alcoholic and I was shoplifting to fund his habit as well. So my life's totally changed. (Michaela, age 34)

> In all honesty, Michaela's been a big positive influence in my life, really honest to God. And it's not just that, she makes me life feel like I'm worth something, you know what I mean? Whereas the last relationship I come out of, I'm being honest with ya, nothing was happening in the relationship, sexual or otherwise for 16 years and that's the God's honest truth. What it was about right is, with me being full gay, I couldn't have children of me own. I could have done probably, do ya get me? … But I knew I was full gay and it just wasn't happening, do ya get me? And I think that's what kept me in that relationship that long; it was the fact of [Shelly's ex-partner's] grandkids. And not just that, with the heroin and everything … I just didn't want them discovering at that age that their nana [was a heroin user] … I didn't want them discovering that and I would have done anything to protect them from that. You know for them not to see that? And that's exactly, to be honest, that's what kept me in the relationship so long,

> I know it did. It was the fact of the children, family orientated and that. Like Michaela's got an eighteen-year-old son and I'm so close to Jack, he's such a lovely lad. I swear to God he's got his head on right and he knows what he's doing ... Honest to God, the whole family have accepted me with open arms, it's just unbelievable. (Shelly, age 53)

For both women, the beginnings of heroin addiction and offending were related to past relationships. Michaela had been connected with the Housing for Northshire (HfN) project whilst in prison because of her history with domestic abuse and she had requested that her new partner, Shelly, a fellow survivor of domestic violence, also be taken in by the agency. Both women had offending histories but supported each other's desistance through their relationship. Shelly and Michaela hoped to get married in the months following the interview, tellingly with Rebecca (Manager of HfN) 'giving them away' at the wedding.

For Heather, her partner represented the 'person who always believed in her' considered in Maruna's (2001) work. Heather's narrative included references to her partner encouraging her to stop drinking and supporting her through suicidal periods in the past. Heather was also engaged to be married at the time of interview. Julie's husband was another example of the angel-type figure who is a constant supporter of the criminalised individual who appears in Maruna's (2001) study. Julie, for example, made reference to her husband being particularly vigilant that Julie did not break her curfew. During the group sessions, a few women also talked about their positive relational experiences. For example, Janet, a former heroin addict at the Easton WC, spoke about her partner wanting her to stop drinking:

> He doesn't like it when I'm drinking. (Janet, Rose Centre observations)

We must treat these seemingly positive relationship experiences extolled by women in their narratives with caution. Particularly where the language of control is present, these narratives may mask an abusive relationship which nonetheless produces a period of non-deviant behaviour (Umberson et al. 1998; Johnson 2006). For example, Karen explained that whilst she was in a relationship she was very 'settled', however this lack of offending actually represented a controlling and abusive, violent relationship:

> When I'm in a relationship, because I was with Tom for five years, I never went out, I'm quite family orientated. You know I had them; I had the dogs. But when we split up and we went to my mum's, because I had my mum on hand, I went out and I was just basically re living my youth … Then when I met Sean and had the kids, for years I was settled down and then… But obviously with the violence, the police were obviously alerted. I didn't press any charges or anything. (Karen, age 36)

Karen's relationships with both Tom and Sean produced periods of non-offending but for dramatically different reasons. The narratives of violence in the lives of many of the women in this study echoe the experiences of violence as described by Emma Humphreys in *The Map of My Life* (Bindel and Wistrich 2003). The often inverse relationship between offending and violence in women's lives should not be underestimated.

Relationships with Men and Offending

Nonetheless, the common romantic relationship experiences described during both observation sessions and interviews were overwhelmingly negative and linked to both the beginnings and continuation of offending. The observation sessions were littered with narratives of relationships (usually with men) being the root cause of the beginnings of offending.

Kelly-Marie had a long history of offending and drug addiction. Whilst she did not blame any of her former partners for the beginnings of her offending behaviour, her relationships marked important 'turning points' in her offending trajectory. Kelly-Marie's first husband introduced her to a world of criminality at a young age, something which Kelly-Marie claimed was new to her:

> And when I got to 16, I left home and I met my daughter's dad, that was Frankie's dad, and I had Frankie. But he were a bit of a bugger. And at the age of 19 I wanted for nothing; I had me own home, as much money as I wanted, clothes, jewellery, cars, you name it, I had it … And I thought that

> was where it were all coming from. And I don't know whether you remember or not but there were a big fraud deal that went down with … cars and hundreds of thousands of pounds worth of cars, well that were my husband. Well anyhow, he obviously had all this money. Well I just had Frankie and the first I knew that he was a criminal were when the police were at my front and the back, and me doors were going in and I'm feeding the baby going, 'what's going on?' Anyhow, they took him away, he's got remanded and big dos and little dos, I weren't too impressed. (Kelly-Marie, age 48)

After splitting up with Frankie's father, Kelly-Marie met her second partner, who she described as a violent and controlling man, father to her second daughter, Emma. During this relationship, Kelly-Marie's offending and drug use decreased. Kelly-Marie eventually escaped this relationship and her offending and drug use again began to increase. However, upon meeting her third and final partner, Johnny, Kelly-Marie's life began to 'spiral out of control':

> I've met a man called Johnny. And I got wi'him and it were all high life and everything, do you know what I mean? It went from amphetamine, to cocaine, to ecstasy, LSD, heroin; you name it, I were taking it … I've got an habit, I've got no job, I've got no money, me family don't agree with Johnny. I'm off the rails, nobody can tell me any different. And I've started committing offences. To the point where he got me … I'd gone and I'd robbed a person, took £25 out of the drawer and he came down the stairs and I remember saying to him, 'I'm sorry but I really do need this more than you right now. And I really don't want to take it.' And I've took it and I've gone. And I've got three years and nine month for that. So obviously, from there onwards, I'd done the sentence, I was still in contact with Johnny. But I loved him. But it weren't him I loved, I think it were the drugs. And that's all our relationship were built on, it were drug orientated. It weren't a normal relationship. (Kelly-Marie, age 48)

Johnny was subsequently 'in and out' of Kelly-Marie's life following this sentence, his entry back into her life always leading to amplifications in drug taking and offending to support their drug use. It was only with final breaks from all the men in her life that Kelly-Marie could focus on desistance:

> Maybe if I had have, not just me, if things had have been picked up sooner and dealt with, maybe I wouldn't have gone down the paths that I've gone down … I've been at every channel and they're the wrong ones, I'm on the right one now. (Kelly-Marie, age 48)

Similar narratives were shared by many of the women. Anna experienced periods of non-offending whilst with her abusive partner and offending acceleration when introduced to other men. Michaela was directly introduced to heroin by her previous abusive partner for whom she would go shoplifting for, and Janet had also been introduced to heroin by a former abusive partner. As well as introductions to offending therefore, male partners also coerced women into offending and drug taking. Domestic violence was such a common experience for women involved in this study that it was referred to by its acronym 'DV' during the group sessions by both staff and service users alike. As previously noted, eight out of the 16 convicted women, and four out of the five staff, told objectively horrific stories of domestic abuse, violence, rape and childhood abuse in their narrative interviews, unprompted by the interviewer (the staff experience will further be considered in Chap. 6). Once again, it is clear that the social bonds desistance thesis, as championed by theorists such as Sampson and Laub (1993) and Laub and Sampson (2003), has neglected to consider the gendered contexts surrounding both the onset and decline of women's criminalisation. Abuse appears as a consistent experience.

Independence and Desistance

Chapter 5 will consider the role of agency and identity in desistance. However, it is worth mentioning here that for many women, rather than being a relational experience, desistance was a largely independent venture. This finding is supported by previous research such as Leverentz' (2014) finding that desistance for women often meant avoiding romantic relationships, at least temporarily. Perhaps this is an unsurprising finding when it is considered that many women were introduced to offending by previous partners or their offending took an upward trajectory whilst in certain relationships. This has been noted above in Kelly-Marie's experience. For

Anna, who was convicted of a joint enterprise offence with her friend, Dave, desistance was synonymous with independence also:

> No, not had a partner for a long time now, no. I think Dave were the closest person that I had from me past. Again, another bloke, someone else that was taken away from me. But I'll always bounce back; they'll never keep me down. I can make mates no problem; do you know what I mean? And I don't need anybody there all the time, me. I'm not one of these people that need a big group of people there… I don't need it, I'm quite happy, as long as I know the kids are happy. That's all I can ask for, that's all I've ever wanted, to do it my way. (Anna, age 36)

The narratives of the majority of the women interviewed were underpinned by an understanding of the linking of independence and desistance. Nonetheless, as claimed by Anna's narrative, this independence was not something which was always socially acceptable:

> And then I fell pregnant off a one night stand [becoming pregnant] with Craig. It were meant to be mates with perks but I found out there were no perks to that situation once I fell pregnant (laughs). The lad [Craig's father] never bothered. He lives two streets away, I walk past him all the time, won't bother about the kid … But the little girl never bothered about her dad, the little boy craves it. He walks round the street going, 'do you want to be my dad?' And yeah the school shout at me and say, 'yeah Craig's problems are down to a lack of men.' But every man that I've managed to find, whether it be friend or whatever had let him down and walked away because I can't give them more or whatever. (Anna, age 36)

According to Anna, her status as a single mother was deviant when considered by wider society including her son's school. Helena Kennedy (1993) has argued that this is something which is reflected in the courts. Conversely, it was this independence which propelled Anna on her desistance journey. Oakley (1981) contended that these 'masculine' traits of independence are often seen by society as deviant (Kennedy 1993). Women, criminalised and otherwise, are too often considered in the desistance literature only in terms of their relational identities—as mothers, partners or daughters. In the process of desistance, women also often discover their independence and this, too, alongside supportive, loving relationships is something which can be promoted through resistance to patriarchal constructs.

Romantic Relationships and the Criminal Justice System (CJS)

A further consideration in the link between relationships and desistance, referred to throughout the women's narratives, is the damage that convictions and their knock-on effects can have on current romantic relationships. This has been considered with women in prison (Scott and Codd 2010) but less so with women serving community penalties. For Katie, the deterioration in her mental health as a result of her conviction for benefit fraud had caused problems in her relationship with her husband:

> But it has been really traumatic, and they [her daughters] can't understand that. And my husband is the same, he blocks things off. And I can't talk to him; he's not the sort of person you can talk to. And he's been a lorry driver since we got married, so he's always worked away. And before that he was in the army. So we've always been away, we're used to being away. So it's not like it's any different but I don't feel like I've got the support there with him that I would have had, if we'd have been close. We're just not close. (Katie, age 60, first interview)

During our second interview, Katie reported that her relationship with her husband had not improved in the intervening months. On top of not being able to talk to her husband, she theorised that the shame brought on by her conviction resulted in less time her husband has spent socialising with friends:

> You know I feel like he doesn't seem to go out, like he used to do with friends and things and I don't know whether they've blocked him off or not because of me (begins to cry). I know it sounds silly … Well I don't think it sounds silly, but maybe I'm imagining it. But that's what I feel like. You know he used to go for a pint with some of his work mates and things or we'd all meet up every now and then together and he's never asked. Or

whether he's asked and he doesn't tell me because he doesn't want to go. I don't know. (Katie, age 60, second interview)

Similarly, Marie related her own relationship problems to her convictions but in a different way. Marie's relationship with her wife, Claire was deteriorating during our first meeting as a result of the driving ban she received as part of her sentence. This ban meant that Marie was unable to 'escape' their marital problems nor provide for her family either through illegitimate means, or through her dog-walking business. I had arranged a second interview with Marie however she called me on the day of the interview to postpone due to 'domestic issues' herself and Claire were having. She did not rearrange another interview but I later found out from one of the other women that Marie and Claire had split up. The negative effects of imprisonment on employment, housing, poverty and relationships are well explored by the literature (Petersilia 2003; Sim 2010; Hattery and Smith 2010). However, even for women serving community sentences, the conviction and its related consequences can have a direct effect on the quality of romantic relationships.

This section has explored the theme of romantic relationships as told from the point of view of criminalised women. As has been seen, there were examples of loving and supporting relationships which were desistance-promoting. However, not every relationship which was desistance-promoting was also loving and supportive. As Karen's and others' experiences highlighted, violent, abusive relationships could also promote desistance for women. Academics and criminal justice practitioners must be very wary not to confuse desistance for positive relational experiences. Many women in this study were introduced to offending by romantic partners. This is not a new finding (Uggen and Kruttschnitt 1998; Jamieson et al. 1999; Rodermond et al. 2016). What it does highlight however is that for many women, desistance was intrinsically linked to independence. Therefore alongside, or in place of, happy, healthy, supportive relationships, desistance may be found in independence. Finally, where there was evidence of positive relationships supporting desistance, the institutions of the punitive state could often destroy these relationships in the same way that it has been known to destroy employment, housing or mental health prospects.

Whilst meaningful employment and romantic relationships emerged as prominent sociogenic themes in this research, further potential 'turning points' which emerged as important included becoming a mother, gaining stable accommodation, changes in friendship groups and communities. In the following sections, these themes will be briefly considered in terms of desistance.

Becoming a Mother

There is much research to indicate that becoming a mother is a significant desistance-inducing social bond for women who break the law (Bersani et al. 2009; Giordano et al. 2002; Graham and Bowling 1995; Uggen and Kruttschnitt 1998; Rutter et al. 1998; McIvor et al. 2011). This argument situates a female's desistance in terms of her relational, gendered identity. Amongst the 16 criminalised women who were interviewed for this study, 13 were mothers and two of these were grandmothers. All offences happened after becoming a mother, indeed eight of the women had lost full custody or completely lost their children to social services or family members due to issues surrounding their offending, their alcohol or drug use, or in Ruth's case, homelessness. The previous chapter has shown how for Holly, becoming a mother indicated a turning point for her friend, Ciara, whilst having her daughter did not produce the same result for Holly. For some women, shoplifting, robbery, fraud or drug supplying were related to being able to provide for their children. Tragically, for Grace, it also meant that her daughter was taken into care. Marie related offending to being able to 'put food on the table'. For these acquisitive crimes, carried out in the main by single mothers, we can see a link to the stereotypically masculine trait of provision for the family.

For a second group of women, offending was not something which was related to their role as mothers, nor their relationship with their children. Paula, for example, noted that neither the threat of loss, nor eventual loss of, her sons encouraged her to stop drinking:

> It's weird really because when you're in the addiction, you're so selfish and you just block out everyone around you. And you see them and you hear

> them and you don't take anything in, even my children weren't enough. And my children got taken to live with their dad, that weren't enough, it was just like 'oh they're not here now; I may as well carry on drinking.' So you're very selfish, but I didn't think of myself as selfish. I suppose at the time I thought of myself as the victim. (Paula, age 36)

Nonetheless, whilst the act of becoming a mother did not produce the required turning point for the women in this study, many did relate their identity as a mother and their desire to become law-abiding to their relationship with their children. It was again not the act which provided the impetus for change, but the identity which helped maintain desistance. Motherhood provided the 'script' (Rumgay 2004) for change in these women's lives. Particularly when considering their hopes for the future, many of the mothers' hopes revolved around their children:

> They're [Ruth's children] the only thing, the only two things, keeping me going at the moment, I haven't got a whole lot to smile about at the minute, as you've been aware. But hopefully something will change, very soon. (Ruth, age 31)

> I'd love to move out of here [Housing for ex-offenders in Southton], start having the children at the weekends and as they're obviously getting older they'll be able to make a decision you know, if they want to stay with me. (Karen, age 36)

Similarly, whilst talking about the decision to begin a methadone prescription, Michaela noted:

> Michaela: 'Cause I have a child that's just turned 18 and I needed to start being a mother.
> Una: So it was to do with that more?
> Michaela: Yeah, for meself and for my son, yeah. (Michaela, age 36)

For Kelly-Marie, whilst having her two daughters and losing custody of her younger daughter, Emma, did not lead to desistance, becoming a grandmother for the first time provided a temporary 'script' for change which was not to last:

> And from Frankie being 16 to me grandson being born, I was in and out of the courts, the cells, prison and just reoffending, taking drugs. And I didn't really give a shit whether I lived or died basically. And Frankie's fell pregnant with me grandson. And I thought, 'right ok, it's time to sort your shit out.' Because even though Frankie had never seen me take drugs, or suffered from me taking drugs, yeah? In my eyes, she hadn't suffered, but she had, yeah, because she didn't have a mum like she should have had. And anyhow, Frankie's had Riley and he's my be all and end all. (Begins to cry). And for seven year I were clean. I got rid of Johnny; I'd moved back near me family and everything were hunky dory. And then Johnny popped up again. And by this time, I let him in, but I'm thinking I'm in control, I'm not taking drugs or anything, I'm clean. But I've gone from one extreme to the other so I'm selling drugs now. And making a lot of money, but I'm spending less time with me grandson. And my granddaughter's come along at the same time. And I'm spending less time with them. (Kelly-Marie, age 48)

Identity and motherhood will be explored further in the next chapter. To base female desistance around women's relational identities however is not only inappropriately stereotypical (Perry 2013), but restricts women's ability to change. Unlike the desistance literature, this study did not find that becoming a mother, nor indeed a grandmother, automatically created a social bond to conventional society. We see in Kelly-Marie's narrative that without addressing other issues such as poverty, relationship issues and drug addiction, desistance will not be forthcoming. For many of the women however, motherhood provided a 'script' (Rumgay 2004) and the 'hook for change' (Giordano et al. 2002) necessary to desist and, importantly, offered hope for a brighter future.

Gaining Stable Accommodation

Perhaps unsurprisingly, inadequate housing was another of the key sociogenic factors recognised by both the women with convictions and the staff of both projects as being conductive to crime and offending. Certainly for two of the women in particular, housing was central to their entry into the CJS. Grace's narrative linked poor housing with inadequate heating directly with her considered 'decision'[9] to begin growing cannabis which would, amongst other financial benefits, help to heat her home. Ruth, on the other hand, who was homeless at the time of interview and had been for 10 months, had been convicted due to her inability to pay off an overpayment of housing benefit. She noted the reasoning of the magistrate in her narrative:

> Ruth: Well they said it was to make me aware that the overpayment was wrong but also it was to open other doors to help me find accommodation because I have been homeless for the last 10 month.
>
> Una: And has it helped you so far?
>
> Ruth: Not so far but I've only been on probation what ... eight weeks so I've got ten month of it left
>
> Una: And have you been getting any help to find accommodation?
>
> Ruth: Not up to now. I mean I've been filling in forms for accommodation through the housing for ex-offenders programme two week ago, so hopefully ... he [Ruth's probation officer] says he doesn't see why not because it's got to be minimum minimal offences to be accepted onto the housing for ex-offenders programme... Mine is the most minimal, it's not as if I'm a reoffender or I'm aggressive. It all takes time; each form you fill in seems to take months to come back to you (Ruth, age 31)

Whilst arguably present in many of the women's narratives, Ruth's narrative highlights a clear example of criminalisation as a direct result of poverty. The court suggested that the only way Ruth can access adequate housing is by her entry into the CJS. Clearly, however, this criminalisation will have wide ranging effects in terms of Ruth's employment prospects, relationships and mental health. McNaughton and Sanders have argued that whilst housing is a crucial aspect in transitions from 'deviant' behaviour to 'ordered lifestyles', 'there is strong evidence to suggest that the conditional welfare services given through the entanglement of the welfare and CJS play a pivotal role in maintaining marginal lifestyles and a cycle of entrapment into social exclusion' (2007: 885). Although the authors here are referencing street prostitution and homelessness generally, the same can be said for women who are criminalised for minor infringements of the law in the guise of support. Whilst Ruth was hopeful for a future which encompassed stable accommodation, she was all too aware of the negative consequences of her criminalisation:

> It's just seemed to have knocked me so far this time, I just want somewhere to live and go back to work. But obviously with this on my record for the next two years, it's … It seems harsh, to give me a criminal conviction over this when I've never been in trouble before. I'm not a reoffender and that's what all these courses are for, all about reoffending … And reoffending isn't what's going to happen. It's not as if I've gone out and done something wrong. But yet I'm paying the price for them overpaying. (Ruth, age 31)

Carlsson (2012) has contended that changing trajectories of offending must come through policies which help 'bond' an individual to the conventional social order rather than through policies which result in isolation, exclusion or punishment. Ruth's case effectively illustrates that even where supposedly well-meaning, criminal justice intervention can create exactly these negative outcomes. The links between the CJS and supporting desistance will be explored further in Chap. 6.

Karen, a 'reoffender' and former heroin addict, had been placed in the housing for ex-offenders accommodation that Ruth was applying to. However, her experience had not been particularly positive. She complained that there was a lack of support to find her somewhere permanent and stable to live. Additionally, on the weekend before her interview, Karen had been visited by her children and she had been told off for them causing noise and disruption which had upset her:

> The system's not really, like, very helpful. They just sort of leave you hanging. It's just like they ignore us, it's like 'oh you're a criminal, you know you've done this, so'… I mean, there's lads in here now, they've signed up for flats and things like that, they're getting to move on. And that's, I hope, a stage I will be at sooner rather than later. So I'll be looking at that, like over the next few weeks… looking at the housing association. Because I spoke to the staff here about that today and said you know, 'Why's my name not down on any housing lists and things like that?' So she's put me forward for things like that, which should have already been done. I feel like I have to tell her what needs to be done, which is really shit really. (Karen, age 36)

In contrast to Ruth and Karen's experience, Shelly, who had been homeless prior to her time spent in prison and had difficulties finding stable accommodation on her release from prison, found that entering the HfN programme run by Rebecca, was the key to both her desistance, and ultimately, survival:

> In all honesty, I'd have gone back to X2 [city Shelly previously lived], I'd have been homeless on the streets, probably be back in jail by now … I'd probably be near dead … I'll be totally honest with ya … Only I met Michaela, she's come to pick me up to Easton. We lived with Michaela's auntie for two weeks, well right it was three weeks altogether because Rebecca had gotten in touch, ya listening? From her agency … that woman honestly is a miracle worker, Rebecca Brown … The help she's given me and Michaela … And not just us, other girls I know that have come out of jail … Her agency, honest to God, is … you just have no stuff like that in X2 and you should have, you should have, honestly. Within three weeks I had … our own home. Like I know it's supported accommodation, it holds up to three women, are you listening? But me and Michaela were the first to go in there. And honestly within three weeks, honest to God… I have a roof over my head. (Shelly, age 53)

This finding supports large-scale quantitative analysis on the particular importance of the link between housing for criminalised women and recidivism (Ellison et al. 2013). For Ruth, Karen and Shelly, securing stable accommodation was central to their desistance pathways. The same was true of Rebecca's other clients, Michaela and Kelly-Marie. However, the experiences of support in securing housing differed vastly. For the majority of the other women involved in this study, securing safe, secure and stable accommodation was part of the 'respectability package' which was related to their desistance. For Bridget, a new house not only meant that she could save money on bills but that she could express her identity by painting and decorating. For Sue, entering new accommodation was important for severing ties to her ex-husband. This research highlights that housing must be central to a female-focused desistance agenda, but homeless women should not be forced into a punitive CJS as a result of punitive welfare net-widening.

Communities, Friendships and Desistance

The linked themes of moving away from friendship groups and communities were final significant social/structural themes which appeared in the narratives of women desisting or attempting to desist. Additional to the idea of securing stable accommodation, many of the women involved in this research expressed a desire to move away from areas in which they lived and had been criminalised. Anna, for example, expressed a desire to move out of the area where she had lived all her life. She believed that the area did not support her desistance because 'you can't change if you're still expected to be the same cow you've always been.' Ironically, however, it was her status as a probationer which meant that she was unable to move out of the area. Anna noted that she was unable to look for somewhere to live as it would have been 'seen as eyeing places up to rob'. Nonetheless, Anna found coping mechanisms to live in the area whilst maintaining her desisting status:

> I've always been alright in the area. I don't mix anymore, I keep my eyes down on me way home, I close myself off… It's the best way to be at the moment with everything going on. I don't want to… I don't want to use it as a big up to myself like most people do. Like I know some of the boys are like, 'look at me, with my tag.' And a lot of the girls in the village and other places love it. Like shorts on 'cause they've got a tag and they've never worn shorts in their life. It's like, 'really, is that what you want? Wow.' And again you have people looking at you, walking around with a tag, what a dick-head. No, I never wanted to be like that. I just wanted to… I don't know… be me. It's a hard thing to be when you're around people who want you to be what they want. But I'll always fight against it and I certainly wouldn't give in now because I feel a bit bullied off the police. (Anna, age 36)

Anna associated the area with her younger 'offending' and her family's reputation (see previous chapter). Her desire to move away from this criminogenic behaviour included a desire to move away from the area and 'be herself', the 'person she was always meant to be' (Maruna 2001). Similarly, Karen noted that when she was young, her family moved from Scotland because her father was becoming involved in the 'gang culture' of the area. Conversely, in her own narrative, however, she experienced rejection from her own community because of her reputation as a heroin user:

> Everybody knows everybody, it's a very close-knit community. But because I started using drugs, that's why I've come away because I couldn't use the drugs I was using on that estate because they wouldn't have it. It's a no on our estate, like a dirty drug sort of thing. (Karen, age 36)

Karen went into supported housing and was on a methadone prescription at the time of her interview. However, her desistance was not as straightforward as moving out of the community and beginning a methadone programme to re-establish social bonds to the area. Karen's desistance also required a 'Road to Damascus' (Soothill and Francis 2009) style conversion whilst in prison and caring for her terminally ill friend, as well as great stores of agency and hope, re-establishing severed bonds with family and overcoming past victimisation.

Many of the women also found support in their communities. Julie found support and comfort in her Church community. Julie had been a regular Church-goer all her life. However, following the discovery of Julie's past alcohol problem and previous arson conviction, by her Church Minister, Julie felt victimised by the Church for bringing up the spent conviction:

> The other biggest person, or people, who have left me as feeling a victim were the Methodist Church. And people ... a lot of people who aren't Christian, or aren't connected with the Church or whatever, cannot believe that I still bother going to Church at all. But it's been my life, and not just that, the fact that there's been someone to rely on and pray to, and I don't know where I'd be without that. And so, I've stuck to that. I don't always get the answers I want. But, you know, I feel that I've been looked after. (Julie, age 59)

By the time of our second interview, Julie and her husband had changed to a different Church:

> We were formally made members of X Church, we transferred our membership. And it's just lovely. It's a little village chapel, but everybody knows everybody. (Julie, age 60)

For Julie, religion and community were interlinked and despite an initial period of rejection, Julie's desistance narrative was based around acceptance by her Church and community.[10] Unlike the majority of the other women, Julie's most recent fraud offence could have been described as a white-collar crime. Julie's narrative centred around acceptance by her community and it was clear that she felt shame about her failure to 'keep up appearances' with family and friends. Julie's status as a middle-class and older law-breaker certainly had an impact on her desistance experience. However, like Anna, Karen and many of the other women, a supportive, orthodox community was an important 'social bond' to conventional life which helped maintain this desistance.

A further key theme was the difference between 'friends' and 'associates' in the women's narratives. This was not only the dividing line between non-criminogenic/criminogenic relationships but also a dividing line between supportive/non-supportive relationships:

> I don't really have any friends, I've had associates but I wouldn't really class them as friends. It's just me, myself and I really. But I've just got to look after myself. Just number one (Karen, age 36)

> I don't have any friends. And they weren't friends; they were just acquaintances, associates. My new friends are to come. I've got two in Rebecca and Josie. Well, I've got another two actually, Shelly and Michaela, yeah? They are friends. (Kelly-Marie, age 48)

> Una: Have any of your friends ever been in trouble with the police and courts?
>
> Michaela: Um, only a couple of them. I don't have that circle of friends, or associates as you'd call them, I just have my normal friends. (Michaela, age 34)

> Other people, obviously, just won't give me the time of day. It's them, what do you call them? Fair-weather friends, they're never there when you need them, too quick to pass judgement. So, I know the people who are around me I know I can trust them. (Paula, age 36)

Not only were supportive friendships important, but the end of certain relationships which were viewed as criminogenic, or non-supportive, were important in desistance-promotion and maintenance. Another important factor were friendships with those who had been through a similar offending/desistance trajectory, as seen in both quotes from Kelly-Marie and Paula above. Katz (2000) noted that friendship groups are important in the desistance of black and minority ethnic women. I have also found this to be the case in the white women I have interviewed. Weaver and McNeill (2014) have explored the relational elements of desistance within a group of desisting males in their 40s. For the women in this study, offending was on the whole not a relational, friendship-based experience, especially with other women. For the more prolific 'offenders' such as Anna, Karen and Marie, offending was partly a consequence of their friendships with male associates but for the rest of the women, offending, and especially desistance, was a largely individual experience requiring stores of agency and resistance against structural inequalities of being a working-class woman. Again it is apparent that on a social bonds level, the Northshire women's desistance was a qualitatively different experience than men's. Friendships and communities were certainly important for women's desistance, but as a result of their offending trajectories and societal reaction to women's offending, these tended to be experienced in different ways.

Conclusion

The 'social bonds' women had prior to their offences were unsurprisingly weak; women's narratives included stories of poverty, unemployment, destructive relationships and communities, domestic abuse, loss of children and homelessness. A telling feature of the lack of social bonds in the lives of the women involved in this research were their apathetic attitudes to politics, particularly in the run up to the general election (see also Farrall 2014). When asked about her political views, Shelly's answer was a typical response:

> You know what, I'm not being funny, the only thing I can turn round and tell ya is this government that are in now… I can tell you I've never felt so strongly about it in my life, this government that are in now have made such a fucking mess of this country, honest to God, they've made such a

> fucking mess of it. 'Cause I'm telling you now, they've taken away… I'm telling you, I mean look what's happening with this bedroom tax and everything. Before you know it how many people are going to be homeless? How many families are going to be homeless on the streets? And that's 'cause of this government. And then you've got to look at it this way; whatever, even if we get them out when we next vote, are you listening to me? How long is it going to take the next ones that get in to clean up the mess they made? Cause I think it's disgusting, food banks and everything? It's disgusting! That's something that doesn't happen in our country, that's something that happens in the 'Third World', that shouldn't be happening here, what's that about? It just makes me so angry. And taking all that money off students to pay tuition fees every year, what's that about? … It just makes me so angry because they're doing it to their own people. They really are. No wonder people are committing crime you know … and you know I don't agree with people selling death, I don't agree with people selling heroin and shit like that, but you know what? I'm not being nasty or nothing but I can understand why they do it, because how the fuck do you live when you want to make money? (Shelly, age 53)

In order to promote women's desistance it is important to not only repair bonds to society but make sure that the harmful circumstances mentioned above—gendered violence, poverty, unemployment, addiction, poor mental health and so on—are not structural features of women's lives in general which lead to criminogenic behaviour. The women involved in this study have complex lives and often their desistance stories can be seen as resilience and survival in the face of expectations of 'normal' [patriarchal, neoliberal] social bonds such as marriage and employment. As well as considering individual social bonds reparation, structural inequalities must be examined; social bonding for the Northshire women, must occur in a society that they wanted to be bonded to. With charity and activist groups such as 'A Fair Deal for Women' and Sisters Uncut highlighting the disproportionate effect of austerity on women, tackling phallocentrism (Smart 1995: 78) in all areas, but particularly in terms of the economic impact of cuts is crucial. In addition, the CJS can be critiqued, particularly where it can be seen as a destructive force on the very social bonds which can act positively influence desistance.

It is important to provide criminalised women with the tools to help themselves. But, women should not be forced into employment which is not meaningful other than as a means of making money, nor should they be coerced into voluntary work on the misplaced, patriarchal assumption that criminalised women in particular have a desire to be generative. Instead, meaningful, rewarding, generative employment should be accessible to women travelling the road of desistance when they are ready to avail themselves of it. Relationships which on surface levels may appear conductive to desistance may be masking violence and coercion. As argued by Pat Carlen,

> Despite previous bad experiences of 'family life', some women, already in trouble with the law, and with a host of other problems stemming from poverty and a generalised feeling of marginalisation, are, none the less, led by existing policies to believe their only way 'back in' again is via men or motherhood. (1990: 122)

Therefore, desistance from crime should not be the only end goal but part of a wider goal of women's equality promotion. As part of this equality promotion, women's desistance should be considered as separate and different from men's, situated in social/ structural circumstances which are often different to men's desistance contexts. We must move beyond the white, male character of 'justice' which pervades liberal societies (Hudson 2006) exposing desistance as a gendered process.

For the women in this study, desistance was about more than changes in work and romantic relationships. As well as the importance of relationships with children, housing, community and friendship groups, cognitive shifts in hope and self-efficacy, shame and remorse, stigma and alternative identities (LeBel et al. 2008) were important in desistance-promotion and maintenance. It is to these subjective-level themes which accompany changes in life circumstances or social bonds that the next chapter turns.

Notes

1. I did not ask a direct question about experiences of abuse but asked the women interviewed to elaborate on any experiences of victimisation.

2. Women are also disproportionately affected by austerity measures (Women's Budget Group 2016).
3. Although some of these women were also involved with voluntary work as part of their licence.
4. Working as a care assistant.
5. Timpson's, a multinational retailer, has been interlinked with prisons to train prisoners and provide employment 'on the outside'.
6. At the WCs and driving courses.
7. See Chap. 6 about Katie's experiences in court.
8. The Joseph Rowntree Foundation (2016) reported that there were over 1.2 million people living in poverty in the UK. 'Destitution' was defined as an income of £140 or less per week per couple with children. It is clear that Holly and Nick fall into this category, as did many of the women involved in this study.
9. See Chap. 5 for more on women's 'choice' to offend and desist.
10. For more on religion, spirituality and desistance, see Giordano et al. (2008) or Schroeder and Frana (2009).

Bibliography

Aresti, A., Eatough, V., & Brooks-Gordan, B. (2010). Doing Time After Time: An Interpretative Phenomenological Analysis of Reformed Ex-Prisoners' Experiences of Self-change, Identity and Career Opportunities. *Psychology Crime and Law, 16*(3), 169–190.

Bersani, B. E., Laub, J. H., & Nieuwbeerta, P. (2009). Marriage and Desistance from Crime in the Netherlands: Do Gender and Socio-Historical Context Matter? *Journal of Quantitative Criminology, 25*, 3–24.

Bindel, J., & Wistrich, H. (2003). *The Map of My Life: The Story of Emma Humphreys*. London: Astraia Press.

Carlen, P. (1988). *Women, Crime and Poverty*. Milton Keynes: Open University Press.

Carlen, P. (1990). *Alternatives to Women's Imprisonment*. Milton Keynes: Open University Press.

Carlsson, C. (2011). Using "Turning Points" to Understand Processes of Change in Offending. *British Journal of Criminology, 52*, 1–16.

Carlsson, C. (2012). Processes of Intermittency in Criminal Careers: Notes from a Swedish Study on Life Courses and Crime. *International Journal of Offender Therapy and Comparative Criminology, 57*(8), 913–938.

Cederstrom, C., & Spicer, A. (2015). *The Wellness Syndrome*. Cambridge: Polity.
Edgar, K., Jacobson, J., & Biggar, K. (2011). *Time Well Spent: A Practical Guide to Active Citizenship and Volunteering in Prison*. London: Prison Reform Trust.
Ellison, M., Fox, C., Gains, A., & Pollock, G. (2013). An Evaluation of the Effect of Housing Provision on Re-Offending. *Safer Communities, 12*(1), 27–37.
Farrall, S. (2002). *Rethinking What Works with Offenders*. Cullompton: Willan.
Farrall, S. (2014). Citizenship Values and Desistance from Crime: Exploring Change Over Time. In S. Farrall, B. Hunter, G. Sharpe, & A. Calverley (Eds.), *Criminal Careers in Transition*. Oxford: Oxford University Press.
Farrington, D. P., & West, D. J. (1995). Effects of Marriage, Separation, and Children on Offending by Adult Males. In Z. Blau Smith & J. Hagan (Eds.), *Current Perspectives on Aging and the Life Cycle* (4th ed.). Greenwich: JAI Press.
Giordano, P. C., Cernokovich, S. A., & Rudolph, J. L. (2002). Gender, Crime and Desistance: Toward a Theory of Cognitive Transformation. *American Journal of Sociology, 107*, 990–1064.
Giordano, P. C., Longmore, M. A., Schroeder, R. D., & Seffrin, P. M. (2008). A Life Course Perspective on Spirituality and Desistence from Crime. *Criminology, 46*, 99–131.
Graham, J., & Bowling, B. (1995). *Young People and Crime* (Research Study No. 145). London: HMRSO.
Hattery, A. J., & Smith, E. (2010). *Prisoner Re-entry & Social Capital*. Maryland: Lexington Books.
Horney, J., Osgood, D. W., & Marshall, I. H. (1995). Criminal Careers in the Short Term: Intra Individual Variability in Crime and its Relation to Local Life Circumstances. *American Sociological Review, 60*(5), 655–673.
Hudson, B. (2006). Beyond White Man's Justice: Race, Gender and Justice in Late Modernity. *Theoretical Criminology, 10*(1), 29–47.
Inquest.org.uk. (2018). *Deaths of Women in Prison|INQUEST*. [online] Available at: http://inquest.org.uk/statistics/deaths-of-women-in-prison. Accessed 27 Dec 2018.
Jamieson, J., McIvor, G., & Murray, C. (1999). *Understanding Offending Amongst Young People*. Edinburgh: The Scottish Executive.
Johnson, M. P. (2006). Conflict and Control: Gender Symmetry and Asymmetry in Domestic Violence. *Violence Against Women, 12*(11), 1003–1018.
Joseph Rowntree Foundation. (2016). *UK Poverty 2016: A Comprehensive Analysis of Poverty Trends and Figures*. London: JRF Analysis Unit.
Joseph Rowntree Foundation. (2018). *UK Poverty 2018: A Comprehensive Analysis of Poverty Trends and Figures*. London: JRF Analysis Unit.

Katz, R. (2000). Explaining Girl's and Women's Crime and Desistance in the Context of their Victimization Experiences. *Violence Against Women, 6*, 633–660.

Kennedy, H. (1993). *Eve Was Framed: Women and British Justice*. London: Vintage.

Laub, J., & Sampson, R. (2003). *Shared Beginnings, Divergent Lives*. Harvard: Harvard University Press.

LeBel, T. P., Burnett, R., Maruna, S., & Bushway, S. (2008). The "Chicken and Egg" of Subjective and Social Factors in Desistance from Crime. *European Journal of Criminology, 5*(11), 131–159.

Leverentz, A. (2014). *The Ex-Prisoner's Dilemma: How Women Negotiate Competing Narratives of Re-entry and Desistance*. New Brunswick: Rutgers University Press.

Maruna, S. (2001). *Making Good – How Ex-Convicts Reform and Rebuild Their Lives*. Washington, DC: American Psychological Association Books.

Matthews, R., Easton, H., Reynolds, L., Bindel, J., & Young, L. (2014). *Exiting Prostitution*. New York: Palgrave Macmillan.

McIvor, G., Murray, C., & Jamieson, J. (2011). Desistance from Crime: Is It Different for Women and Girls? In S. Maruna & R. Immarigeon (Eds.), *After Crime and Punishment: Pathways to Offender Reintegration*. Willan: Cullompton.

McNaughton, C., & Sanders, T. (2007). Housing and Transitional Phases Out of 'Disordered' Lives: The Case of Leaving Homelessness and Street Sex Work. *Housing Studies, 22*(6), 885–900.

Oakley, A. (1981). Interviewing Women: A Contradiction in Terms. In H. Roberts (Ed.), *Doing Feminist Research* (pp. 30–62). London: Routledge & Kegan Paul.

Perry, E. (2013). 'She's Alpha Male': Transgressive Gender Performances in the Probation 'Classroom'. *Gender and Education, 25*(4), 396–412.

Petersilia, J. (2003). *When Prisoners Come Home: Parole and Prisoner Re-entry*. New York: Oxford University Press.

Richards, G. (2018). What It's Like Growing Up as a Working-class Girl in the UK. *The Conversation*. Available at: https://theconversation.com/what-its-like-growing-up-as-a-working-class-girl-in-the-uk-93403. Accessed 27 Dec 2018.

Rodermond, E., Kruttschnitt, C., Slotboom, A. M., & Bijieveld, C. C. J. H. (2016). Female Desistance: A Review of the Literature. *European Journal of Criminology, 13*(1), 3–28.

Rumgay, J. (2004). Scripts for Safer Survival: Pathways Out of Female Crime. *The Howard Journal, 43*(4), 405–419.

Rutter, M., Giller, H., & Hagell, A. (1998). *Antisocial Behaviour by Young People*. New York: Cambridge University Press.

Sampson, R. J., & Laub, J. H. (1993). *Crime in the Making: Pathways and Turning Points Through Life*. London: Harvard University Press.

Sampson, R. J., Laub, J. H., & Wimer, C. (2006). Does Marriage Reduce Crime? A Counterfactual Approach to Within-Individual Causal Effects. *Criminology, 44*(3), 465–508.

Schroeder, R. D., & Frana, J. F. (2009). Spirituality and Religion, Emotional Coping, and Criminal Desistance: A Qualitative Study of Men Undergoing Change. *Sociological Spectrum, 29*, 718–741.

Scott, D., & Codd, H. (2010). *Controversial Issues in Prisons*. Maidenhead: Open University Press.

Sim, J. (2010). Punishing the Poor: The Neoliberal Government of Social Insecurity. *British Journal of Criminology, 50*, 589–593.

Sim, J. (2018). We Are All (Neo-)Liberals Now: Reform and the Prison Crisis in England and Wales Justice. *Power and Resistance, 1*, 165–188.

Smart, C. (1995). The Woman of Legal Discourse. In *Law, Crime and Sexuality: Essays in Feminism* (pp. 186–202). London: Sage Publications.

Soothill, K., & Francis, B. J. (2009). When Do Ex-Offenders Become Like Non-Offenders? *The Howard Journal, 48*(8), 373–387.

Uggen, C. (2000). Work as a Turning Point in the Life Course of Criminals: A Duration Model of Age, Employment, and Recidivism. *American Sociological Review, 67*, 529–546.

Uggen, C., & Kruttschnitt, C. (1998). Crime in the Breaking: Gender Differences in Desistance. *Law and Society Review, 32*, 339–366.

Umberson, D., Anderson, K. L., Glick, J., & Shapiro, A. (1998). Domestic Violence, Personal Control and Gender. *Journal of Marriage and Family, 60*(2), 442.

Verbruggen, J., Blokland, A. A. J., & Van Der Geest, V. R. (2012). Effects of Employment and Unemployment on Serious Offending in a High-Risk Sample of Men and Women from Ages 18 to 32 in the Netherlands. *British Journal of Criminology, 52*(5), 845–869.

Warr, M. (2002). *Companions in Crime*. Cambridge, UK: Cambridge University Press.

Weaver, B., & McNeill, F. (2014). Lifelines: Desistance, Social Relations, and Reciprocity. *Criminal Justice and Behaviour, 42*(1), 95–107.

Women's Budget Group. (2016). *Rethinking Austerity Is Overdue: It Has Hit Women and Ethnic Minorities Hardest*. Available at: https://wbg.org.uk/media/rethinking-austerity-overdue-hit-women-ethnic-minorities-hardest/. Accessed 27 Dec 2018.

5

All in the Head? A Feminist Critique of Subjective Theory

The previous chapter considered the 'social bonds' (Sampson and Laub 1993; Laub and Sampson 2003) which proved effective or otherwise at encouraging desistance. It was concluded that many of the social bonds present in the male desistance literature tended also to be salient in the female experience. However, when female narratives are considered, it emerges that many of the social bonds which have proven persistent in the male desistance literature are problematic. The realities of patriarchal capitalism mean experiences of discrimination, abuse and material deprivation are common. As has been noted by desistance theorists in the past (Maruna 2001), what the social bonds approach also tends to neglect is the agentic actor and the subjective cognitive discourses which accompany these social changes or act independently to produce change.

It is important to study desistance from the point of view of those experiencing desistance attempts in order to open what Farrall (2002) terms the 'black box' of terminating offending. When we consider the silencing of the female experience, it is particularly important to allow women the agency to explain their own thoughts, emotions and cognitive processes post-criminalisation (Clarke and Chadwick 2018). Whilst there are limitations to the narrative method, it is also the most

Ú. Barr, *Desisting Sisters*, Critical Criminological Perspectives,
https://doi.org/10.1007/978-3-030-14276-6_5

useful methodology for studying subjective experiences of desistance. Particularly where women's voices have been silenced and side-lined, storytelling approaches, as have been employed in this book (for more see the Appendix), allow women the power to narrate their own experiences.

As noted in Chap. 2, LeBel et al. (2008) highlighted four interrelated subjective-level themes which they contended emerged as most buoyant when considering the desistance experiences of male property offenders: Hope and Self-Efficacy; Shame and Remorse; Internalising Stigma and Alternative Identities. This chapter will also examine these themes, finding some concordance with the male literature. Whilst structural inequalities have created a fissure between hope and self-efficacy, both appear to be as important for women as men in their experiences following entry into the Criminal Justice System (CJS). Shame, remorse and stigma, however, should be treated with caution. Much of women's lives in general are replete with shame and stigma. When they break both the social and gender contracts, this is amplified and problematic to the living of lives free from harm and social exclusion. The final subjective-level theme of identity change is particularly poignant in the narratives of the women involved in this research. Women generally are often categorised in terms of their roles as daughters, partners or mothers. Simultaneously, those within the CJS are categorised as 'offenders', 'victims' or 'survivors' (Mills 2015). In each case their identity is connected to an 'other' person (usually a male) or traumatic or harmful event. This chapter moves beyond these limited relational or stigmatised identifications to consider women as bricoleurs of their own desistance, resisting the structures which constrain their identities. Again it is clear that subjective desistance theories are gendered in their approach and do not take note of the systemic inequalities faced by criminalised women attempting to desist.

Hope and Self-Efficacy

Feelings of hope and self-efficacy were often present in the narratives of the Northshire women. These elements have salience in the male literature (Maruna 2001; Bottoms et al. 2004; LeBel et al. 2008; Burnett and

Maruna 2004; Farrall and Calverley 2006) as well as female-based studies (Rumgay 2004). Distinguishing between hope and self-efficacy, theorists have suggested, can be divided into 'the will' and 'the ways' of achieving change (LeBel et al. 2008).

The hopes of the women were, on the whole, 'everyday' hopes in an age of austerity and encompassed family, housing, education and employment. These hopes were not only associated with desistance but also the onset of offending. Many of the women related the beginnings of offending to finding a more stable and ordinary life, a far cry from Jack Katz's (1988) moral and sensual attractions of committing crime. The 'thrill' of crime described by Katz was largely absent from the women's narratives. The psychological processes for the Northshire women did not surround wild desires or heightened emotions but were aligned with their everyday hopes and worries. In general the women's hopes had not modified significantly from their pre-criminalisation desires:

> Well, I'd like my health to be better. I'd like, if possible, to have some sort of employment, even if it was only charity, charitable work. Maybe we might move because I think as time goes on we're going to need a bungalow rather than a house, and something smaller. And, well, I mean, I'm not looking at winning the lottery, well I wouldn't ever do that because I don't even buy tickets (laughs). But, yeah, just a nice home that was suited to what Kenneth and I require because probably by then, I'd like to see Daniel [Julie's son] happily married, if I could. And then, I'm not asking for loads of anything, just what we need and if I can have a job where I either earn money or just do something voluntarily for somebody else, and decent health. Those are really the priorities. (Julie, age 59, first interview)

> I'm hoping to sort meself out, get this operation done and behave meself, make enough money to plod on. I don't want a lot, I'm not asking for a lot. I'm happy with my house and that. I've got everything I need in my house. I need to crack on with this business but obviously it's [Marie's conviction] put me back a lot now. (Marie, Age 48)

Una: So what are your hopes for the future?
Michaela: Just to stay focused on being abstinent from illegal drugs really
Una: Sure. And where do you see yourself in five years?
Michaela: Hopefully with a job (laughs)
Una: What would you like to do?
Michaela: Anything. A job's a job to me, do you know what I mean? There's nothing specific. (Michaela, age 34)

I don't really look too far into the future 'cause I live for the here and now and I can only deal with … I haven't got any long-term plans to you know have a cottage in the country with a little rose-framed fence around it. I'd like to, you know, go back to a bit of writing more or less when the project is embedded and running itself, Paul and I to take a step back and relax a little bit. (Rebecca, age 46)

I want Rebecca [Brown, Housing for Northshire Project manager, quoted above] to stay my landlady and she's going to get me and Michaela a two bedroomed house or two bedroomed flat, right? And she's going to continue support and like I said, next year me and Michaela are getting married on [date] and Rebecca's giving us away. It's my birthday, yeah so we're planning to get married then. So I turned around and said to Paul before, 'I don't know about Rebecca giving us away, she'll be fucking throwing us away!' (Laughs). So that's what I will be doing, yeah, that's my ambition in life, yeah. (Shelly, age 53)

These ordinary hopes and desires reflected the findings of the 'Sheffield study' (Bottoms and Shapland 2011). However, there was a gap between 'the will' and 'the ways' in some of the women's narratives. Grace, for example, situated her hopes in extending her education and moving to a new house. She noted, 'I know what I want and I know where I want to end up, I'm just not sure about what's needed in between.' This statement was typical of the women's subjective experiences and highlights a gap which had the potential (Merton 1957) to lead to further criminalisation. There was clear room for supporting Grace in this example, yet austerity measures meant she was unlikely (as she appeared to be aware of) to find the educational and housing support required.

Not all the women had such straightforward ambitions, however. For both Heather and Katie, self-efficacy was situated abroad. Both women had been failed so completely, both on an intimate, relational level (which can nonetheless be understood as a product of patriarchal capitalism) and a structural, State level, because of their status as criminalised women and the linked harms, that the only option they saw as being available to them was to leave the country completely[1]:

Heather: [I want] … to get better, to have a better life really and start afresh in a different country
Una: Do you think that moving away will help?
Heather: I do, I really do yeah, 'cause it's something new, it's a new experience, something I've never done before and I just think I'd be better really going somewhere else (Heather, age 24)

> We have really good friends in [Spain]. We said we were going to move over there a few years ago but we didn't. And they said they'd help us get property and everything, so I do know I could get help if I do go over there. But it would be abroad definitely. I do not want to stay in this country a minute longer than I have to do to be perfectly honest … I've never voted because there's nobody who I would have wanted to vote for. And after this experience, as soon as I can, live in another country than England… I'd rather get somebody else's nationality. And I'd rather be Spanish or something than English. I just think it's not a just place… (begins to cry) (Katie, age 60, first interview)

Despite these hopes, both women had various relational ties and caring responsibilities in England; Heather had a younger sister who she wanted to look after[2] and Katie had her granddaughter, Natalie, who in the intervening months between interviews had developed a chronic illness. Heather narrated her messy, internal process of change in hope relating to external circumstances:

Heather: I feel like it's [her life] in turmoil at the moment, it's neither good or bad it's just in the middle
Una: Why do you feel like that?
Heather: Because it's like when things start to settle down, something always goes wrong if you know what I mean? Like at the moment with my sister, I'm trying so much to support her 'cause she's been through a lot, and she's falled out with her boyfriend recently, it was on Friday, and she had to go to the hospital and things like that. And I had to go with her and it was a nightmare. It was horrible (Heather, age 24)

Karen's narrative contained perhaps the most significant lack of hope and especially self-efficacy. Yet whilst in prison, Karen experienced what Aresti et al. (2010) would term a 'defining moment' which impacted significantly on her feelings of confidence and ultimately agency:

This time, in custody, my friend's got terminal cancer and she was dying. She got moved to X prison, to be closer to home, to die really. The Home Office wouldn't pardon her, because of her offence. And it wasn't actually her, it was one of those Joint Enterprise charges… In a couple of months, it ate away at her, you know, it went to her brain, all over her body, you know when she went for scans. You know when she had these seizures, she was scared to go to sleep, you know, scared she wouldn't wake up. Now when they asked about being resuscitated she'd said that she didn't want to be… When she had the seizure, it changed her mind, she said she did want to be resuscitated. The prison were humming and hawing about this and talking to Macmillan[3] and saying you know… And it was like she died…. And basically because I'm like I am, basically I was like having none of it, causing uproar. And one of the governors took a liking to me and basically said he respected the fact that I was sticking up for Louise because she used to be a very feisty woman, but she was unable to do it for herself at that time. So her medication got put up and things like that. She was more comfortable and that. And it made me take a big, big look at my life. I watched her kids come to see her, and her twelve-year-old daughter, her youngest, you know, she had to tell her daughter on a prison visit, you know, 'I'm dying.' And you know, it was horrible. (Karen, age 36)

This incident is reminiscent of Faith's (2011) work on the bonds women make with other prisoners as a form of resistance, resisting 'prisonisation' and maintaining dignity. Additionally for Karen, this damascene moment had a powerful, initial influence on her personal desistance. Not only did she experience her own agency, but she experienced a 'wake-up call' regarding her drug use and linked crime. Poignantly though, once outside of prison, the realities of the harm caused by her criminalisation to practicalities such as housing and employment, as well as the damage done to her relationships became clear. The damaged relationships with her former abusive partner, her accommodation providers, and her mother and children, when combined with her heroin addiction, diminished all self-efficacy which emerged from this 'defining moment'. Like the other women, Karen's narrative contained modest hopes. Yet, like Grace, the chaos of her life, the harm caused by prison, and the lack of support she felt once released, meant she could not see a way of achieving her goals. She distinguished herself from 'normal women':

> I'd love to move out of here, start having the children at the weekends and as they're obviously getting older they'll be able to make a decision, you know, if they want to stay with me. But my mum is very strict, my mum actually wants to see me get accommodation, live properly, go shopping, live a normal life, do things that normal women do. I don't seem to have that in me, I just feel, you know, incomplete. (Karen, age 36)

Whilst Karen's manifestations of hope were indeed aligned with those of 'normal women', she saw herself as an outcast, buying into the idea of her own 'double deviance' and taking on the responsibilisation rhetoric of the punitive justice system (Hart 2017). She used the terminology of 'choice' in her narrative, in particular about her 'choice' in her offending behaviour:

> I choose my paths. You know, I went seeking this different life, you know. When I first split up from my eldest son's father I sort of like went off the rails then as well … I know the choices I've made have had a domino effect on me and everyone around me, my whole family and friends. And I realise that now but it's a bit too late, I can't take those memories back for the kids,

> you know… I've not been seeing them now because my mum doesn't like me seeing them, they get upset, they don't want me to go, and then they just take it out on my mum. Because they remember me and my mum arguing because my mum doesn't like me drinking. I'm quite confrontational when I've had a drink. So my mum kicked me out basically. And my kids were aware of that, they were hearing things, so they resented my mum for that. She's done so well. She's done an amazing job. The kids are great. My eldest son, he's at his dad's mums', and he's spoilt rotten. The conservatory is his games room, he's got a big 50 inch TV. But he doesn't want that, he wants to be with his brothers, he wants the family, and I've took that away from them through stupid choices I've made. (Karen, age 36)

Karen's experience shows that where both hope and self-efficacy are eroded away by injustices and victimisations, further harm can often lead (especially when combined with addiction) to criminalisation.

The follow-up interviews with Julie and Katie exposed the importance of hope and self-efficacy in the promotion of desistance, as well as their wavering temporal effects. Julie was more hopeful in the first interview than Katie and could see the 'light at the end of the tunnel' in her hopes for getting her electronic tag removed in the coming months. It is this prospective turning point around which Julie believed her life would revolve. She noted how her tag would be removed around her 60th birthday and she planned a party around this time. However by the time of our second interview, Julie had turned 60 and had her tag removed but she had also been hit in the meantime with legal aid fees which caused her mental health to deteriorate once again. Nonetheless, with the help of her daughter, Julie maintained her sense of self-efficacy even though this required maintenance when challenged:

> And I said to my husband, 'When this tag isn't on, I think I might feel like dancing in the garden before seven o'clock in the morning.' But it's just that you know, that feeling of things being better. But that's how I view it all. (Julie, age 59, first interview)

> I had [a panic attack] last week when I woke up and I'm thinking about these blimming bailiffs and I'm thinking, 'Oh, crumbs.' And I decided that when I was in the house I would lock the front door, I would lock the back

door and then if anybody came I could hide. But then I thought, 'Well that's not going to do any good is it?' You've got to address this and try and sort it out and that's what I've been doing. But you've got to get yourself into that frame of mind. And my daughter's very good, she sends emails back and says, 'Why don't you try this and that.' And I'm thinking, 'That's the sort of thing I would have said to people years ago.' But now, trying to focus on it, when it is you, is not easy. But anyway, we're getting there, we're getting there slowly. (Julie, age 60, second interview)

Katie, meanwhile, was less optimistic in her outlook during the first interview and the glimmers of hope in her narrative emerged only in her desire to escape and move abroad to start a new life. Her experiences, not least her arrest and conviction, had led to serious mental health problems including attempts at taking her own life. By the second interview, however, things had changed; her granddaughter's serious illness was something that she could not have predicted and, in her mind, dwarfed her own problems. Her hopes for the future became centred around her granddaughter's health. This focus provided her with the self-efficacy required to 'carry on':

I don't feel much about my life; I don't feel like I have a life because I'm trapped indoors really because I'm frightened of going out because I'm looking behind me all the time thinking, 'has somebody got a camera? Have they got it in their handbag? So I don't go out, I don't go to any family dos or functions, I don't go out for a drink. The odd time the kids will drag me out for a meal or something; I have a friend who comes and takes me out sometimes and gets me lunch … But I just don't feel like I have anything in my life whatsoever. (Katie, age 60, first interview)

I just carry on, I just carry on and try and get through every day separately, you know like, every day as it comes … [My hopes are] just that Natalie gets better, you know, these episodes are fewer and further in between because they said that every time she has an episode it damages part of her brain. And when they did the scan, there's five parts of her brain that have been damaged with this, you know with her speech and her writing and things like that. Her mobility. So I just want things to sort themselves out and get back to normal. (Katie, age 60, second interview)

Subjective experiences change over time; what a person feels on one day can be different to the next. Changes in social circumstances naturally affect stores of hope and agency. Each interview conducted and each group meeting observed as part of this research provided only a snapshot into each woman's life. Symbolic interactionist theorists (Mead 1934; Matsueda and Heimer 1997; Giordano et al. 2002; Uggen et al. 2004; Carlsson 2012) would argue that every piece of research is coloured by the women's daily experience and interaction. Adding to this, the women involved in this research had chaotic lives compounded by criminalisation. Desistance for them, as Carlsson (2012) would argue, was a constant process of maintenance. Any move towards desistance, and subsequently a life free from harm, should be celebrated whilst any setbacks should be examined and addressed. Hope was an important factor in their desistance because when there is nothing to lose, criminalisation is more likely to occur.

Hope increased for the women in particular when they saw others successfully desisting and resisting criminalisation. For example, Holly's hope was increased by her brother's successful desistance negotiation and Rebecca, Kelly-Marie, Shelly and Michaela each inspired hope in the other. Self-efficacy occurred when the women experienced positive social bonds, from good relationships, meaningful employment, supportive agencies, stable housing and so on. As will be discussed in the next chapters, criminalisation makes these results unlikely. Kelly-Marie's narrative confirms the power of hope and self-efficacy when they come together. The contrast in Kelly-Marie and Grace's narratives (see above) were stark. This subjective-level theme (which, for Kelly-Marie, was initiated by her involvement in Rebecca's agency and her improved relationship with her mother) can be the turning point needed for change:

> I've gone full circle, there's nothing else can come at me now. I had to do it for me, and I had to be ready for me and I'm just fortunate enough to have me family and still have me mum… And well, I wake up every morning and I smile 'cause I've got something to wake up for. And that's it basically, I just take each day as it comes, ***I know where I'm going, I know what I want and I know what I need to get there***. Do you know what I mean? And I'm in recovery, I interact with [the drug recovery team] and they're

> trying to get me involved in doing recovery work there, working as a peer mentor, but I'm not ready for that. And if I'm more honest with meself, I don't think I really want that. Because I want to pull meself away from the addiction and what goes on with it 'cause you can quite easily slip back down the road. And I don't care whether you're a recovery worker or whatever; they say 'once an addict, always an addict.' Well that's not true, once in recovery, you're in recovery for the rest of your life. And I don't want reminding for the rest of my life, do you know what I mean? There is something else out there for me, and when the time's right it'll be there. (Kelly-Marie, age 48)

Shame, Remorse and Internalising Stigma

The next cognitive-level themes which LeBel et al. (2008) considered to be important to desistance are shame and remorse. However, the authors noted that shame and remorse do not always lead to desistance but can have the opposite effect in terms of the 'doomed to deviance' (Maruna 2001) script, as represented in Karen's narrative. This was particularly evident in Karen's use of the discourse of 'choice' as noted above. This difference in the positive and negative effects of shame and remorse links to the third theme considered by the authors, internalising stigma. John Braithwaite (1989) draws the distinction here between re-integrative shame, where the law-breaking act is regretted but the internal self-worth of the individual is preserved, and stigmatising shame, where both the act and the actor are degraded. According to Braithwaite (1989) these distinctions emerge in criminal justice reactions. However, I would extend this definition to include the internal processes and reactions to shame as imposed by the CJS or from other sources such as the media and local communities. Probyn (2005) argues that shame is gendered, particularly for women who experience abuse. Probyn argues that this shame is located in 'women's enduring, historically diverse and multi-dimensional experiences of subordination' (2005: 83). In Karen's narrative, above, it was clear that the effect of the shame and remorse about her past actions resulted in stigmatising shame. The process of 'double deviance' for Karen had been particularly effective (Heidensohn and Silvestri 2012;

Worrall 1990; Leverentz 2014). Karen stigmatised herself for her actions as both a mother and a citizen. This stigma was a reflection of her interactions and was reinforced in internal cognitions. Probyn (2005) argues that those who experience shame in early life are likely to re-experience it later, and this again was particularly clear in Karen's narrative.

The difference between stigmatising and re-integrative shame is important. Whilst re-integrative shame has desistance-inducing potential, stigmatising shame effectively blocks desistance journeys, constructing barriers between criminalised women and their future 'good' selves. Stigmatising shame does not provide the glue for the social bonds to society described in the last chapter, whilst re-integrative shame arguably can do. Katie, for example, differentiated between the stigmatising shame she felt from her family and the re-integrative shame she felt from her friend, related to her mental health difficulties following her conviction:

> So we [Katie and her friend, Rose] went out for lunch and it was really nice. Yeah we caught up on things and we said we'd do it more often, go out once a month at least and so we can have a talk. And she's really good, she's a really good friend and we've known each other since I was nine, so it's nice. She's there if I need her you know, she's told me to ring her, if I need her she'll come over. So that's nice to know that I've got somebody there besides the family that doesn't judge me. My family seem to judge me and, 'oh pull out of it, stop being so daft.' You know, if I keep saying I feel really down today, [they say] 'oh don't be so silly.' It's like they don't understand. So she's got lots of patience, Rose has, and it's nice. (Katie, age 60, second interview)

Shame also moved from the stigmatising to the re-integrative for other women. Kelly-Marie described her shame surrounding her past behaviour, towards an acceptance of the behaviour as part of the 'person she used to be' which had in turn helped her become the person she 'is'. Her narrative strongly resembled Maruna's 'desisting scripts' (2001):

> My eyes are open wide and it's time to move on. Yeah? My grandchildren are getting to an age now where I don't want their friends saying, 'Oh your nan's always getting in trouble with the police.' I don't want that. I mean I brought the embarrassment on my daughter and my family. There's another

generation there … I want them to be able to come and visit their nana, and their children to come and visit because they don't know any of this. They don't know any of their nana's life. And what life I have got left, I want to find something out there, to get a career or maybe carry on with me beauty and hairdressing, whatever comes up, do you know what I mean? (Kelly-Marie, age 48)

Paula's narrative was similar to Kelly-Marie's; whilst her offending was not as consistent (she described the theft as a 'one-off'), the re-integrative shame she felt as a result was central to avoiding future offending and maintaining sobriety:

It's just not the kind of person I am. And now that I'm out of addiction and the guilt and shame of it all. And my family, the children, it's just not a good thing to do. And prison is not a nice place to be. I was only there for 6 days luckily. But not an experience I ever want to do again. (Paula, age 36)

Paula's experience of re-integrative shame was such that her new partner's reaction to the disclosure of her conviction would be a decisive turning point for their future. Stigmatising shame on his behalf would result in the ending of the relationship. Paula was more concerned with her own desistance than a romantic relationship:

But it's still early days. At the end of the day, I think I spoke to someone in here [the Women's Centre] about it, and it's just one of them isn't it? If they're a keeper they're not going to be bothered. (Paula, age 36)

Rebecca's narrative also had strong themes of re-integrative shame throughout. Rebecca described hope and self-efficacy; shame and remorse; internalising stigma and alternative identities in her internal journey from stigmatising shame to more useful re-integrative shame through her work on her project:

So the sentence on my life, it wasn't even a sentence, it was my own behaviours. You know I started beating myself up a lot. You know … 'cause that's what guilt is, it's turning the knife inwards, I do believe that. And I started

> really, really doubting myself as a person … And you know it wasn't … a behavioural act, it was something that I choose to do and was with intent … You're typing in somebody else's name that isn't your name, that's intent. I intended to defraud, even though she didn't have to pay anything financially, because it was all written off, that's not the point. You know, I stole her identity. And that should never have happened, regardless of my personal feelings towards her; that is crime, it's a criminal act and it impacted my life deeply. Very much so. That the only way I would ever have come to terms with my criminal behaviour was by doing something for 'the criminals'. That was the only way I could come to terms with it. And my work today has enabled me to come to terms with that. (Rebecca, age 46)

The shift from stigmatising to re-integrative shame for Rebecca was also intimately connected with her relationship with her partner; whilst stigmatising shame had a negative effect on her relationship, when her past behaviours were acknowledged and accepted, the relationship also changed:

> So when I was going through, because I didn't tell him [Paul, Rebecca's partner] what I'd done, he knew something was wrong and thought I was an online gambler or I was having an affair. So, you know, eventually it just threw us apart because I couldn't actually bring myself to [tell him] … and that was the guilt. So I justified my lies with never having to feel the guilt but that's how the guilt was dribbling out and he could obviously see and he thought, 'Well she's just lying, she's this,' and when it all did come out, he said, 'well if only you'd told me because I was thinking ….' He said, 'Well is that all?' (Laughs) But we've come through that time and obviously you know he's supported me in getting this [her agency] off the ground, because he knew for the … for my own piece of mind that I had to do it. (Rebecca, age 46)

For many women involved in this study, stigmatising shame was the lasting effect of criminalisation. Even Katie, who maintained her innocence in the benefit fraud she had been convicted of throughout our meetings, described the stigmatising shame she felt. Katie's conviction had also been featured in the local media:

Katie: Yeah I just feel like everybody's looking at me (begins to cry) and they aren't, they probably don't even remember it, or they never saw it. I just feel like when people do look at me, they're seeing a criminal. I know it's silly, it's silly thinking that … but ….

Una: What does make you think that?

Katie: I don't know, I think how I'd be with somebody. Like my daughter's husband, he's in prison for murder. And I think … I look at him and I think … I don't believe he did it, I think he had some involvement in it, I really do, but I don't think he actually did anything to it … But I look at that now and I think, that's you know … people are going to know you for that, I mean I know it was murder and things. But that's how I think, is somebody going to look at me and think, you know you've taken all this money of the state and … (Breaks down) … you're a criminal. You see it just goes through my head that. I just want to shout, 'I haven't done anything wrong.' (Katie, age 60, second interview)

Katie's stigmatising shame was so profound that she equated her own transgressions (unwitting benefit fraud) with those of someone convicted of murder. Negative effects of criminal justice intervention will be explored further in the next chapter. However, for many women, sources of shame did not solely emerge from criminalisation. Kelly-Marie, for example, described her deep shame at falling pregnant with her second child to her abusive partner:

Anyhow, it's got to two weeks before I was supposed to go for the IVF and I told him I weren't going. He said, 'I've paid all that money, what do you mean you're not going?' I said 'I don't want to,' I said, 'If I can't have one naturally, then it's not meant to be.' I didn't want to be able to… He said to me, 'You're pregnant you.' I said, 'Don't talk stupid.' Anyhow I'd gone and got all these tests just to piss him off 'cause I'd spent all his money, this that and the other, and I took two into the doctors and they'd all come back positive. Well my gynaecologist couldn't believe it 'cause there were no way that I should have got pregnant naturally. So I've gone up there, had the scan and he's over the moon. But I wasn't. And I felt so guilty and so shameful all the way through that pregnancy. And it were me baby I were feeling for 'cause I'm tied to this man for the rest of my life now. I'm going to be abused and battered and where's me life going? Anyhow, there you are. And I'd made a few attempts at taking my life. (Kelly-Marie, age 48)

Kelly-Marie's stigmatising shame here emerged from what she saw as her inability to be a 'good mother' to her second child. The impact of the ideology of motherhood is clear here (Rich 1996). Again the 'double deviance' of women is a feature even in the absence of transgressions of the law. Women are deemed deviant even when they are abused but cannot fulfil the prescribed mother role. There are clear links with Karen's narrative of her inability to be a 'normal woman' (see above). In both cases, gendered expectations are synonymous with shame when they are unmet.

For Holly, shame was a feature of her relationship with her mother's drug use. This taking on of parental shame was also evident in Jenny's (a member of staff at the WC) narrative. Holly's narrative was replete with references to gender roles. Jenny described her shame at not being able to provide for her siblings. Again her shame resulted from her inability to live up to gendered expectations around caring roles:

Holly: A lot of people ask me and stuff like about my family and my mum and I tell them she's on drugs but I won't go into it like this. Like my probation worker, she knows and like people like that, but I don't really speak about it because people who really know me know about my background, so …

Una: Do you mind talking about it?

Holly: Not really, 'cause I've gone through it now haven't I? So, it don't bring it back up just I wish it could have been different but in a way 'cause like my mum left me through like drugs and that and my grandma's… In a way I think about it and I go mad at my mum, but I can't really go mad at my mum 'cause I left my little child, well my grandma had to take her 'cause of domestic violence, but in a way with me going out and smoking the cannabis, I'm doing exactly the same as her, not like through drugs, but through different circumstances, so I don't really go mad at her no more 'cause I try my best to get my daughter back and stuff and stop going mad at my mum 'cause I've done it for the past… like, she's been there the past twelve months and stuff. (Holly, age 24)

> The kids got taken off my mum and given to me and my nan. And I think what happened because of that, we knew it was bad 'cause she was using drugs, but we didn't realise just how bad the neglect was. And I think that, 'cause I kind of stopped going to my mum's because I … that was my way of dealing with it. It was all that guilt had built up and I had to have … it was kind of like post-traumatic stress. So I had to have counselling for it but I did become really, really depressed to the point where you know I couldn't even make eye contact with people in work, you know 'cause I was that anxious about stuff and I'd be crying all the time and I was in a very bad relationship as well. It's surprising how easy people can sniff you out when you're vulnerable. (Jenny, Group Leader, Women's Centre)

Skeggs (1997) notes that white, working-class women often construct systems of meaning to negate the symbolic systems of denigration and degeneracy they are marked with. For Holly and Jenny, these systems of meaning emerged in their personal lives. For Holly, as is seen above, this was in her desistance and her ability to care for her daughter. For Jenny, this meaning was found in her generative employment at the WCs. In this way, Jenny's experience mirrored Rebecca's attempts to overcome stigmatising shame, despite Jenny not having a conviction:

> But yeah I've got a really good relationship with them [her parents] now, which I think is really important for my own personal development personally and in my career 'cause if I can't lay things to rest, I don't think I could do the job that I do which is so intense sometimes. So I think I had to do that for my own personal and career development. (Jenny, Group Leader, Women's Centres)

It is clear that, even in the absence of convictions, women deal with stigmatising shame in their day to day lives. Shame, remorse and stigma are important cognitive-level themes which emerge in women's desistance narratives just as they do men's (LeBel et al. 2008). Yet even in the absence of offending pasts, women's narratives often also contain these themes. Women involved in the CJS are often 'doubly demonised' (Heidensohn and Silvestri 2012; Worrall 1990; Leverentz 2014) as a result of their imagined moral transgressions in the eyes of the CJS and wider society in general related to their positions as mothers, daughters and partners. On top of this, women experience levels of shame and stigma attached to other 'deviant' behaviour, particularly related to these roles, or even engulfing shame related to the deviant behaviour of others.

Identity

Maruna notes that 'to desist from crime, ex-offenders need to develop a coherent, pro-social identity for themselves' (2001: 7). Maruna argued that those who successfully desisted from crime had high levels of self-efficacy, meaning that they saw themselves in control of their futures, and had a clear sense of purpose and meaning in their lives, that is, 'the ways' (discussed above) to enable desistance. They also found a way to 'make sense' out of their past lives and often found some redeeming value in lives that had often been spent in and out of the CJS. Implied here is the suggestion that, in order to desist, former law breakers must consider themselves not in terms of self- or socially imposed offending identities. The 'offender' term carries with it, not only a description of the past, but a presumption of the future. Feminist research has argued that often women do not fall easily into the artificial 'victim/offender' binary (Ferraro 2006; Stubbs and Tolmie 2008; Prison Reform Trust 2017). This approach suggests that for women, (and indeed for many men) desistance therefore is not just about overcoming 'offender' identity but also may be about overcoming a self- and socially imposed victim identity which may also be linked to past offending behaviour. This is not to suggest that those with an identity associated with victimhood are unable to desist, but high levels of self-efficacy and feelings of control do not usually emerge from those who continue to self-identify as victims. What follows is an examination of the various identities considered by women involved in this research, moving beyond the victim/offender binary to consider desisting women as survivors and bricoleurs (Levi-Strauss 1962) of their own fate through various alternative pro-social identities.

Offender/Ex-Offender Identities

Chapter 2 included references to women and men as 'offenders' and 'ex-offenders'/'former offenders', as criminalised individuals are often termed in the desistance literature. Whilst for some the term 'ex-offender' can be associated with positive connotations related to self-change, for others the term situates identity in past actions, mistakes and, indeed, victimisations (Aresti et al. 2010). Some researchers and people with convictions have gone as far as to describe the term as dehumanising (O'Neill 2017), a term which describes a person in terms of past behaviour or actions and nothing else. Both the Women's Centres (WCs) and Housing for Northshire (HfN) project also found these terms problematic. Rebecca articulated her feelings on the terms on behalf of herself and her clients at the HfN Project. Similarly, Christine, CEO of the WCs, contended that her project did not situate women's identities in terms of their 'offences':

> I never refer to myself as an offender or a former offender. I see myself as a citizen of society that leads a law-abiding life. So I don't ever describe myself as a former offender or an offender … I don't see myself or any of our members as criminals, former offenders, ex-cons or anything. We've got the experiences that we've got and I think it's important, just like any other area, that our narratives are given in order to you know make a bit of change, at least a small dent in it. (Rebecca, CEO of Housing for Northshire Project)

> We don't differentiate someone being an offender or not an offender. They come and the reason they get access is because they seem to be all unique stories but similar stories, similar themes. (Christine, CEO of the Women's Centres)

Perhaps ironically, some of the methodological difficulties I faced when recruiting women for this study included a tendency for women at the WCs to argue that, as they did not see themselves as 'offenders' or 'former offenders', they would not be good candidates for interview. Whilst this resistance was important in their desistance journeys, at times, it also effectively formed part of the societal reaction for other women who *did* consider themselves 'offenders' or 'former offenders'. It was the societal and criminal justice reaction to their offences which caused some of the women, including Anna, to consider themselves as 'offenders':

> In reality I'm gonna have to see myself as an offender now because of the charges that are over me head and me name. I keep denying it but I'm going to fight it… I did drive away but I didn't realise there was something in the back of me car. I did know things weren't right. (Anna, age 36)

Nonetheless, within Anna's recognition of her status in the eyes of others, there was a resistance; she acknowledged that she had been denying the label but was now going to 'fight' it. This resistance to criminalisation was evident in many of the women's narratives:

> I've never been in trouble with the police [prior to her current offence]. I just made a massive mistake. It's not like I got caught in the act, I actually handed myself in for it. So, no. I don't know, I think I'm just one of those people who messed up. (Paula, age 36)

> I do joke about being a criminal, yes. Well, no I don't to be honest because really it is just circumstantial. For me, it's obviously, it's an emotional issue. I'm looking to do an emotions course actually in Northton in September because I think I need to address that, because that's when things seem to go a bit pear shaped. So, yeah, I'm just trying to do what I can really. (Sue, age 40)

> If I did it purposely, I'd hold my hands up and go, 'Yes I did, I am an offender, I've learned my lesson.' But it was just a mistake you know. (Heather, age 24)

For Heather, Paula and Sue, their identity was not related to their criminalisation; for these women, their transgressions[4] were blips in otherwise law-abiding lives. The lack of a pattern of behaviour clearly changes the identity dynamics. Particularly for Sue and Paula, offending was recognised as something which was separate from their identity. Yet they did not deny the transgression, but tried to take something positive from it. Essentially, much like Maruna's (2001) 'desisters', these women saw themselves as fundamentally good people who had nonetheless made a mistake. This finding also reflects the conclusions of Radcliffe and Hunter's (2013) research into the positive reinforcement effect of women's community services (these will be discussed further in Chap. 6). However, particularly in Heather's case, but also in Katie's and Ruth's narratives, there was a sense that the 'offender' identity was something which had been imposed on them unjustly. In these cases, it was difficult to 'make sense' out of their convictions and supposed past errors.

Some attempting to desist did find the 'ex-' or 'former-' label useful nonetheless. Some of the Northshire women such as Kelly-Marie found their identity situated in a recognition of past behaviour, but more prominently in their attempts to move beyond historic behaviour:

> I think of myself as somebody that's been rehabilitated, yeah? I'm a work in progress, yeah? I'm not running before I can walk, I'm not biting off any more than I can chew; I just take each day as it comes. (Kelly-Marie, age 48)

Kelly-Marie had one of the strongest 'desistance' (rather than 'ex-offender') identities amongst the women involved in this study. This identity was also present in Michaela and Shelly's narratives as well as Rebecca's. It was perhaps their status in the HfN Project which caused this desisting identity to be so strong. The women were faced on a daily basis with their past offending selves. They constantly confronted this identity in an attempt to move past it. In comparison, the women attending WC meetings were only likely to confront this aspect of their past behaviour formally on a weekly basis.

Societal reaction was a key feature in the construction of identity. As noted, many of the women drew distinctions between themselves and other 'proper offenders' and this helped in the construction of their 'non' or 'lesser' 'offender' identities. Marie, for example, drew a distinction between her own offences of robbing flag stones and burglar identity:

> I don't see myself as… last time I got arrested the sergeant says to me, 'Oh it's Dodgem the burglar.' And I went 'wow' I said, 'I'm not a burglar.' He went, 'Yeah I remember when you got done last time.' And it were an allotment

thing, I met this lad there, went to pick the trailer up for him. He'd nicked a whole lot of stuff and I were basically the wheels behind it again. Got caught; but it were classed as burglary within a non-dwelling. But I wouldn't class myself as a burglar. And then I were up on a burglary charge for one of my customers when I were dog walking, and I were looking at five year for that. Anyway I won it 'cause I took it to court and everything 'cause I'm not a burglar, it's not something I do. I can't do it. I'd have a heart attack on the spot. It's a bit different than… I know it's not right and the police don't see it like this, but I'll go to an old farm, on me own, middle of nowhere, night time, and fill the car up with slate, sell it the next day. That's where I need to step back and think, 'no that's wrong, that belongs to someone.' It obviously belongs to someone, I don't know who. But… it might not, I dunno (laughs) it belongs to the quarry doesn't it? But I don't know; it's hard really to… I wouldn't go and pinch something out of someone's house or anything, I can't do that. I'm not like that. (Marie, age 40)

It could be argued that this propensity to recognise her offence as somewhat victimless was a factor barring Marie's desistance journey. This was a feature of many of the women's narratives. For example, during a WC observation session of a group session on victimisation, a woman in the group, Sarah, noted that she did not know who the victim of her shoplifting offence really was:

See this is where I have a problem, I can't see who the victims of my crimes are … There's no way that if all shoplifting stopped tomorrow there would be a massive drop in the price of clothes… They have insurance. (Sarah, Tulip Centre)

This was something which was raised time and again in the victimisation sessions and something which the group leader also found problematic:

Their insurance prices will go up after they've claimed. Although I know what you mean, it does seem to sometimes be like a grain of sand on the beach to those big companies. (Jenny, Group Leader, Tulip Centre)

Again there is a link here between the 'offender' identity, victimisation and desistance. Where there was an absence of an identifiable victim, it could be difficult to promote desistance. At these times, both the WCs and the HfN Project promoted individual self-improvement as an end in itself. This raises questions about the individualisation of the structural harms created by both patriarchy and neoliberalism.

A further issue in identity change processes, which emerged in the narratives, was the social construction of identities which occurred prior to and following criminalisation. For example, the identities of Julie and Holly can be compared. Julie was more resistant to the 'offender' identity, situating her offence in the context of her mother's death and stresses at work, whilst avoiding mentioning previous offences.[5] Holly immediately accepted herself as an 'offender' and was upfront about her past shoplifting and marijuana use. For social constructionists what is important is the presentation of the 'self' in comparison to others. As argued by Nils Christie,

> Crime does not exist. Only acts exist, acts often given different meanings within various social frameworks. Acts and the meanings given to them are our data. Our challenge is to follow the destiny of acts through the universe of meanings. Particularly, what are the social conditions that encourage or prevent giving the acts the meaning of being crime? (Christie 2004: 3)

Although both women had essentially been convicted of crimes, Julie's rejection of the 'offender' identity can arguably be accounted for by Julie's middle-class, older, religious identity which, in neoliberal Britain, is not usually associated with criminalisation. In comparison, Holly's acceptance can be related to her working-class, younger identity and her relationships with other 'offenders'. In many ways, however, this will make Julie's desistance pathway a more difficult one to travel; without a public recognition of past mistakes, it will be difficult to move past them. Julie cannot find the 'something good' in her past offending which Maruna (2001) found can be central to identity transformation. For example, Julie would almost certainly shy away from the public post-criminal justice intervention 'graduation' ceremonies advocated by Maruna and LeBel (2003) whilst Holly would be likely to embrace them.

When considering desistance it is clear that we must take into account socially constructed identities which are not only gendered but class, 'race' and culturally based.

The importance of socially constructed 'offender' identities was clear in Katie's narrative. As noted above, there was a sense in Katie's narrative that the 'offender' identity was unjustly imposed upon her. Nonetheless the socially constructed identity was an important one:

> I feel like I've got 'criminal' tattooed on my forehead. That's how I feel. And I mean I know it's not murder or anything, it's not child abuse or anything like, but it's still… I've still fraudulently claimed from the government. (Kate, age 60, first interview)

Whether a woman took on the master status 'offender' identity had as much to do with her offence and her own self-perception, as to the societal reaction and support she received. Desistance occurred not only in the change in women's behaviour and actions, but also in society's reaction to this change. This was also clearly evident in the narratives of Marie and Shelly; both had been accused of something of which they were later found not guilty, but in both cases it was the women's status as 'offenders' which caused the suspicion around the offences. Shelly was tried for a theft from a person offence. She had pleaded not guilty but nonetheless was denied a place in a hostel whilst she was on trial because of her perceived 'offender' identity:

> And I'd put a 'not guilty' plea in; remember in the magistrates court? He's [the magistrate] then gone like that, 'no I'm not giving her bail because I believe she'd reoffend.' So as far as I'm concerned, you found me guilty before, I've just told you I'm not guilty, me plea's not guilty, you found me guilty already. (Shelly, age 53)

Similarly, Marie was convicted of a burglary offence for which she was later found not guilty. Shelly's and Marie's not-guilty case studies starkly highlight how reaction to past offences can have negative consequences in terms of escaping the 'offender' label. In addition, societal reaction can act in more subtle ways by denying women alternative identities. Labelling theory has salience here as the state's reaction can affect deviant identities. As was noted by Howard Becker, 'deviance is not a quality that lies in a behaviour itself but in the interaction between the person who commits an act and those that respond to it' (1963: 14). Reactions are clearly important in 'offender' identity construction and deconstruction. A good example of how societal reaction can promote 'offender' identity deconstruction happened after my interview with Bridget. Bridget's mentor, Fran, spoke to me and said, 'She's not a bad person, she's just easily led and people take advantage.' This rhetoric clearly affected Bridget's opinion of herself and fed into her desire to want to 'go straight' so that she would not let Fran and others down. Relationships between staff and service users will be explored further in the next chapter.

The women involved in this research tended to travel one of three pathways in terms of the 'offender' identity; either they took on this identity which proved to make desistance more difficult; they rejected the identity completely which again tended to make desistance arduous (unless they had very minimal offences, see Sue, for example) or thirdly, like Maruna's (2001) desisting group, they accepted this identity as something which was part of their past, which they learned from and built upon, developing an alternative pro-social identity as they went.

Alternative Identities

Summarising the differences between male and female desistance pathways, Matthews et al. (2014) argued that there were four factors which can explain the difference. Firstly, informal relations and supports were more important for women. Women were also more likely to seek conventional roles of a partner or parent. Thirdly, women were more concerned with seeking roles with social approval. And finally, women appeared to be able to change their lifestyle more quickly than men. This section will focus on the second and third of these purported differences which build upon Rumgay's (2004) finding that women use 'scripts' during desistance to exit offending behaviour. Beverley Skeggs (1997) has argued that although white, working-class women are inscribed and marked with the symbolic systems of denigration and degeneracy, they manage to create systems of value and attribute respectability and high-moral standing to themselves. This labelling system was even more prominent for the white, (largely) working-class women with convictions involved in this study. Some of the women were able to create similar systems of respectability and high-moral standing. One way in which criminalised women used alternative systems of meaning and identities in their narratives was to compare and contrast their offences and 'offender' identities with imagined other, more serious or prolific offenders/offences:

> I'm not a naughty, naughty girl, I wouldn't go and burgle someone or owt like that, I've got an heart do you know what I mean? (Marie, age 40)

> I have seen other people who have gone to court with far, far more serious situations and got off very lightly, well in my view. (Julie, age 60, first interview)

> And when I've had my benefit it's not like I've lived a fancy lifestyle or anything. You know, it's not like you see some people where they've claimed thousands or over half that I've done and they just do it openly. (Katie, age 60, first interview)

Whether these techniques of neutralisation (Matza and Sykes 1957) are conductive to desistance, however, is questionable. Maruna (2001) noted that for his desisting group, those who successfully navigated identity change incorporated elements of their former offending selves into their new personality. Where this behaviour was denied or downplayed, desistance became difficult. Yet, as found by Jamieson et al. (1999), females were more likely to downplay their offending and attach a moral element to non-offending behaviour, highlighting the social control element of patriarchal structures. Therefore whether or not offending was incorporated into the women's identities, the social structures in which this cognition takes place (as well as the intended audience of the change or otherwise) must be taken into account.

Nonetheless, for women, like Karen, who still saw themselves in terms of an offending identity, desistance was extremely arduous:

> I'm living day to day at the moment, I'm not even thinking about the future. You know I was thinking about this the other day, you know when I was younger and little girls used to say, 'when I'm older and I get married and ….' I never had that in my head, I never dreamed of getting married and things like that. And I just feel like, my path was set out at a young age and I followed it, and here I am now, you know, in a train wreck. (Karen, age 36)

For Karen, all hope had gone, her identity as a 'normal woman' was destroyed before it had a chance to exist. As a result of her offences, Karen's gendered, pro-social identity was stripped away. She linked her offending identity to a fatalistic sense of self. Despite being a mother, once her children were removed from her care, Karen had no alternative pro-social identity to conform to. For Karen, the 'offender' and mother identities could not coexist with each other and so she resigned herself to a criminalised identity. She contrasted her sister's experience who she felt had 'chosen' a different path and conformed to the alternative identities which Karen felt were out of her grasp:

> She's got everything that I wanted. At 36 I feel like I'm not going to get it now. My kids… I feel like I've lost them through the domestic violence. I wasn't strong enough to make a choice you know. They put me in refuges, in Bridgetown and things that. But I just blocked it out. I just got involved with bad things, I felt like to punish myself, I felt I deserved it. I felt like I let my kids down. You know the choice I made to let my kids go to my mum's, I made that choice because it was best for them. If I had have dragged them from house to house… Sean was smashing houses up. The kids were very close together. Two of them are the same age now, they're both 7 but they're not twins. So… age 3 and under, you know it was hard work and then with him [Sean] on top. So for years you know I was, you know, family orientated and then when it all crumbled, I just went back to what I was like. (Karen, age 36)

Karen had taken on the 'offender' identity to the extent that it sequestered her sense of self-worth. She felt 'doomed to deviance' (Maruna 2001). The rhetoric of choice in her narrative highlights the damaging effects of the lack of help and support available which made Karen unable to draw a distinction between the victim and 'offender' identity, leading to a continuation of offending and self-punishment. Again the dichotomy of 'offender/normal woman' within Karen's narrative highlights how for women, even for the 'offender' themselves, offending is not a 'normal' identity. Again this reflects Jamieson et al.'s (1999) finding that women tend to underplay their offending identity as compared to men and tend to seek hyper-moral (Matthews et al. 2014) roles when travelling the road of desistance in order to compensate for this supposed past transgression against their gender, to account for their 'double deviance'. This is also reflected in Perry's (2013) argument that the CJS often associates desisting identities with traditional 'feminine' roles.

As has been seen in the previous chapters, the gendered 'script' of motherhood did, for some of the women, provide a route out of offending. For example, Anna found doing 'the perfect mum shit' as a script she could follow to protect herself from offending behaviour. Similarly, Ruth, Karen and Michaela all related their attempts at not offending to their roles as mothers whilst Kelly-Marie linked non-offending and her identity as a grandmother. Rebecca provided a clear example of Maruna's (2001) desisters when she described how her past behaviour had affected, but not subsumed, her essentially pro-social identity:

> But you know, my morals had gone, all my moral fibre, but my values never changed; I always knew deep down that I have got values and they never changed. I was still a mother, I was still a daughter, I was still a sister, I was still a friend. And you know, I was still the same person I was that had been loved and had a successful career before I went down that road. (Rebecca, age 46)

Rebecca's identity therefore was not only rooted in her perpetual relational identities as mother, daughter, sister and so on, but also in her hyper-moral (Matthews et al. 2014) subsequent actions. Other women also found their pro-social identity in generative roles. For Grace, the possibility of an alternative identity based in motherhood was removed when her daughter was taken into care following her arrest. This was clearly an extremely difficult experience for Grace; nonetheless she managed to find strength and the possibility of an alternative identity through her volunteering work:

> Yeah, well, like as I say, I went from being a full time mum to being like nothing. It kept me occupied, it kept my mind off things and they're [the voluntary shop staff] very nice, they talk to you, you know, and I get along with all of them there. (Grace, age 31)

Julie meanwhile found her alternative identity rooted in a renewal of her religious identity and an increased involvement in charitable fundraising. She described raising money by asking for charitable donations instead of gifts for her 60th birthday:

> I got £150 and I was told, Sunday just gone, that the money just gone to a lady that's in Sierra Leone who suffers from polio but has been given two children to foster who have lost their parents to Ebola. And the £150 will give them food, rice and will feed them for 6 months. 6 Months! Without her having to beg… Really, it's not a huge amount of money is it? But it can make such a difference so I thought, 'Oh that's really good.' So that was nice. (Julie, age 60, second interview)

As was seen in the previous chapter, for many women it was their relational roles as partners and mothers which provided either the route into, or the maintenance of, their offending. This was highlighted clearly in one of the observation sessions when one woman, Janet, described, without shame, her part in covering for her son's offending, something which she and others felt was part of her motherly duty:

Janet:	My sons have been in trouble with the police before so when there was stolen stuff in the house, I took the blame
Christine:	That just shows you're a good mum (Rose Centre)

When desistance literature suggests that women change much faster than men, this may mask inequalities and social expectations of what it is to be a 'good woman'. Although Matthews and colleagues note that women exiting prostitution tend to be attracted to relational and generative alternative identities, 'not all women aspire to or are able to achieve such roles. This raises the issue of whether women ascribe to these roles because of the lack of viable alternatives on offer: or as we have seen in relation to exiting, for example, the limited emphasis that is placed on finding alternative forms of employment' (2014: 136). In addition to constricted employment identities, within the Northshire women's narratives, there was a limited access to additional alternative identities other than those relational, gendered roles of mother, partner and so on.

Victim Identities

As has been seen in previous chapters, the women involved in this research did not easily fall into the 'victim/offender' binary often portrayed by the CJS and traditional criminological research (Ferraro 2006; Stubbs and Tolmie 2008). As well as being women who had a history of transgressing the law, the women in this research were also victims of domestic abuse, poverty and poor mental health. The 2014 Prison Reform Trust Report has confirmed that these are the common experiences of women in prison in England; it is evident that this can extend to women serving community penalties also. The Northshire women were also victims of the violence of the CJS (explored further in the next chapter), the media and the punitive welfare system, particularly in the context of austerity. Their punishments included removal of children from their care. Throughout the research it was clear that criminalised women included victims of childhood and gendered abuse, rape, forced prostitution, violence, theft, robbery, fraud, assault and other harms. In a collection of essays, Rebecca Roberts noted, 'the overlapping nature of law breaking and victimhood where women with experience of abuse, assault and sexual violence are frequently swept up in the CJS as "offenders"' (2015: 9). Nonetheless, victimologists maintain that labels, including victim labels, much like 'offender' labels, are socially constructed (Walklate 2007). Similar to criminalisation, processes of victimisation are selective. Christie (1986: 18–19) for example, argued that there are five attributes of the 'ideal victim'. Christie noted that the ideal victim is weak, carrying out a respectable project, where she could not be blamed, whilst the 'offender' is 'big and bad' and unknown to the victim. Certainly many of the women did not easily align with this socially constructed notion of the 'ideal victim', restricting both the ability of the state, and themselves, to see them as such. Within many of the narratives of the women involved in this research, there was often a resistance to the 'victim' label:

> It was me who did the wrong, so no; I wouldn't describe myself as a victim. (Paula, age 36)

> I suppose I do feel hard done by, yeah, I feel it's one of those things, why me? But I know lots of things happen to lots of people, probably worse than me. But I think with me it's just sort of being a constant… Hopefully now, I can just sort of have some stability. (Sue, age 40)

> I'd never describe meself as a victim. I've overcome all that. (Anna, age 36)

The reasons for resistance to this label varied, but for all, resistance to victimisation was central to desistance. Whilst, for some women, resisting victimisation was about becoming the person they always knew they were (Maruna 2001), for Anna, the former victim identity was associated with transgressive behaviour. Following abuse at the hands of her former partner, Anna described how she became 'a bully, a drinker, a rebel'. Anna's desistance therefore was related to overcoming both her victim and 'offender' identities in a very direct way. Conversely, Holly adopted the rhetoric of the offender/victim binary when she separated her own victimisation and offending identities. However, part of Holly's desistance inevitably involved support for her experiences of abuse:

> Una: And would you describe yourself as a victim?
> Holly: No. Well not any more. I were like last year, from my ex-partner and that. Obviously people are victims like where I've stolen from shops and stuff like that, that's a victim isn't it? (Holly, age 23)

Shelly recalled her past experiences of domestic violence in much the same way as Maruna's (2001) desisting group spoke about their past offences. For Shelly, desistance was about not only coming to terms with and learning from past offending experiences but also past victimisation experiences:

> I would never accept myself as a victim at one time. But now, yeah. Because when I look back, 'cause I used to think of it as a weakness and I never ever seen myself as a weak person. But you know what I mean. Michaela just makes me see things in a different light. 'It doesn't mean you're a weak person Shelly.' 'You should have fucking said something Shelly, you should have spoke out at the time.'... But I do now, yeah, [see herself as a victim in the past] yeah of course. I do now. I've still got the scars to prove it, trust me. (Shelly, age 53)

For Shelly, part of her desistance was about addressing and overcoming past victimisations. As has been seen, many, if not most, criminalised women are victims (Prison Reform Trust 2017). However, where women's victimhood stems from criminalisation itself, (Smart 1977; Kennedy 1993; Jordan 2004; Davies 2011) it is clear that it was difficult for them to associate the label with anything positive, and particularly difficult for women to match this victimisation up with moves towards desistance. Principally, in the narratives of Katie, Ruth and Heather who struggled to view their transgressions as offences, the victimisation at the hands of the CJS was particularly harmful as it was so brutal and yet emerged from a previously trusted source (the State). Speaking about her conviction, Katie noted:

> It's like you're in a dream and you're standing outside and thinking, 'No that's not me; nobody'd do that to me.' (Katie, age 60, second interview)

Kelly-Marie also struggled to come to terms with her victimisation at the hands of the CJS and square this with any moves towards desistance, particularly in regards to the short prison sentences she served:

> They [the short sentences] were pathetic 'cause I were crying out for help and they just thought, 'Just put her in prison.' So I were drying out, coming out and just doing it all over again. (Kelly-Marie, age 48)

Much like the reaction to the 'offender' identity, those who fully accepted the victim identity, seeing it as their master status, faced barriers to desistance. This identity, like Kelly-Marie's past attempts show, was not conductive to feelings of hope, self-efficacy and agency. Women who denied their past victimisations also had trouble travelling the road of desistance. They were unable to address the issues which often led to their offending in the first place. Nonetheless, there is a difference here between denial and resistance. Resistance meant a recognition of past victimisations and acceptance of them as part of the make-up of their current identity. Yet it also included a rejection of the identity as their master status. This final group were often further along their desistance journeys. Women who were able to resist both offending and victim identities can be described as survivors and/or bricoleurs. This identity will now be examined.

Survivor/Bricoleur

Where women resisted the labels of both 'offender' and 'victim' and yet had experience of both the harms of the CJS and wider gendered harms, they often adopted the identity of 'survivor'. This research has found that desisting women were more than survivors, they were bricoleurs of their own desistance, using what limited resources they had in their attempts to travel the desistance pathway.

Anna described her entry into the criminogenic world her brothers and father had inhabited. Once she entered this world of fraud, robbery, drugs and violence, however, and established her dominant offending identity, she found it was difficult to escape:

> And then do you know how hard it is to get out? It's easier to get in! And it has taken me all these years to finally be able to walk around my own area without getting dirty looks and the fucking comments. But I've done it so… It's one of them isn't it, life goes on. It's got to… (Anna, age 36)

Nonetheless, Anna did make her way out of this world. Her most recent offence was characterised in her narrative as a blip in an otherwise deviance-free journey, a result of where she lived, her family's notorious identity and the social expectations of those surrounding her. As a result of this most recent conviction, Anna described a breakdown in her relationship with her children which she believed was a consequence of what she saw as the interference of social services, resulting in constant paranoia that her children would be removed from her care:

> I felt like my world had crumbled. Do you know what? They've knocked my confidence and everything. Me and my kids haven't been getting on since it all because I'm looking at them going right, every time they're late for school I panic.... I look at my daughter, Stacey, she's a teenager, she's fourteen .... They text me the other day from school saying that she's been late, so she comes home, I'm screaming at her so she went 'Mum phone 'em, phone 'em, phone 'em', do you know how late she was? Three minutes. And I was nearly slapping her, I was going, 'you're lying to me!'... It's ruining my life, you're [the school] ruining the family right? (Anna, age 36)

Anna could succumb to her status as a 'deviant mother' as she felt was portrayed by the school and social services. Nonetheless, she resisted both the 'offender' and victim identities; she recognised these identities as part of her past but was ready to move beyond them, using resources provided by the WC, her relationship with her children, along with great stores of hope and self-efficacy to attempt to travel her own desistance journey. Maruna (2001) found that desisting narratives include an intervention from 'someone who always believed in them'. This was not, on the whole, the experience of the women involved in this research. Instead desistance was a lonely experience which often required great stores of agency. Anna was determined to move on, even against others expectations:

> How can I try and move past it? I am though and I'm going to do the volunteering at the women's centre... I'm going to do it just to prove I could, to myself. I'm just trying to keep myself busy. (Anna, age 36)

We can see here Anna's identity change beyond the offender/victim binary using both social and psychological bricolage to construct her desisting identity. Levi-Strauss (1962) argued that bricoleurs use any limited materials available to them to solve new problems. When cultural (or social or psychological) materials are limited, bricoleurs reuse tried and tested methods. Sue discussed a similar use of psychological and social bricolage to help herself; things she did not find conducive to desistance she disregarded, but she took on the advice of others, as well as doing things for herself, to help her cut down on alcohol consumption, moving beyond the 'offender' and 'victim' identities towards desistance:

> I mean I've done a lot myself. I went on a self-esteem and assertiveness course at the women's centre, I've had counselling .... She [the counsellor] really, really helped because we did a similar thing to what we are doing now; we started right from the beginning and went through right to the present day. The advice she's given is... you know the thing is with me, I always like to get things done quickly, you know I'm an organised person. So what she's said to me now is, because you're on your own now, just take a step back, take it a day at a time and things will just happen when they happen. (Sue, age 40)

Conversely, Karen was in the very early stages of her identity change and had very limited support, social bonds or psychological reserve available to her; she had no fixed accommodation, was in a drug rehabilitation project, had lost her network of friends or associates, as well as custody of her children. The guilt and stigmatising shame Karen felt by not living up to the constructed idea of an 'ordinary woman' was something which was difficult to move past. Karen struggled to take on her past offending and victim identities and lost the possible alternative 'mother' script:

> I go to see my probation officer and she says, 'Oh take deep breaths in the morning and don't think about it.' But if you're taking deep breaths not to think about it, you're thinking about it. And it's there all the time, it's always at the back of my mind. It just won't go away (starts crying). I keep thinking, 'how long is it going to be for me?' Because I keep thinking, 'what could I have done differently that I hadn't already done?' (Karen, age 36)

The desistance journey continued to be redrawn for the women. When they found something (whether this was a cognitive process, a new identity, a relationship or voluntary employment etc.) which worked for them, they tended to build on this, discarding what did not work for them along the way. Desistance also meant the construction and reconstruction of identities; generally, what tended to work for women was a recognition of past offending and victim identities but a resistance also to allowing these to become their dominant identities or master status. In some ways, the talking therapy provided by the interviews provided some of the women with the opportunity to recognise past offending and victimisation, as well as pinpointing factors which had helped in desistance and those which had not. In addition, for some of the women, the interviews provided a generative opportunity (in their opinions) to 'give back' through the sharing of their own experiences with the researcher:

> I'm glad I've helped, I'm really glad I've helped. And I hope it helps somebody else, I really do.... thank you very much for letting me speak about it, it does help, you know talking to somebody about it and I'm just glad I've helped you. (Katie, age 60, second interview)

> I knew it had to be talked about... well I think I probably needed to offload it anyway. (Karen, age 36)

Christine, the CEO of the WCs, considered the construction of identity around the offender/victim/survivor binaries as often detrimental to women's desistance journeys:

> I see very often people defining themselves in those roles [ex-offender, victim or survivor] somehow and it feels like that is something that's difficult to move away from. I also seem to find that people define themselves as being 'in recovery' for a very long time and you see that amongst different communities. And they will, 'I'm in recovery, I'm a recovery champion.' And it becomes their identity and you know I would say, 'I'm Christine' you know 'I'm good and bad and full of hope and stability and bad habits, and all those sorts of stuff.' I wouldn't describe myself as polarised. (Christine, CEO of Women's Centre)

The narratives of desistance highlighted by this research, can in many ways, be viewed as narratives of resilience. In the previous chapter, it was contended that desistance can mean resilience in the face of social expectations; in this section on identity, it has been noted that desistance can also mean resistance to the offender/victim binary. Women who successfully negotiate and resist the offender/victim binary can be seen as bricoleurs of their own fate, using whatever limited resources they have to hand to desist in spite of patriarchal capitalism. Clearly as Maruna (2001) found, identity change was a key element in desistance. Women who transgress the law are portrayed as 'doubly deviant' and are therefore 'doubly damned' (Lloyd 1995) in terms of their treatment at the hands of the CJS, the media, social services, at intimate relationship level and by wider society in general. When this was combined with the fact that criminalised women are likely to be victims of domestic and childhood abuse, mental health issues, poverty and addiction, it could be difficult to see beyond the offender/victim binary into which women with convictions are generally placed. Nonetheless, the Northshire women who were successfully desisting from these harms saw themselves as bricoleurs of their own fate, using resilience, stores of agency and whatever resources they have to hand to resist their 'victim' and 'offender' identities.

Conclusion

Thomas LeBel and colleagues argued, 'the idea that rehabilitation involves changes in an individual's thinking and personal outlook is among the oldest ideas in corrections. What are relatively new are systematic efforts to uncover just how desisting ex prisoners think and how these thinking patterns differ from those of active offenders' (2008: 136). The authors proposed that previous research suggested there were four interrelated themes which were salient in the subjective literature; hope and self-efficacy, shame and remorse, internalising stigma and alternative identities. The 'Oxford Recidivism Study' involved a ten-year follow-up of 130 male former prisoners who had been convicted of property offences (LeBel et al. 2008). The authors quantitatively measured the desistance-inducing potential of these themes and concluded that there was an argument for a 'subjective-social' model for desistance. Subjective states before release from prison had a direct effect on recidivism and indirect effect on social circumstances following release which proved important when predicting desistance. The current study examined the same cognitive themes prospectively and qualitatively from the narratives of criminalised women, based in Northshire, who may or may not have spent time in prison for a range of offences (although the majority were property-based), concluding that cognitive processes are similarly important in the desistance scripts of women with convictions.

What is missing from LeBel et al.'s (2008) study however is both an interrogation of what hegemonic understandings of rehabilitation mean and, importantly, an acknowledgement of the social structures which shape cognition. When considering desistance from a female point of view, it is important that the realities of women's lives are considered. The structural constraints and political systems which criminalise their behaviour require examination and, as has been shown, these systems are evident in their cognitive processes. The research found levels of hope and particularly, self-efficacy, to be important factors in the narratives of criminalised women. In general the Northshire women's hopes were modest and surrounded families, homes, health and employment. Interestingly these hopes were generally similar to pre-conviction hopes. Hope and self-efficacy, however, were found to be qualitatively different factors; many women had hopes and dreams but had no idea about where or how to begin achieving them.

A further key distinction in cognitive-level themes was found in the difference between re-integrative and stigmatising shame (Braithwaite 1989). In a patriarchal society, women are stigmatised on a daily basis for not conforming to socially constructed gender norms when they resist or fail in their roles as mothers (Rich 1996), daughters and partners. Furthermore, Goffman (1968) argued that stigma occurs when a person does not conform to desired socially constructed roles. When we consider women as 'offenders', not only have they resisted gender norms but they have also violated moral and legal norms (Kennedy 1993). Desistance can involve a negation of both these harmful stigmatising effects and the role was not only confined to the criminalised individual but should involve a wider programme of social change.

Finally, cognitive shifts were deeply related to identity constructs. Criminalised women are often constructed as falling within the offender/

victim dichotomy. This study has found this to be problematic. When women self-identify as 'offenders' or 'ex-offenders', this can result in either a self-fulfilling prophecy or a positive move towards desistance depending on the availability of alternative meaning structures. When women are socially identified as 'offenders', the result tends to be the former. Yet when women are constructed solely as victims, they are pathologised, their agency disappears; they are sometimes relieved from blame regarding their offences but also their ability to desist. Similarly, when women with convictions are identified as survivors, it could be difficult to move away from the past as this is where their identity is constructed from. When women fail in or reject stereotypical care-giving or relational identities, further stigma is often the result. On top of this, it was often these very identities which were the catalyst or maintainer of deviance. Instead, this research has shown women who resist these identities are bricoleurs of their own fate; they made do and mended with what resources and cognitive processes were available to them and constructed their own desistance pathways, with the help of positive relationships and other social bonds.

What is clear is that when women are doubly demonised, cognitive processes require reinforcement. Alternative systems of meaning (Skeggs 1997) and non-gendered scripts for safer survival (Rumgay 2004) must be readily available for women attempting to desist from crime and harm. Hart (2017) has noted that the responsibilisation discourse prevalent in the CJS hinders women's attempts to live a crime free life. Additionally, she notes, that without social, cultural, economic and symbolic capital, women will be unlikely to desist. The Northshire research reinforces these findings, adding that often structures of patriarchal capitalism serve to reinforce responsibilisation whilst restricting the capital available to criminalised women. Yet we must not underestimate women's ability to change their own lives, to hope against all odds, to resist stigma and reconstruct shame and above all to be bricoleurs of their own fate.

Maturational, sociogenic and cognitive explanations for desistance have now been considered. In doing so some concordance with the male literature has been found, and each perspective has been somewhat helpful in shedding light on the how and why of female desistance. However, the unique, yet plural, perspectives of criminalised women in patriarchal capitalism has shown that much of what is 'known' about male desistance journeys cannot be applied to women's experiences. Women are often criminalised for one-off offences or, later in life, their offending and desistance often occur in situations of deprivation and abuse; their journeys are intimately linked with feelings of shame, lack of self-efficacy and a limited prospective of alternative identities. With these caveats clear: can justice and social agencies effectively promote and encourage desistance journeys? It is to this theme that the next chapter turns.

Notes

1. For more on Katie and Heathers' experiences see the next chapter.
2. Heather's sister attempted suicide the weekend prior to our interview whilst she was staying at Heather's house.
3. Macmillan Cancer Support who provide support and advice for individuals who have cancer in prison.
4. It is worth remembering that Heather in particular denied any awareness that 'ticking the wrong box' was morally or legally 'wrong'.
5. During the first interview, Julie had mentioned a statement from the council in the local press and advised me to look this up. Upon doing so, I came across another article which suggested Julie's involvement in an arson attack in 1999. The article suggested Julie had set fire to the car of the boyfriend of a teenage girl she had become 'obsessed with' through some voluntary work. The article also suggested Julie had mental health issues and problems with alcohol. When I brought the incident up, Julie accepted this was herself. 'I still to this day do not remember. I underwent treatment at X rehab centre and it was apparently an attempt on somebody's car. But I … I don't know, I was told I was lucky that I hadn't killed myself.' This revelation also indicated that Julie was becoming more comfortable with our relationship and the trust between us had grown. Julie's story also indicated the importance of multiple meetings as part of a research methodology.

Bibliography

Aresti, A., Eatough, V., & Brooks-Gordan, B. (2010). Doing Time After Time: An Interpretative Phenomenological Analysis of Reformed Ex-Prisoners' Experiences of Self-change, Identity and Career Opportunities. *Psychology Crime and Law, 16*(3), 169–190.

Becker, H. (1963). *Outsiders*. New York: Free Press.

Bottoms, A., & Shapland, J. (2011). Steps Toward Desistance Among Male Young Adult Recidivists. In S. Farrall, M. Hough, S. Maruna, & R. Sparks (Eds.), *Escape Routes: Contemporary Perspectives on Life After Punishment*. London: Routledge.

Bottoms, A., Shapland, J., Costello, A., Holmes, D., & Muir, G. (2004). Towards Desistance: Theoretical Underpinnings for an Empirical Study. *The Howard Journal, 43*(4), 368–389.

Braithwaite, J. (1989). *Crime, Shame and Reintegration*. Cambridge, UK: Cambridge University Press.

Burnett, R., & Maruna, S. (2004). So Prison Works, Does It? The Criminal Careers of 130 Men Released from Prison under Home Secretary, Michael Howard. *Howard Journal of Criminal Justice, 43*, 390–404.

Carlsson, C. (2012). Processes of Intermittency in Criminal Careers: Notes from a Swedish Study on Life Courses and Crime. *International Journal of Offender Therapy and Comparative Criminology, 57*(8), 913–938.

Christie, N. (1986). The Ideal Victim. In E. Fattah (Ed.), *From Crime Policy to Victim Policy*. Basingstoke: Macmillan.

Christie, N. (2004). *A Suitable Amount of Crime*. Abingdon: Psychology Press.

Clarke, B., & Chadwick, K. (2018). From 'Troubled' Women to Failing Institutions: Necessary Narrative Shifts in Decarceration of Women Post-Corston. In L. Moore, P. Scraton, & A. Wahidin (Eds.), *Women's Imprisonment and the Case for Abolition: Critical Reflections on Corston Ten Years On*. London: Routledge.

Davies, P. (2011). *Gender, Crime and Victimisation*. London: Sage Publications.

Faith, K. (2011). *Unruly Women: The Politics of Confinement and Resistance*. New York: Seven Stories Press.

Farrall, S. (2002). *Rethinking What Works with Offenders*. Cullompton: Willan.

Farrall, S., & Calverley, A. (2006). *Understanding Desistance from Crime* (Crime and Justice Series). London: Open University Press.

Ferraro, K. (2006). *Neither Angels nor Demons: Women, Crime, and Victimization*. Boston: Northeastern University Press.

Giordano, P. C., Cernokovich, S. A., & Rudolph, J. L. (2002). Gender, Crime and Desistance: Toward a Theory of Cognitive Transformation. *American Journal of Sociology, 107*, 990–1064.
Goffman, E. (1968). *Stigma: Notes on the Management of Spoiled Identity*. Harmondsworth: Pelican Books.
Hart, E. L. (2017). Prisoners Post-Release, The Need for a Critical Desistance. In E. L. Hart & F. J. C. Van Ginneken (Eds.), *New Perspectives on Desistance*. London: Palgrave Macmillan.
Heidensohn, F., & Silvestri, M. (2012). Gender and Crime. In M. Maguire, R. Morgan, & R. Reiner (Eds.), *The Oxford Handbook of Criminology* (pp. 336–369).
Jamieson, J., McIvor, G., & Murray, C. (1999). *Understanding Offending Amongst Young People*. Edinburgh: The Scottish Executive.
Jordan, J. (2004). Beyond Belief? Police, Rape and Women's Credibility. *Criminology and Criminal Justice, 4*(1), 29–59.
Katz, J. (1988). *Seductions of Crime: Moral and Sensual Attractions in Doing Evil*. New York: Basic Books.
Kennedy, H. (1993). *Eve Was Framed: Women and British Justice*. London: Vintage.
Laub, J., & Sampson, R. (2003). *Shared Beginnings, Divergent Lives*. Harvard: Harvard University Press.
LeBel, T. P., Burnett, R., Maruna, S., & Bushway, S. (2008). The "Chicken and Egg" of Subjective and Social Factors in Desistance from Crime. *European Journal of Criminology, 5*(11), 131–159.
Leverentz, A. (2014). *The Ex-Prisoner's Dilemma: How Women Negotiate Competing Narratives of Re-entry and Desistance*. New Brunswick: Rutgers University Press.
Levi-Strauss, C. (1962). *The Savage Mind*. Oxford: Oxford University Press.
Lloyd, A. (1995). *Doubly Deviant, Doubly Damned: Society's Treatment of Violent Women*. London: Penguin Social Sciences.
Maruna, S. (2001). *Making Good – How Ex-Convicts Reform and Rebuild Their Lives*. Washington, DC: American Psychological Association Books.
Maruna, S., & LeBel, T. P. (2003). Welcome Home? Examining the "Re-entry Court" Concept from a Strength Based Perspective. *Western Criminology Review, 4*, 91–107.
Matsueda, R. L., & Heimer, K. (1997). 'A Symbolic Interactionist Theory of Role Transitions', Role Commitments. In T. P. Thonberry (Ed.), *Advances in Criminological Theory, Vol. 7, Developmental Theories of Crime and Delinquency*. New Brunswick: Transaction.

Matthews, R., Easton, H., Reynolds, L., Bindel, J., & Young, L. (2014). *Exiting Prostitution*. New York: Palgrave Macmillan.
Matza, D., & Sykes, G. M. (1957). Techniques of Neutralization: A Theory of Delinquency. *American Sociological Review, 22*(6), 664–670.
Mead, G. H. (1934). *Mind, Self, and Society from the Standpoint of a Social Behaviourist*. Chicago: University of Chicago Press.
Merton, R. K. (1957). *Social Theory and Social Structure*. New York: Free Press.
Mills, H. (2015). Addressing Violence Against Women Beyond Criminal Justice. In H. Mills, R. Roberts, & L. Townhead (Eds.), *Empower, Resist, Transform: A Collection of Essays* (pp. 7–9). London: Centre for Crime and Justice Studies.
O'Neill, D. (2017). *Film as a Radical Pedagogic Tool*. New York/London: Routledge.
Perry, E. (2013). 'She's Alpha Male': Transgressive Gender Performances in the Probation 'Classroom'. *Gender and Education, 25*(4), 396–412.
Prison Reform Trust. (2017). *Why Focus on Reducing Women's Imprisonment?* London: Prison Reform Trust.
Probyn, E. (2005). *Blush: Faces of Shame*. Minneapolis: University of Minnesota Press.
Radcliffe, P., & Hunter, G. (2013). *The Development and Impact of Community Services for Women Offenders: An Evaluation*. London: The Institute for Criminal Policy Research, School of Law, Birkbeck College.
Rich, A. (1996). *Of Woman Born – Motherhood as Experience and Institution* (3rd ed.). New York: W. W. Norton & Company.
Roberts, J. (2015). *'It Was Do or Die' – How a Woman's Experience of Domestic Abuse Can Influence Her Involvement in Crime: A Qualitative Investigation of the Experiences of Community-Based Female Offenders*. Doctoral Thesis, University of Leicester, Leicester.
Rumgay, J. (2004). Scripts for Safer Survival: Pathways Out of Female Crime. *The Howard Journal, 43*(4), 405–419.
Sampson, R. J., & Laub, J. H. (1993). *Crime in the Making: Pathways and Turning Points Through Life*. London: Harvard University Press.
Skeggs, B. (1997). *Formations of Class and Gender: Becoming Respectable*. London: Sage Publications.
Smart, C. (1977). *Women, Crime and Criminology: A Feminist Critique*. London: Routledge.

Stubbs, J., & Tolmie, J. (2008). Battered Women Charged with Homicide: Advancing the Interests of Indigenous Women. *Australian & New Zealand Journal of Criminology, 41*, 131–161.

Uggen, C., Manza, J., & Behrens, A. (2004). Less Than the Average Citizen: Stigma, Role Transition and the Civic Reintegration of Convicted Felons. In S. Maruna & R. Immarigeon (Eds.), *After Crime and Punishment: Pathways to Offender Reintegration* (pp. 261–294). Cullompton: Willan Publishing.

Walklate, S. (2007). *Handbook of Victims and Victimology*. London: Routledge.

Worrall, A. (1990). *Offending Women: Female Lawbreakers and the CJS*. London: Routledge.

6

(In)Justice Systems

'Would you tell me, please, which way I ought to go from here?'
'That depends a good deal on where you want to get to,' said the Cat.
'I don't much care where—' said Alice.
'Then it doesn't matter which way you go,' said the Cat
—Taken from *Alice in Wonderland* by Lewis Carroll, also
on the wall of the Daffodil Centre in Northton,
where group meetings were held

Desistance theory has often been presented as a battle between agency and structure (McNeill 2012; Hart and Van Ginneken 2017). Agency, as represented by the conversation between Alice and the Cat in Lewis Carroll's famous book, was evidentially a main concern for the Northshire Women's Centres (WCs) also. Personal ownership of desistance outcomes was a key concept and this was also reflected in observations of the group-work at the centres. However, the structures and institutions of the Criminal Justice System (CJS) and the state more widely must also be examined for their place in desistance-promotion (or otherwise). As Clarke and Chadwick (2018) have argued, the increasing neoliberalisation of state institutions, including, but not limited to,[1] the CJS, has

Ú. Barr, *Desisting Sisters*, Critical Criminological Perspectives,
https://doi.org/10.1007/978-3-030-14276-6_6

resulted in a responsibilising agenda which can be challenged. The role of the CJS, and the increasing marketisation within it, was particularly salient at the time of research because of the changes under the 'Transforming Rehabilitation' (TR) programme (and with it, the system of 'Payment by Results' [PbR]), which many authors have argued has had, and will continue to have, significant detrimental impacts on women attempting to desist.[2] Annison and Brayford (2015) argued that much of PbR and TR will reverse recommendations made by the 2007 Corston Report. Women are a minority within any part of the CJS; under the TR agenda, Community Rehabilitation Companies (CRCs), in times of austerity, are likely to concentrate their funds on the majority male clients, as this is where they can concentrate on reducing reoffending. Broad and Spencer (2015) also argued that policy 'silences' around women's rehabilitation will be likely to persist, amplified by austerity cuts to services. However, Annison and Brayford (2015) noted that this also opened the possibilities for Women's Centres becoming CRCs, specifically focused on the needs of their female clients. Yet, swayed by the forces of neoliberalism, this was later found to not be the case (The Howard League 2016). Additionally, commissioning decisions under TR have been happening from November 2014 under a binary measure of reoffending rates. This decision has been criticised by academics studying the link between gender and desistance (McDermott 2012; Radcliffe and Hunter 2013; Barr 2018) as lacking recognition of the complex pathways of desistance that women travel and devaluing the incremental moves they may make towards desistance. Certainly much of what has been shown in this study so far reinforces these points. Desistance for women can be a multifaceted process involving setbacks and disappointments, situated within hostile environments, not least of these, cuts to women's services.

This chapter examines the role of parts of the justice system in the process of desistance both from the perspective of women attempting to desist and from that of women attempting to enable and empower them to. The various dimensions of desistance, as explored in the previous chapters, often coincide with women's experience of the CJS. This chapter in particular examines the multifaceted role of prison, probation and community alternatives such as the WCs and the Housing for Northshire

(HfN) project (an overview of each project is available in Chap. 1) in enabling or preventing desistance. It must be noted that desistance academics in general argue that desistance can be supported but not controlled by interventions or services (Clinks 2013; Graham and McNeill 2018) and therefore (generally) steer clear of formulating a generic guide for effective practice. This chapter takes a similar approach and does not aim to produce a guide for practitioners working with women. Instead, this chapter examines what service users and staff have found to be useful or otherwise in supporting desistance. It critiques the harmful effects of the risk-needs-responsivity approach. It finds that particular community alternatives can provide 'interstitial strategies' (Hart 2017) to help resist neoliberal, patriarchal concepts of responsibilisation, shame and stigma. Importantly, this chapter stresses the importance of shared experiences as promoting the relational aspects of desistance and resistance to criminalisation.

The Risk-Need-Responsivity Approach

Prison

The UK CJS has been described as a system built on 'risk' and 'needs' (Drake et al. 2018). Particularly since the implementation of TR, the CJS has become increasingly risk-focused. Yet, desistance theorists have long suggested that programmes for sentenced individuals should have as their basis a 'desistance paradigm' (Burnett and McNeill 2005). This section will examine the extent that this is a feature of the current risk-need-responsivity approach of the CJS. Turning first to the prison service, the mission statement of HM Prison service is: 'to keep those sentenced to prison in custody, helping them lead law-abiding and useful lives, both while they are in prison and after they are released' (Gov.uk 2018). Whilst there is no direct reference to desistance here, the aim of law-abiding and useful lives contains an implicit aim of encouraging a move away from offending. The vast majority of criminological research now widely acknowledges that time spent in prison does not reduce recidivism but in many cases actually has a criminogenic effect (Cullen et al. 2011; Drake 2012). Prison has also been recognised as an 'expensive and ineffective way of dealing with many women offenders' (House of Commons Justice Committee 2013: 4), something which was also made clear in the 2007 Corston Report and the 2018 Strategy for Female Offenders (Ministry of Justice). Prisons are harmful places of monotony and routine and also violence and pain (Drake and Scott 2017).

Although the Northshire research was firmly set within the community context, as discussed in Barr (2018), the women's narratives were replete with references to imprisonment. Seven out of the 16 women interviewed about their offences had spent time in prison. An additional three women had male family members with prison experience; Anna's father, brothers and male friends had spent time in prison, Holly's partner had recently been released and Katie's son in law was in prison during our interviews. The women were most familiar with short sentences; Paula, for example, served six days before her appeal was granted; Michaela served a total of 22 sentences throughout her life, her longest sentence was five-and-a-half months; and Shelly claimed she had 'lost count' of the number of prison sentences she served in her early life which she largely related to shoplifting to fund her heroin addiction 20 years previously:

> Shelly: To be honest with ya, I had a heroin problem so I had to fund it didn't I? So I was in and out of jail every six weeks starting a new prison sentence, every six weeks right? For shoplifting. Every six weeks I was back because then if you'd been nicked for shoplifting, on the third time you were nicked, you were back obviously it was an automatic prison sentence. So every six weeks I was back in jail (laughs).
>
> Una: How many times were you in prison?
>
> Shelly: Aw Jesus, God that was … loads (Shelly, age 53)

Kelly-Marie had served multiple prison sentences including two long sentences of three years and nine months and another for seven years, both for burglary. She served five shorter sentences, firstly for non-payment of a fine, three for shoplifting and finally a 28-day recall for not attending probation meetings. Kelly-Marie articulated her feelings about the shorter sentences:

Kelly-Marie:	The little sentences, they were hard work. I don't like little sentences. I don't like long, but the short sentences are a lot harder than a long one.
Una:	What do you mean by that?
Kelly-Marie:	Because your head's still out the gate, you can't get your head into what you're doing. Whereas, if you're on a long sentence, you've got things put in place; you've got your sentence plan and things that you need to do like TSP[3] or drug programmes … or whatever, yeah? You've got things that you've got to put in place and you've got to deal with your issues. Whereas on short sentences, you're just a statistic, basically. You go in one gate, you come out the same gate and you're still the same. (Kelly-Marie, age 48)

According to this perspective, short sentences had none of the elements of support as claimed by other interventions, but all the futility of separation from relationships, particularly with children. Michaela reiterated Kelly-Marie's sentiment:

> I just think that women need a lot more support in prison than they do get. You know 'cause some people do come out homeless, some people don't want to go out of prison because they've got no life to go back to, or their life's not good. They just need more support in prison, yeah. (Michaela, age 34)

Shelly also recalled the futility of imprisonment for many women. She recalled women she met in prison who had received jail for shoplifting a bottle of lemonade, and another for shoplifting a sandwich. The punishment of the poor was clear from Shelly's narrative. Many of Shelly's former fellow prisoners had been imprisoned for failing to keep probation appointments. The introduction of 12-month supervision periods following prison has compounded this problem. The majority of the former prisoner group discussed the detrimental impact of imprisonment on their children.[4] They also talked about the impact on their own mental health. Karen talked about women being introduced to drugs in prison. Additionally, Michaela discussed the lack of 'through-the-gate' support for women in prison. This finding has been replicated in an Australian study by McIvor et al. (2009) as well as in Aresti et al.'s (2010: 169) male former prisoners phenomenological accounts of 'doing time after time'.

The detrimental impact of women's imprisonment as related to both support and reconviction and particularly women's short-term imprisonment is well known in research (Gelsthorpe and Morris 2002; Prison Reform Trust 2014; Player 2014) and has become clear particularly a decade on since Corston's proposed reforms (Hogarth 2017; Moore and Wahidin 2018; Women in Prison 2017), of which only 2 of 43 have been implemented. In 2016, a decade after the deaths of 6 women in Styal prison, which prompted the Corston Report, the deaths of women in prison reached a record-breaking high when 22 women died in custody (INQUEST 2018). As noted by Chris Tchaikovsky, founder of charity and campaigning group Women in Prison,

> Taking the most hurt people out of society and punishing them in order to teach them how to live within society (is) futile. Whatever else a prisoner knows, she knows everything there is to know about punishment because that is exactly what she has grown up with. Whether its childhood sexual abuse, indifference, neglect, punishment is most familiar to her. (Women in Prison website)

Prison is a harmful environment which does not promote desistance. Carlton and Seagrave (2011) argue that imprisonment should be viewed as an extension of traumatic events in the lives of those incarcerated who are likely to experience interventions of the punitive state at all turns. Yet imprisonment is an increasingly probable perspective for women attempting desistance. In addition to the part privatisation of probation and the introduction of PbR, TR also imposed a 12-month supervisory period on those who had been sentenced to less than a year in prison following release. This has particularly impacted women who are more likely to serve shorter prison sentences, putting them in danger of recall following breeches of their licence. Increasing use of suspended sentence orders and the ongoing decline in the number of community orders compound this issue. Abolitionist perspectives, therefore, marry well with desistance theory (Hart 2017; Barr 2018; Clarke and Chadwick 2018; Sim 2018) and the abolition of women's prisons is often seen as a first step to abolition of the prison industrial estate (Carlen 1990). Those seeking to support desistance—theorists, practitioners and activists alike—are well placed to support decarceration campaigns[5] and end the harm inflicted on women and others by the prison industrial complex.

Probation

Probation also featured heavily in the women's narratives and indeed during observations; offender managers often had brief meetings with the women before or after their group sessions. Probation was often a topic which emerged in group sessions. Some studies have positively linked formal probation with encouraging desistance. Farrall et al. (2014), for example, noted the long-term desistance potential of probation supervision, which the authors found could have a reinforcing and re-encouragement effect in the long term which supported their male sample's desistance journeys. Many of the women also had positive probationary experiences, which they elaborated on in the course of our meetings. On the whole, the positive probation experiences were related to good relationships with offender managers and flexibility in their approach. Shelly's experience was typical of a 'good' probation experience:

> You know what I've got one of the top probation officers … I swear, he goes like that to me, he goes, "you know what Shelly? You're very punctual and you're always here when I tell you," he went, "but if there's ever a time, for whatever reason," he went … "if you can't make it for whatever reason, give me a ring, or get Rebecca's [Housing for Northshire manager] office to ring … "If you haven't got any credit, please get Rebecca to give me a bell … He went, "I'm not going to breach you," he went, "I'm not going to get on your case over it." He's dead good, my one, honest to God. (Shelly, age 53)

Shelly compared this current experience with former probation experiences which she did not feel were as useful. However, Shelly recognised that this poor relationship was also a result of her own mental state at the time, drawing on the reinforcing effects of agency and structure:

> In X2 [city Shelly previously lived], I wouldn't give a shit. I must have been a probation officer's worst nightmare, I must have been. 'Cause the moment they said, "Shelly's at reception", that woman's [Shelly's former probation officer's] nerves must have been in bits. I'd go in there, I'd be steaming drunk, I couldn't give a fuck. And I'd say to her, "excuse me, you going to help me, or am I going to sleep on the streets again tonight? What you going to do for me?" (Laughs), I goes, "because yous are full of shit, that's what I'm thinking, yous are full of shit." And she'd just sit there like that … She gave me loads of black coffee and everything, I'd still go like that, "Now what are you going to do?" … And like when I was waiting to be transferred over to here to Easton, you know, probation wise, she obviously stayed in touch with me on the phone. She'd ring me up and go, "I can't believe it's you I'm speaking to, Shelly, you sound so accomplished, so happy and full of life," she went, "I can clearly tell that you've not been drinking or anything." "Well there's no need," I went, "it was that ex-partner and everything. And X2 stressing me out." (Shelly, age 53)

Karen also had a good relationship with her probation officer. For Karen, the guilt she felt at past actions was reflected in the attitude of her probation officer; nonetheless, Karen felt this is what she 'needed' to maintain her desistance and abstinence from heroin:

> My probation officer has been amazing, she's firm but she's fair, she gives me a good kick up the backside when I need it. But I still feel like I've failed and I can't take back that time. (Karen, age 36)

What was important to both Shelly and Karen was the time taken to build a positive relationship with their offender managers. Within the neoliberal CJS, there has been concern that the relationship element, central to the foundations of the Probation System, has been eroded over time (Burnett and McNeill 2005; Annison and Brayford 2015; Barr 2018). Most narratives which indicated a negative probation experience noted this lack of concern with their well-being and criminal justice trajectories (Barr 2018). Furthermore, it appeared that the erosion of the time to build relationships had a knock-on effect on the consideration given to the particular status of working, single mothers. Marie remembered an incident, for example, where her probation worker was 15 minutes late to an appointment, during which time Marie's daughter was waiting outside. As the officer kept Marie 15 minutes late, this also had an effect on Marie's employment as a dog walker. She was particularly concerned that the probation officer did not apologise for this disruption to her life, something that she noted she could have been severely punished for, had the tables been turned. Anna recalled a very similar instance showing the lack of flexibility on the part of her probation worker to note her caring responsibilities:

> Probation have just … I was weekly but she's dropped me down to monthly. But she said I wasn't interacting … I don't have any problems with her, but she went on holiday right? And she knocked on my door when I was going out with Craig [Anna's son], and I said, "I'm always here, if I'm not here just text me, you'll always get a text". And she's … I don't know what's going on, I got bollocked yesterday for it. And I'm like, "really? I've not missed one" … And then I think, like I said, "I'm on the phone, I'm on the mobile." […] And I've even turned up with my little boy, "listen I'm not lying, he's really poorly, what do you want me to do?" (Anna, Age 36)

In both the above situations Marie and Anna felt that the respect they were expected to show was not reciprocated and resulted in an unequal relationship. This in turn added to feelings of victimisation at the hands of the CJS, which created feelings of defiance and barriers to desistance. This was not an unusual finding about women's experiences of the CJS (Smart 1977; Kennedy 1993; Jordan 2004; Davies 2011). The lack of awareness or encouragement of the 'social bonds' (Laub and Sampson 2003) required to maintain desistance was also present in Rebecca's narrative when she described not being allowed to continue her community service (which she had been enjoying) by probation for reasons which were unknown to her. Further problematic elements of probation provision present in the women's narratives were the lack of women-only probation space which, for Anna, resulted in intimidation and an unwanted reconnection with men from her past offending experiences. Furthermore, there was concern amongst staff in both the Housing for Northshire (HfN) Project and the WCs that the TR agenda (which was just under way at the time of the research), and particularly the PbR element, would result in an objectification of probationers where they are seen as statistics rather than individuals with holistic support required for desistance (see Barr 2018).

Punishment of the Poor

Harm caused by the CJS not only emerged in narratives surrounding probation; harm created by the state was present in every aspect of contact with the CJS, from relationships with the police and courts, to solicitors and prison staff. This was particularly poignant in the narratives of Katie, Karen, Ruth and Heather who espoused various levels of innocence regarding their recent convictions, but also in the narratives of Shelly and Marie which contained examples of past convictions for offences of which they were later deemed innocent. Both Katie and Heather had been convicted for benefit fraud offences. In both cases the women maintained that they were unaware they were committing fraud. Nonetheless, both their lives were harmed by what they felt was the unnecessary involvement of the CJS in their lives:

> Because to do what they [the police] did … if they sent me a letter! You know to send people a letter to say, "Can you come in? We need to have a meeting", I'd have gone, I wouldn't have said, "Oh I'm sorry I'm not coming." And when I've had my benefit, it's not like I've lived a fancy lifestyle or anything … I've thought I've done everything I should have done. Even the job centre said, "You've done what you should have done, you're on it [the benefit] indefinitely. This shouldn't be happening." And I thought, "Would they have gone to court and said that? Or would they not have been able to?" … I would have said, "Right, I'm sorry, I'm working. It's my fault. I will sort it out." And that's it … I can believe that I'm not the only person this has happened to. (Katie, age 60, second interview)

> I filled in a little section wrong, I put an "X" instead of actually not doing, that's all I did … Yeah, 'cause it says, "Does your partner work?" I just put an "X" there instead of saying anything. And that's why I got … It would be good if they could have rang me and asked, you know, "You filled this in a bit strangely, does your partner work or not?" (Heather, age 24)

Heather's and Katie's narratives had more in common than a feeling of victimisation at the hands of the police and courts. Both women experienced severe mental health issues following their convictions and both made attempts to take their own life, which they related to their convictions. Additionally, both Heather and Katie had been given advice to 'go guilty' by legal and mental health professionals; and both regretted the 'decision' to do so, although both felt they did not have much choice:

Heather: Well when I was trying to explain to my solicitor, he just said, "Well, other people won't believe that, they won't believe you." And he were quite nasty really with me, he just said, "There's no point wasting your time 'cause they won't believe you." So I just felt really low then, I was just like, I have to basically say that I've done it on purpose, just so that I can do, do you know what I mean?

Una: So was that his advice, to plead guilty?

Heather: Yeah. It was basically … in a way it felt like he were threatening me 'cause he said, "if you don't plead guilty, it's going to go on forever, they're going to be really harsh with you, you're going to have to pay more money", and all this, so it's like I had no choice. (Heather, age 24)

And then, when we went round to court, I spoke to the barrister … He said, "I've got your case, we'll go and have a talk." I said, "right", I told him everything and I said, "but I want to plead guilty." He said, "why?" I said, "I've had this nervous breakdown. I'm seeing a counsellor at the minute, she said she doesn't think I'm well enough to go through a court case, it could make it worse, she said, because I'm classed as high risk for suicide" … "And she said it'd just make it worse for me … 'if you plead guilty, it'll all be done away with, it'll be over with and that's it. It's done. It'd be dragging on', she said, 'and you'd have to go to court, and there would be people there who'd done statements, they'd have to say things that you wouldn't like.'" … He said, "Look, I'd rather you plead not guilty, because, everything here, you've got a really good case …" … I said "I can't, I can't. I can't go through it; I'll just be a wreck, a nervous wreck. And I don't think I'll make it through, I think I'll do something stupid …" So that's how it happened … Well I stood there and they said, "Well, how do you plead?" And I said, "not guilty." And everyone turned around and they looked, and I said, "Oh, I mean guilty." And they were all looking at me and I were thinking, "Oh my goodness." I were that confused. (Katie, age 60, first interview).

Katie narrated how her voice was effectively silenced as a result of this advice. Indeed, it was arguably because of this silencing that Katie was so determined to narrate her experience to me:

> And then they told me, I heard one of the magistrates say to the others, "she's been on this benefit for a long while and she's been working for five years." And I thought, "I haven't been working for five years, I've been working for two and a half years that's all." And she said, "She knows she's doing something wrong." And I wanted to stand up, and I weren't allowed to do. I wasn't allowed to say anything. The solicitor took down words that I wanted to say. And I said, "look, I want them to know." He said, "There's only so much I can say with you pleading guilty, because if you're pleading guilty, why are you saying, 'oh I shouldn't have been arrested', you've got to accept that if you're pleading guilty, you can't do a thing." I thought "oh crikey." I kept thinking, "Am I doing the right thing? Should I plead not guilty? Should I go through this?" And I thought, "I can't". It were awful, I was sat there crying all the time I were in court. (Katie, age 60, first interview)

Despite their experiences arguably not being linked with processes of desistance from crime, the harmful, distressing experiences of Heather and Katie at the hands of the CJS deserve recognition here. Whilst neither Katie nor Heather arguably had desistance journeys to travel, their experiences of ill mental health, poverty and terrible treatment by the CJS mirror many female potential desisters experience. The myth of the 'benefit scrounger' within the media and the CJS runs deep (Grover 2010). It is particularly noteworthy that the reason given for the women's treatment in court was their fragile mental states (according to their narratives, from Heather's solicitor and Katie's counsellor). In many ways women who are sentenced are not only doubly demonised but they are doubly harmed precisely because of the hardships and inequalities that they face (poor mental health and poverty in these cases). The punitive practices of the CJS are unlikely to abate at any time soon, despite any amount of liberal reform (Sim 2018). A 2012 government White Paper provides insight into current criminal justice thinking; the paper promises 'swift' and 'sure' judgement within courts with an emphasis on punishment and redress. The reforms proposed by the paper were 'designed to secure guilty pleas earlier in the prosecution process, improving efficiency, reducing paperwork and process times and alleviating some of the burden on witnesses and victims of crime' (Ministry of Justice 2012: 6). Mary, a member of staff at the Women's Centre, noted that this kind of rhetoric was unlikely to be helpful for women attempting to desist from crime.

Another woman who described being brought into the CJS 'for her own good' was Ruth. Ruth became homeless following a relationship breakdown. Ruth's offence was also related to her benefits; she had been overpaid housing benefit, council tax and income support and had been paying this back over time. When she could no longer pay, she was given a 12-month probation order. Ruth stated that the court passed the sentence to 'make me aware that the overpayment was wrong, but also it was to open other doors to help me find accommodation'. Whilst Ruth's entry into the CJS had a moral element to it, this net-widening of the CJS to include a social services role is reminiscent of Foucault's statement:

> The carceral objectives of resocialization through work, through the family and self-culpabilisation, are now no longer localized in the closed space of the prison, but are being extended and diffused throughout the whole of the social body. (1976/2009: 16)

Ruth's experience shows that even seemingly progressive, welfare-focused strategies can lead to further criminalisation by net-widening. It is also worth noting that at the time of our meeting, eight weeks into her supervisory experience, Ruth was no closer to gaining accommodation. Yet she was now the recipient of a criminal record, which she was acutely aware would create difficulties in gaining employment. Jamieson et al.'s (1999) finding that women are routinely failed by the CJS and other systems—doctors, solicitors, teachers, social services, and so on—is particularly poignant here. The authors found that individuals who claimed to have been treated unfairly by the CJS were most likely to reoffend.

Certainly, in the cases of the women mentioned here, the CJS, through a focus on 'swift' (and consequently unconsidered) 'justice', has done much more harm than good in supporting desistance. Even where there is a seemingly progressive objective, women's inequality within the neoliberal, patriarchal, social body is best addressed outside the harmful CJS.

As has been noted in Barr (2018), the traditional institutions of the CJS have found to be harmful, both to women's well-being and to their desistance potential. Arguably, the prominence of agency rather than structure in the desistance literature has assisted this harm. The Corston Report (2007: 2) placed emphasis on the individual responsibility for women in developing 'resilience, life skills and emotional literacy' to adapt to the harm caused by the structured inequalities (patriarchy but also class and racialised structures) which they face, and which have been highlighted in this and previous chapters. Yet even the liberal recommendations considered in Corston (2007), despite initial enthusiasm, have not found political backing (Hogarth 2017; Women in Prison 2017). The pairing of abolitionist and desistance work has found support within Hart (2017) and is reinforced by the Northshire research. Additionally, probation work under TR (as was beginning to happen during the research period) has been found to be problematic, in the absence of relationship building, and has been shown to be lacking in awareness of the gender-specific support requirements of desisting women.

Social Justice and Desistance

This book argues for a prison-abolitionist approach to desistance. Yet the 'net-widening' of the CJS through punishment in the community (Moore et al. 2018; Balfour et al. 2018) should also be critiqued. Nonetheless, community-based approaches have enabled women to fight their criminalisation. To some extent, projects can enable this by being aware of both the evidence-based research around desistance theory for women and the importance of challenging and resisting structural inequalities. In Barr (2018) I set out how the Northshire Women's Centres and the Housing for Northshire Project were enabling and supporting women's desistance through providing a holistic, women-only service which addressed and supported the social bonds required for desistance, avoided labelling of women, and overcame stigma and shame using talking methods. Importantly, these services provided women with hope for change. However, the emphasis, particularly within the WCs, on responsibilisation (Hart 2017) was problematic. This, for example, was reflected in the Alice in Wonderland quote at the beginning of this chapter. If there are barriers in one of Alice's potential courses—tree roots, stinging nettles and dangerous creatures—the choice may be taken from her. In the same way, if the structural forces of neoliberalism and patriarchy and their consequences; poverty, homelessness and domestic violence amongst others, stand in the way of desistance for criminalised women, no amount of individual agency and responsibility will be likely to build a safe path towards it. There has been an increased blurring of lines between neoliberal, punitive, criminal justice and supportive, liberating social justice under TR and related practices, particularly evident in the power of the WCs to breech women for non-compliance. Indeed, the contradictory dual status of the WCs as somewhere where women received support but were also at risk of being returned to prison was palpable during the research.

Yet, the support available in the WCs was clear from quotes like Holly's. Holly particularly emphasised the time taken to build relationships and provide practical help to avoid criminalisation:

> Holly: Yeah it's helped, the Women's Centre, 'cause like they're giving me a course in January so it's helping, that. They should do that, they should get you voluntary work or something, probation, just to make sure you're not going out during the day and doing crime and stuff like that.
>
> Una: So if you could change anything about your sentence what would you change?
>
> Holly: Just my probation, like come to the women's centre instead of all the times I were meant to go there, like twice a week. (Holly, age 24)

Whilst selection bias[6] must be considered, it appeared during observations that both the Women's Centre provision and Housing for Northshire programmes were, on the whole, enjoyed and appreciated by the service users. This was evident from both the conversations with the service users and also during the observation period at the WCs. I noted in my field notes that group settings were largely friendly, inclusive and welcoming spaces.

One of the crucial elements of the Women's Centre provision was the flexible support provided. Bridget was a 27-year-old mother of two. She was one of only three women I met during the course of this research who had, at any point in their life narratives, been arrested for violent offences. She had spent two short sentences in prison. Bridget had severe learning difficulties. She was mentored by Fran, a WC volunteer. When we met, Bridget had finished her specified group activity requirement at the WC but was continuing to attend weekly group meetings. She met with Fran on most days. The other women in her group evidently 'looked out for' Bridget and during one of our meetings when Bridget was running late, there was a fear amongst the group that she was not going to turn up. When she eventually did turn up there was a palpable sense of relief amongst the women. Bridget talked about her desire to move away from her friends who were 'a bad influence' on her. It was evident both in the actions of the women and in Bridget's narrative, that in Fran, the other WC staff, and her fellow group members (criminalised women) she had found an alternative, prosocial relational bond. On top of this, Bridget attended money management programmes and was in the process of finding a new house to rent with Fran's help. Although Bridget had recently breached her licence and tag, the WC was in contact with the police and magistrates to negotiate not returning to prison. There was an acknowledgement of the harmful and criminogenic features of the prison from both the staff and Bridget. Bridget described the prison environment as 'stressful … I got picked on in there [prison]'. The close and flexible relationship with Fran and other WC staff was only possible through an effective women-only provision. Healy (2012) has noted the importance of beyond-programme help. Carlsson's (2012) rhetoric around intermittency is also pertinent here. The support provided by the WC enabled Bridget to resist further criminalisation and its associated harms.

Farrall (2002) noted that there was a fissure between the social bonds rhetoric of desistance and the actions (or inactions) of the CJS. It is this fissure that the WC and HfN Projects have been particularly positive in bridging. As a very brief overview, women involved in this research accessed counselling services, domestic violence support services, debt management programmes, art and exercise workshops, volunteering experience, college courses, housing, full-time jobs and mental health services through initial contact with both the WC and HfN programmes. The HfN programme was particularly prudent in involving the women's families in their desistance journeys. Kelly-Marie, for example, forged a new and improved relationship with her mother following encouragement from Rebecca.

> Anyhow I got introduced to the Housing for Northshire Project and Rebecca Brown and my life's finally turned round. I've gone full circle, there's nothing else can come at me now … I'm just fortunate enough to have me family and still have me mum. I mean, me and me mum have sat down, we've talked. But what we've also done is interact; they've got somebody to interact with me mum to explain to her, from a drug addict's point of view. And they've involved her in my recovery and I feel like I've got a totally different mum now; I feel like I've got the mum I should have had years ago. (Kelly-Marie, age 48)

Maintaining connections with the community was also a focus of the HfN provision. Shelly discussed informal soup kitchens and provisions for community members who were struggling, set up by Rebecca and helped by the other women. Michaela was also preparing to begin volunteering at the local community café where we held our interviews. Here it was clear that the HfN Project was providing a safety net for those suffering under violent austerity conditions and maintaining a sense of community by resisting neoliberal individualism.

Both HfN and the WCs also provided support for cognitive-level moves towards desistance; for example, as previously noted, neither service labelled women as 'offenders'. The approaches of the services were strengths-based, encouraging women to focus on their future rather than 'offending' pasts. Additionally, the WC group sessions provided the women with a sense of hope for change, seeing their fellow group members and staff as positive role models. Stigma and shame were overcome by talking methods in both projects. Stories were, on the whole, shared openly and honestly and often shared experiences were noted with shock.

Nonetheless, the provisions of both community projects were not perfect. Although the HfN Project was able to work with the family and community, the same was not the case for the WCs. Weaver and McNeill (2014) have highlighted the relational aspects of desistance; where these are missing from formal systems, this may be problematic. The volume of women in the WCs as compared to the HfN service meant that this could not be catered for on the whole. WC staff would, for the most part, deal with women in a group setting and could not, for example, provide homeless women with housing directly. This, as Ruth's narrative previously highlighted, was often a laborious process. Mary, Criminal Justice Project Manager at the WCs, found housing to be one of the project's central issues. Her experience highlighted stable housing as a crucial element in desistance, yet something, in times of austerity, which the WCs were slow to find recourse to:

> We can't find emergency accommodation, but we do often find ourselves in the situation where we are running round like headless chickens trying to find somewhere for women to stay. (Mary, Criminal Justice Project Manager, Women's Centre)

Another consequence of cuts to funding of the WCs, the group provision of the WC sessions, was criticised, even amongst staff members, for not being suitable for every woman. For example, Maria talked about probation referring a woman with dementia and the difficulties this posed for the group setting. Many of the women, Maria noted, required more one-on-one mentoring than the WC was often able to provide in the two-week induction and conclusion. Certainly, I witnessed group sessions where one or two women in the group did not contribute to the group for two weeks. Jenny, a fellow group leader, also noted that the structure of the provision was problematically rigid; women had to go through the motions of all the different courses. For example, many of the women were enrolled on a comprehensive education and employment course provided by the WCs yet also had to cover this topic as part of their specified activity requirement. Sometimes the women confided in me that they found some of the sessions irrelevant to their lives, or covered topics which they found to be common knowledge. To this end, the WCs were responding to this criticism, and Mary outlined developments which were forthcoming:

> The plan is, obviously you still need your induction session, but to make, rather than eight sessions, some that are a bit fluffy … put it into six sessions, condense it a little bit and make it more meaningful and make the add on support, like the housing and debt, the access to benefits; which is a massive thing 'cause everything's got to be done online, equipping people with those kind of skills, and the counselling. And [making] the other move on groups more a part of it in those six sessions really, more of an engagement tool, helping them recognise what the issues are 'cause they may not well know what their own issues are. Because everything just becomes a big bubble of loads of issues and how do we address that? So just making it more condensed, more meaningful, to give an added value to the add on support as well, that's kind of what we're looking at. (Mary, Criminal Justice Project Manager, Women's Centre)

This flexible approach from the WCs meant that it was adaptable to change and able to recognise and amend its faults in a meaningful way. Yet austerity affected both the provision of its own services and that of its partners. Simultaneously, increasing inequalities meant that their clients were often suffering with a number of interlinked finance, housing, employment and other problems. Whilst staff were positive about the future, there were times it was clear they felt they were fighting an uphill battle.

There were only three women interviewed who were clients of the HfN Project, as well as two members of staff. The project was very small and to take a sceptical position would be to suggest that it was because of this small sample number that there were no critiques or complaints about the service from either staff or service users. On the other hand, the focused, one-on-one mentoring, housing model as provided by the service was difficult to critique. As Shelly noted, Rebecca was available for her clients 24/7. Certainly the service would not be suitable for all women with convictions. Many of the WC group were minor or one-off 'offenders', on the most part with housing and fairly good community and/or family support. Nonetheless, for repeatedly criminalised and/or homeless women, the support offered was crucial to desistance, and the secondary desistance narratives of Shelly, Michaela and Kelly-Marie are testament to its successes.

The main challenges faced and anticipated by staff in both projects were surrounding cuts to community service funding and the linked TR and PbR. Although funding for the WCs came partly from the local CRC, Christine sensed that this would create a worrying potential for them to be swept into the system of putting a price on the head of each potential desister. In this way, it appears that drawing the line between the 'well-being-focused' elements of alternative community provision and punitive traditional justice system was becoming increasingly difficult:

> I think as far as barriers [to desistance] go, there is danger that we increasingly become part of the system. And I think the contract environment pushed us towards that, we're much more target focused, data focused, measurement focused. I would say, as a manager, there's benefits to that; it helps us get control of the process, really look at what's working and what isn't working, you know grow the skill set of the practitioners. But it can feel that there's more assessments and those can be barriers, and questions asked of women can be barriers. (Christine, CEO, Women's Centre)

Overall, both programmes provided women-only 'desistance structure' or 'space' by engaging with structural, social and cognitive-level themes which have been shown to be conducive to desistance journeys. The importance of engaging with the social/structural as well as the cognitive was summarised by Jenny, a group leader in the WC:

> It's very rare that you would find a woman that goes out and thinks, "You know what I'm going to go out and I'm going to punch someone in the throat." No they don't do that, they don't go out and think, "I'm going to go out and rob summat". No, there's always an underlying issue. And whether that is housing, accommodation, substance misuse problems, mental health problems, you know a bad relationship, and things like that, there's usually something underlying that needs dealing with. (Jenny, Group Leader, Women's Centre)

Through providing a holistic, women-only service, these two projects were helping to 'deal' with exactly the issues outlined above. Whilst neither project was perfect for all women, there was a recognition of some of these issues and attempts to overcome them. The ability to be flexible was evident in both projects and meant that assisted desistance (Rex 1999) was possible to some extent. To repeat Baroness Corston's (2007) finding, community-based approaches tailored towards the gendered needs of women enable women to feel supported at turning their lives around. Whilst there are clearly problems with Corston's recommendations (discussed in Moore et al. 2018), much of the structures the Report was trying to build can be gleaned from the WCs and HfN provisions. On the whole, the projects studied in this research provided a tonic to the male-focused, punitive, traditional system. The structural conditions blocking women's desistance were also the structural conditions preventing the projects to carry out their assisted desistance. Resistance to neo-liberal and patriarchal conditions, therefore, was central to informing the continuation of these projects' praxis in order to support meaningful desistance.

Staff Narratives of Resilience, Survival and Resistance

All women experience gendered inequalities to varying extents. When considering desistance, these inequalities could provide a relational bond between staff and service users which could provide resilience for desistance attempts. Certainly, the staff interviewed and observed during the course of the Northshire research experienced gendered inequalities which reflected those experienced by the criminalised women. Indeed, in all staff narratives there was a constant theme of 'it could have been me ….' For Rebecca, Housing for Northshire project manager, it *was* her; she did experience the CJS for herself. She truly represented Maruna's (2001) concept of the 'professional ex'. Many of the other staff had experienced the CJS inadvertently through experiences of friends and family members. The staff in both the WC and HfN displayed resilience which reflected the desistance experiences of their clients. The shared gendered inequalities enabled many empathetic and supportive relationships between staff and service users. Shelly, Michaela and Kelly-Marie had such a close relationship with Rebecca that they all referred to her as a friend. Whilst this relationship did not suit every woman or staff member, I witnessed WC group sessions in which leaders would hug women who broke down after discussing mental health problems or, on the other hand, chatted to them about their children, reality TV programmes, makeup or the local council. Empathy was central in these relationships.

Much like the majority of the women interviewed for the Northshire research, staff members experienced low-level offending during youth and young adulthood, something which they largely matured out of as they got older:

> Not that I ever really did anything massive. I don't know … it's all a part of it, I suppose. I smoked a bit of weed and stuff like that with that kind of group of friends. And one of my friends that was quite a bit older than me took me shoplifting. And I did that once and nearly got caught and was so scared that I never did it again. Not anything like major. That, and just smoking a bit of weed. (Mary, Criminal Justice Project Manager)

Mary's trajectory differed from that of Holly's and Anna's, for example, because of the social capital she had in place with supportive family and friends. Nonetheless, as has been established, the women in this study experienced a range of offending trajectories; unlike the staff, many of the women such as Sue, Heather or Katie did not get involved in offending until later life. However, the experience of offending at any stage did create empathy between the women. For example, Claudia, a group leader in Easton, explained during a group session how she had been convicted of shoplifting at the age of 18 and was questioned about this during her interview for working at the WCs. Staff often shared negative experiences of the CJS or social services. This connection enabled the women to open up about their own experiences and discuss the perceived injustices of the CJS and wider structural inequalities. The staff were not viewed as 'other' as a result.

The social makeup of the lives of the staff was also not dissimilar to their clients'. Many of the staff discussed mental health issues such as anxiety and depression both in group scenarios and during interviews; they talked about alcohol and drug abuse, poverty, failed relationships and job opportunities due to pregnancies and caring responsibilities. Of the six women interviewed as 'staff members', five had suffered mental, physical and/or sexual abuse at the hands of former partners. Josie, a volunteer at the HfN Project, talked about years of violence and emotional abuse at the hands of her ex-husband and father to her six children. Whilst Josie had no experience of offending, she felt her life experience enabled her to do her generative, volunteering work as she could see the parallels between her life and the lives of the women she worked with; she felt she was in a position to enable them to get to 'where they're going' much like she enabled herself:

> But I always wanted, I wanted to go down the route of being a support worker like say with women who've had DV 'cause I've been there meself and I know meself when you go into there, and there's services … you've got to want to do it from your heart. You can't go in to do it financially 'cause it won't work because you are vulnerable and you don't want to open up to people. And you've got to trust people before you start opening up. And you do have some people, and they treat you like you've done summat wrong in a way. Well "no, it's not my fault I'm in here; I'm in here for whatever reason" … So I thought … 'cause I can't patronise anyone and I would never judge anyone, do ya know what I mean? So I want to give summat back. I started a course in January … and then I found out about the Housing for Northshire Project. So I had an interview with Rebecca and like I said to Rebecca, 'I can't understand the drug part of it, because I've never took drugs. And I can't … obviously I've never worked with people in prison, I've never been in prison meself, I've never committed a crime." ***But it was about helping women get back from where they was to where they're going***. And I do think, I think along the lines, or somewhere in there, there's something happening in their lives where they choose to go off the rails and say, "I don't care," I mean I know meself, I would probably have done the same if I didn't have the kids. I mean I can sit here and say; If I didn't have them two girls [two of Josie's children moved with her when she eventually moved out of the home she shared with her husband] with me, I wouldn't even be here now. (Josie, volunteer, Housing for Northshire Project, my emphasis)

This generative narrative was evident throughout the stories of staff in both projects; they often wanted to 'give back' what they had learned from their own experiences. For Jenny, group leader in the WCs, this came from her experience as carer to her younger brothers and sisters, as her parents were both heavy drug users throughout her childhood. As the oldest girl in the family, Jenny felt both internal and external pressure to take on a parenting role. When Jenny could not conform to this 'mother role' expected from her, she experienced guilt and post-traumatic stress. She linked her recovery to her work within the WC and her supportive colleagues. Jenny received counselling from the WC. Throughout the group meetings, Jenny and other group leaders would relate the topic back to their own life narratives; this encouraged the women to tell their own stories related to the given topic. Furthermore, this sharing of narrative encouraged validation. In these cases, the validation was not just of the emerging prosocial self, but also of the offending, victimised or non-conforming 'ideal female' past or current self. This enabled a sense of resistance to the stigma surrounding offending and the sense of double deviance experienced by criminalised women.

Staff members, therefore, could also be viewed as 'offenders', victims or survivors. However, the victimology narrative was largely absent or contested in the narratives of the staff to a greater extent than the women with convictions. Relating her experiences of abusive relationships and neglectful parents, Jenny stated,

> I would never think of myself as a victim 'cause then that is accepting that it's had triumph over you, and it's not. But then if I were like, "yeah I'm a victim", that's victimising myself. I was a victim of circumstance, but I don't have to be now. I've got the, you know, power to change that, so I don't see myself as a victim. (Jenny, Group Leader, Women's Centre)

This agency and self-efficacy was often missing from the prospective desistance narratives of the women with convictions. Perhaps this is unsurprising; staff members were able to come to terms with their past victimised self, much in the same way their clients were trying to. For criminalised women, their victimised identities were compounded by self- and socially imposed 'offender' identities. Nonetheless, the staff narratives of survival, resilience and resistance to patriarchal norms were available as bricolage for the women. It was clear that these narratives were sources of self-efficacy and agency. When the overlapping labels of women as offenders and women as victims are considered, Maruna's (2001) 'professional ex' concept can extend to staff members in another way which enables them to be role models and mentors. In many ways, the narratives of staff members interviewed as part of this research overlap with narratives of desistance, survival and resilience of the women with convictions. Women cannot 'desist' from the structural and gendered inequalities of being a woman. Staff members had narratives which contained much of the same gendered harm as those of the criminalised women. As a result of this, they were able to act with empathy and understanding. This was central to the assisted desistance experiences of many of the criminalised women and, simultaneously, the desistance narratives of the criminalised enabled a move towards survival. When we consider the relational element of desistance as considered recently by Weaver and McNeill (2014), the overlapping and reciprocal supportive relationships between staff and service users in community-based projects cannot be overlooked. Burnett and McNeill (2005) have previously highlighted that the role of relationships in probation declined during the 1980s and 1990s, a reflection of the managerialism arising from Thatcherism and the target-driven approach to budgetary restraint, as well as 'just deserts' punitive penal policy. Yet austerity measures and the new TR and PbR agenda have led to a further and increased diminution of this relationship role. If women's desistance is to be promoted, challenging and resisting neoliberalism on the part of academics, activists, practitioners and criminalised individuals alike must inform a central part of this promotion.

Conclusion

Jock Young, in his explanation of left realist approaches to crime control, noted that 'crime cannot be simply explained in terms of crime control agencies, and … the agencies involved in crime control are much wider than in the CJS' (1991: 152). Nonetheless, this chapter has noted that 'control agencies' can play a central role in the encouragement and containment of desistance journeys (Österman 2018). Traditional justice systems, this research has found, do more harm than good in enabling women's desistance. Beginning with the police and courts, this research has found a worrying lack of understanding about the contexts of female offending. This misunderstanding about mental health, particularly within magistrates' courts, can have severe consequences, as Heather and Katie's narratives illuminate. Just deserts and punitive rhetoric are not the way forward (Radcliffe and Hunter 2013; Barr 2018). Certainly, prison can have a detrimental impact on desistance. Particularly, short sentences for non-violent offences—the most common sentences served by women—are more likely to have a particularly detrimental effect on desistance attempts. Relationships with probation officers, where they are flexible and encouraging, with an understanding of the social barriers to desistance, can be a source of hope nonetheless. Yet, whilst there is no one-size-fits-all relationship model, there is a continual worry amongst practitioners and academics alike (Annison and Brayford 2015) that the changes under the TR agenda are making flexible and supportive relationships less likely where the focus is on a binary measure of results which does not recognise incremental moves towards desistance. The number of women recalled to prison following release doubled in the four years from 2014 (Prison Reform Trust 2018), which researchers (ibid) have related directly to the imposition of 12-month supervision by CRCs under TR and their risk-focused practice which has meant women being recalled for failure to keep in touch. This net-widening of criminalisation must be a concern for anyone worried about desistance, as the harmful effects of the punitive system are abundantly clear. The Northshire study has not found that punishment can produce positive change.

What would a 'desistance paradigm' (Burnett and McNeill 2005) for criminalised women look like? In the first place, it is clear that most of these women's needs are best addressed outside the CJS. For desistance to truly have meaning structures and institutions must change. Clarke and Chadwick (2018: 64) have argued,

> Agency and empowerment of women is not simply a statement of 'women making better choices' or having responsibility to 'turn their lives around' but a collective abolitionist strategy demanding the changes necessary in

> communities and (where possible without compromising visionary abolitionist goals) within state institutions to address the marginalisation and the disproportionate criminalisation of women.

When women are referred to (community) services, this research has highlighted that flexible, holistic, women-only, strengths-based services with post-programme support would go a long way to producing assisted desistance (Rex 1999). These services, against all odds, often provide the 'interstitial strategies' (Hart 2017) needed to resist criminalisation. Programmes which wish to promote desistance, therefore, should be aware of the social circumstances in which desistance from crime does or does not take place, whilst recognising and applauding incremental moves towards desistance. Some of these features reflect what has already been considered as part of a male 'desistance paradigm' and it is clear the male system can learn much from female successes, including the implied resistance of hegemonic systems. Additionally, many of these features are present in both the work of the WCs and the HfN Projects studied as part of this research. Whilst neither programme is a panacea and neither provides a one-size-fits-all model, the acknowledgement of what is 'known' about both desistance and women's criminalisation provides community-based projects with a template to work from. However, with increased marketisation of these programmes there is a deepening of the hostile environment which leads to the punishment of the poor, increase in responsibilisation as an outcome, and curtailment of support for social justice projects. Chapter 8 therefore considers what a desistance-focused feminist jurisprudence might offer.

The Offender Rehabilitation Act 2014 requires the Justice Secretary to make arrangements to meet the needs of women with convictions, and many of these needs could be gleaned from the above-mentioned projects. Yet in times of austerity where women's services and mental health services are first on the line to go, alongside 'crackdowns' on benefit fraud and reductions of the welfare system, women are increasingly likely to be criminalised due to poverty, abuse and mental health issues. As the staff narratives highlighted in this chapter show, these issues are not only confined to women with convictions but are gender-wide issues of inequality and subjugation. The staff and service user narratives provide bricolage for desistance and survival. Whilst the promotion of individual mentoring successes related to individual workers and clients should be cautioned against as another reflection of neoliberal responsibilisation, the sharing of structured inequalities through sharing of narratives can be productive in terms of a powerful form of resistance. These issues will be considered further in the next chapter which draws together some of the theoretical findings of the research analysis.

Notes

1. For example welfare, education and health policy and practice.
2. See Annison and Brayford (2015) for a detailed examination.
3. Thinking Skills Programme.
4. For a theoretical overview see Scott and Codd (2010).
5. Such as the campaign to reclaim the former Holloway prison site for a Women's Centre and social housing.
6. The women interviewed were contacted through the services and may therefore have been more likely to take a positive view of them.

Bibliography

Annison, J., & Brayford, J. (2015). Context; Transforming Rehabilitation: Implications for Women. In J. Annison, J. Brayford, & J. Deering (Eds.), *Women and Criminal Justice: From the Corston Report to Transforming Rehabilitation*. Bristol: Policy Press.

Aresti, A., Eatough, V., & Brooks-Gordan, B. (2010). Doing Time After Time: An Interpretative Phenomenological Analysis of Reformed Ex-Prisoners' Experiences of Self-change, Identity and Career Opportunities. *Psychology Crime and Law, 16*(3), 169–190.

Balfour, G., Hannah-Moffat, K., & Turnbull, S. (2018). Planning for Precarity? Experiencing the Carceral Continuum of Imprisonment and Reentry. In A. Sarat (Ed.), *After Imprisonment Studies in Law, Politics and Society* (Vol. 77, pp. 31–48). Bingley: Emerald Publishing Limited.

Barr, U. (2018). Gendered Assisted Desistance: A Decade from Corston. *Safer Communities, 17*(2), 81–93.

Broad, R., & Spencer, J. (2015). Understanding the Marketisation of the Probation Service Through an Interpretative Policy Framework. In M. Wasik & S. Santatzoglou (Eds.), *The Management of Change in Criminal Justice: Who Knows Best?* Basingstoke: Palgrave Macmillan.

Burnett, R., & McNeill, F. (2005). The Place of the Officer–Offender Relationship in Assisting Offenders to Desist from Crime. *Probation Journal, 52*(3), 247–268.

Carlen, P. (1990). *Alternatives to Women's Imprisonment*. Milton Keynes: Open University Press.

Carlsson, C. (2012). Processes of Intermittency in Criminal Careers: Notes from a Swedish Study on Life Courses and Crime. *International Journal of Offender Therapy and Comparative Criminology, 57*(8), 913–938.

Carlton, B., & Seagrave, M. (2011). Women's Survival Post-Imprisonment: Connecting Imprisonment with Pains Past and Present. *Punishment & Society, 13*(5), 551–570.

Clarke, B., & Chadwick, K. (2018). From 'Troubled' Women to Failing Institutions: Necessary Narrative Shifts in Decarceration of Women Post-Corston. In L. Moore, P. Scraton, & A. Wahidin (Eds.), *Women's Imprisonment and the Case for Abolition: Critical Reflections on Corston Ten Years On*. London: Routledge.

Clinks. (2013). *Introducing Desistance: A Guide for Voluntary, Community and Social Enterprise Sector Organisations*. London: Do It Justice.

Corston, J. (2007). *The Corston Report: A Report by Baroness Jean Corston of a Review of Women with Particular Vulnerabilities in the Criminal Justice System*. London: Home Office.

Cullen, J. T., Jonson, C. L., & Nagin, D. S. (2011). Prisons Do Not Reduce Recidivism. *The Prison Journal, 48*, 485–655.

Davies, P. (2011). *Gender, Crime and Victimisation*. London: Sage Publications.

Drake, D. (2012). *Prisons, Punishment and the Pursuit of Security*. Basingstoke: Palgrave Macmillan.

Drake, D., & Scott, D. (2017). Build Communities Not Prisons [Blog]. *Centre for Crime and Justice Studies*. Available at: https://www.crimeandjustice.org.uk/resources/build-communities-not-prisons-0. Accessed 27 Dec 2018.

Drake, D., Havard, C., & Muncie, J. (2018). The Dubious 'Science' of Risk Prediction in Criminal Justice. [Blog] Centre for Crime and Justice Studies. Available at: https://www.crimeandjustice.org.uk/resources/dubious-science-risk-prediction-criminal-justice. Accessed 27 Dec 2018.

Farrall, S. (2002). *Rethinking What Works with Offenders*. Cullompton: Willan.

Farrall, S., Hunter, B., Sharpe, G., & Calverley, A. (2014). *Criminal Careers in Transition: The Social Context of Desistance from Crime*. Oxford: Oxford University Press.

Foucault, M. (1976/2009) Alternatives to the Prison: Dissemination or Decline of Social Control? Theory, Culture and Society, 26(6), pp. 12–24.

Gelsthorpe, L., & Morris, A. (2002). Women's Imprisonment in England and Wales: A Penal Paradox. *Criminology and Criminal Justice, 2*(3), 277–301.

GOV.UK. (2018). *HM Prison Service*. [online] Available at: https://www.gov.uk/government/organisations/hm-prison-service. Accessed 27 Dec 2018.

Graham, H., & McNeill, F. (2018). Desistance: Envisioning Futures. In P. Carlen & L. Ayres França (Eds.), *Alternative Criminologies*. London: Routledge.

Grover, C. (2010). Social Security Policy and Vindictiveness. *Sociological Research Online, 15*(2), 8.

Hart, E. L. (2017). Prisoners Post-Release, The Need for a Critical Desistance. In E. L. Hart & F. J. C. Van Ginneken (Eds.), *New Perspectives on Desistance*. London: Palgrave Macmillan.

Hart, E. L., & Van Ginnekin, E. F. J. C. (2017). Introduction. In E. L. Hart & F. J. C. Van Ginneken (Eds.), *New Perspectives on Desistance*. London: Palgrave Macmillan.

Healy, D. (2012). *The Dynamics of Desistance* (2nd ed.). New York: Routledge.

Hogarth, L. (2017). *Trapped in the Justice Loop? Past, Present and Future of the Woman-Centred Services at the Heart of the Systems-Change Called for in the Corston Report* (Briefing 18). London: Centre for Crime and Justice Studies.

House of Commons Justice Committee. (2013). *Women Offenders After the Corston Report: Second Report of Session 2013–2014*. London: The Stationery Office Limited.

Inquest.org.uk. (2018). *Deaths of Women in Prison|INQUEST*. [online] Available at: http://inquest.org.uk/statistics/deaths-of-women-in-prison. Accessed 27 Dec 2018.

Jamieson, J., McIvor, G., & Murray, C. (1999). *Understanding Offending Amongst Young People*. Edinburgh: The Scottish Executive.

Jordan, J. (2004). Beyond Belief? Police, Rape and Women's Credibility. *Criminology and Criminal Justice, 4*(1), 29–59.

Kennedy, H. (1993). *Eve Was Framed: Women and British Justice*. London: Vintage.

Laub, J., & Sampson, R. (2003). *Shared Beginnings, Divergent Lives*. Harvard: Harvard University Press.

Maruna, S. (2001). *Making Good – How Ex-Convicts Reform and Rebuild Their Lives*. Washington, DC: American Psychological Association Books.

McDermott, S. (2012). *Moving Forward: Empowering Women to Desist from Offending*. London: The Griffins Society.

McIvor, G., Trotter, C., & Sheehan, C. (2009). Women, Resettlement and Desistance. *Probation Journal, 56*(4), 347–361.

McNeill, F. (2012). Four Forms of Offender Rehabilitation: Towards an Integrated Perspective. *Legal and Criminological Psychology, 17*(1), 18–36.

Ministry of Justice. (2012). *Swift and Sure Justice: The Governments Plans for Reform of the CJS* (CM 8388). London: Ministry of Justice.

Moore, L., & Wahadin, A. (2018). The Post-Corston Women's Penal 'Crisis' in England and Wales: Exploring the Failure of Reform. In L. Moore, P. Scraton, & A. Wahidin (Eds.), *Women's Imprisonment and the Case for Abolition: Critical Reflections on Corston Ten Years On*. London: Routledge.

Moore, L., Scraton, P., & Wahidin, A. (Eds.). (2018). *Women's Imprisonment and the Case for Abolition: Critical Reflections on Corston Ten Years On*. London: Routledge.

Österman, L. (2018). *Penal Cultures and Female Desistance*. London: Routledge.

Player, E. (2014). Women in the CJS: The Triumph of Inertia. *Criminology and Criminal Justice, 14*(3), 276–297.

Prison Reform Trust. (2014). *Transforming Lives: Reducing Women's Imprisonment*. Stockport: Soroptimist International.

Prison Reform Trust. (2018). *Broken Trust: The Rising Numbers of Women Recalled to Prison*. London: Prison Reform Trust.

Radcliffe, P., & Hunter, G. (2013). *The Development and Impact of Community Services for Women Offenders: An Evaluation*. London: The Institute for Criminal Policy Research, School of Law, Birkbeck College.

Rex, S. (1999). Desistance from Offending: Experiences of Probation. *The Howard Journal, 38*(4), 366–383.

Scott, D., & Codd, H. (2010). *Controversial Issues in Prisons*. Maidenhead: Open University Press.

Sim, J. (2018). We Are All (Neo-)Liberals Now: Reform and the Prison Crisis in England and Wales Justice. *Power and Resistance, 1*, 165–188.

Smart, C. (1977). *Women, Crime and Criminology: A Feminist Critique*. London: Routledge.

The Howard League. (2016). *Is This the End of Women's Centres?* London: All Party Parliamentary Group for Women.

The Offender Rehabilitation Act. (2014). Available at: http://www.legislation.gov.uk/ukpga/2014/11/contents/enacted. Last Accessed 12 Mar 2019.

Weaver, B., & McNeill, F. (2014). Lifelines: Desistance, Social Relations, and Reciprocity. *Criminal Justice and Behaviour, 42*(1), 95–107.
Women in Prison. (2017). *Key Facts*. Available at: http://www.womeninprison.org.uk/research/key-facts.php. Accessed 25 Sept 2017.
Young, J. (1991). Left Realism and the Priorities of Crime Control. In K. Stenson & D. Cowell (Eds.), *The Politics of Crime Control*. London: Sage.

7

Making the Invisible Visible

The previous chapters have examined desistance as experienced by a group of Northshire women, viewed through the lens of what is already 'known' about it—largely taken from the dominant white, heterosexual, male literature perspective, but increasingly with relevance to the theoretical perspectives which have considered women's experiences. Ontogenetic, sociogenic and subjective theoretical arguments have been analysed in turn, giving voice to the women's experiences. Additionally, the role of criminal and social justice institutions has been considered. Whilst there are overlaps, for example, in the importance of relationships, work, hope and shame—there are also areas in which the female desistance experience was distinctly different from the literature in the area: women can experience abusive relationships, yet appear to be desisting; gendered social control can mean women are inappropriately assumed to have generative desires which result in an overreliance on volunteer work to encourage desistance; hope may be experienced differently; and shame is such a factor in women's day-to-day lives that it can halt desistance and cause harm at every turn.

Some of the themes which have emerged from feminist research will be brought together in this chapter. There are four interrelated points to be

Ú. Barr, *Desisting Sisters*, Critical Criminological Perspectives,
https://doi.org/10.1007/978-3-030-14276-6_7

made. Firstly, the argument is made that the realities of criminalised women's lives before, during and after criminal justice contact reveal the harm and trauma generated by living in a society dominated by heteropatriarchal and capitalist social relations. Desistance from *crime*, therefore, can be reframed, theoretically and in practice, as desistance from *harm*. Next, the concept of agency will be interrogated through a feminist lens. The overreliance on a restricted definition of agency within desistance literature has led to an individualisation of structural harms and the bolstering of responsibilisation as political rhetoric and criminal justice practice. Yet feminist understandings of agency provide important analytical perspectives for desistance. To suggest that women's offending is *never* the consequence of rational choice is to deny women their agency. Women display resilience and agency both in situations where they are desisting and in situations where they are not. The arguments of abolitionist feminism are drawn together in the third section. The radical alternatives set out by anti-carceral theorists and activists can be productive to desistance praxis, moving forward to promote desistance from harm in all its forms. Finally, the conclusion points to the question of the personal and the political. The personal relationships, trauma and interactions considered in the previous chapters are contextualised within the question of power and the struggle for gender equality. Desistance struggles therefore intersect with wider political struggles for equality. The structures of heteropatriarchy and neoliberalism have thus far been invisible in desistance research. It is a central purpose of this book, through analysis of the Northshire women's experiences, to make that which has thus far been invisible, visible.

Social Harm

The concept of social harm emerged from a critique of criminology which was developed by Paddy Hillyard et al. (2004). The authors argued that criminology is a problematic discipline for a number of reasons. For example, it perpetuates the myth of crime, which has no ontological reality. Historically, criminology has excluded serious harms such as state and corporate harm, whilst legitimising the expansion of crime control which inflicts pain. The authors also maintained that criminology legitimises and reinforces hegemonic power relations. Providing a new lens through which to view injustices, the authors argued for a move from the study of crime to the study of harm, including physical harms, financial/economic harms, emotional and psychological harms and cultural safety.

Criminalisation, and particularly imprisonment, has been related to 'social death' by prison theorists (Price 2015). This theoretical development has been particularly inspired by the work of those conceptualising slavery (Patterson 1982) who argued that social death involved three main elements: systematic violence, humiliating treatment and 'natal separation', where one experiences enforced separation from families, communities and social networks. In particular, Joshua Price relates the concept of social death as experienced by the formerly imprisoned. He notes:

> The formerly incarcerated do not generally gain or regain their civil and social status as full citizens. Rather, they are relegated, often permanently, to the status of despised and excluded subordinate, contemplated by the rest of the society with suspicion and hostility, and forced to live a life grounded in an uncertain, unstable future. This seals rather than undoes their marginalization. (2015: 112)

This description can also be related to post-criminal justice contact in all its forms, including following community punishment. The Northshire women's narratives, as detailed in previous chapters, were littered with experiences of abuse, neglect, drug and alcohol addiction, mental health problems and poverty *prior* to becoming criminalised. Following criminalisation, these experiences often continued, worsened or became more entrenched. This was particularly harmful to the Northshire women whose experience of social death was particularly intensified because of their womanhood which was imbued with patriarchal constructions of what it is to be a 'good woman'.

Patriarchal and neoliberal understandings of the good life only enable women to desist *in a certain way.* Desistance from crime can mean a curtailment of law breaking. It also can mean a life of poverty including a lack of state support, reinforced by social stigma, shame and the fear of male violence and coercive control. Desistance is a powerful theoretical concept which shines a light on the positive changes individuals make in the face of adverse life experiences. However, without a simultaneous challenge to structural inequalities, it can mean (re)conformity to a life filled with injustice.

Victoria Browne (2014) argued that second-wave feminist understandings of the harms of patriarchy remain ever pertinent to the present-day experience of women in the UK. This argument is made with a particular focus on Operation Yewtree.[1] However, a myriad of current state and sociocultural activity and resistance can also be noted that can explain patriarchy's ongoing relevance as an analytical framework, for example, the #MeToo movement, ongoing abortion restrictions in Northern Ireland and state-sanctioned deception of women activists and campaigners. Browne makes use of the work of feminist writers such as Kate Millet, Gillian Howie and Sylvia Walby to argue that a theoretical understanding of patriarchy is necessary to capture 'the depth, pervasiveness and interconnectedness of different aspects of women's subordination' (2014: 3). She notes that a practice or institution is patriarchal when it contributes to the systematic subordination of women's interests. She refers to the theoretical importance of Walby's (1990) six sites or structures that form patriarchy—patriarchal modes of production, patriarchal relations in paid work, patriarchal relations in the state, patriarchal relations in sexuality, patriarchal relations in cultural institutions and male violence. It is clear that each of these structures is present, and yet analytically absent, in normative conceptions of desistance theory. Patriarchal structures shaped the lives of the criminalised Northshire women involved in this research prior to, during and following contact with the Criminal Justice System (CJS).

As has been already established, desistance theory has been based on an analysis of the male experience (Rumgay 2004; Carlton and Baldry 2013; Matthews et al. 2014; Rodermond et al. 2016; Österman 2018). It is not surprising, therefore, that a structural analysis of patriarchy has been absent in theoretical analysis. This dearth has led to a focus, in the literature, on the idea that women mature faster than men (Gottfredson and Hirschi 1990; Matthews et al. 2014) whilst ignoring the conditions which create the feminisation of social control. It has also led to the sustaining and, indeed, bolstering of, historical, patriarchal institutions such as marriage and patriarchal relations in paid work, including the gender pay gap. At the same time there is an absence of a critical analysis of male violence, in providing the social backdrop to desistance experiences (Laub and Sampson 2003). Additionally, patriarchal assumptions form the basis of cognitive theories which have led to an individualisation of cognitive processes of change, inevitably leading to the responsibilisation of vulnerable women to make 'better' life 'choices' in the future (Pollack 2013; Haney 2004; Hart 2017; Clarke and Chadwick 2018).

Within patriarchal state relations, criminalised women are judged, by the CJS and wider society, as being 'doubly deviant' (Heidensohn and Silvestri 2012). For this reason, their desistance pathways, as illustrated by narratives of the Northshire women, can be even more arduous and demanding than those of their male counterparts (Rumgay 2004). Not only have these women broken the imagined, idealised, social contract, but they are also in violation of the gender contract to which every woman is an automatic signatory (Worrall 1990). They have not only broken the law but they have 'committed'[2] the crime of abandoning the roles assigned to them by breaking the stereotypes of 'woman' which are structured around notions of family, femininity and compliance. Compounding this, Rumgay (2004) notes that the life histories of criminalised women include victimisation, parental neglect, incomplete education, and lack of access to economic and social capital, all of which limit their ability to sustain an alternative identity outside of offender/former offender. These experiences have been central to the life narratives of the Northshire women. The process of restoration which desistance involves, therefore, can be tremendously difficult in a society laden with stereotypical ideals of a woman's behaviour.

Social control mechanisms have been found to have a positive effect on female desistance in the sense that awareness of peer, familial and societal disapproval is felt to a greater extent by women than their male counterparts (Weaver and McNeill 2010; McIvor et al. 2011). Whether these social controls are positive because of their desistance-inducing potential or problematic because of their patriarchal origins should be a central concern of desistance theorists. This is discussed more fully below.

David Harvey, tracing the development of the neoliberal state since the 1970s, described neoliberalism as the dominance and influence of capital in all areas. Neoliberal theory 'holds that the human good will be maximised by maximising the reach and frequency of market transactions, and it seeks to bring all human action into the domain of the market' (2007: 3). Reiner (2007) has argued that neoliberalism influences both the commission and the recording of crimes in various ways and the intensification of punitive penal policies, alongside the weakening of social welfare support. Poverty is criminalised and neoliberal praxis has led to the intensification of, and confinement within, poverty for many. In turn this has been linked to the inequality created by the pursuit of neoliberalism with rising prison populations and in the proliferation of a culture of control (Wilkinson and Pickett 2010; Dorling 2015; Carlen 2012). Carlen (2012) persuasively makes the case that the rehabilitation industry serves to reinforce this inequality and reframe it as risk, which in turn becomes profitable:

> And it could be argued that, more often than not, it is desirable for governments, markets and capital accumulation that the poor and the powerless should be kept "in their place" – and the rich in theirs. (2012: 3)

For those poor and powerless who manage to desist, conceptions of the good life are intimately linked with materialist and acquisitive values, individualisation and self-reliance. Perhaps unsurprisingly therefore, Hart (2017) argues that considerations of desistance which promote reform of the CJS 'are framed by the wider neoliberal context that promotes responsibility, meritocratic ideals and increased surveillance and control' (p. 273).

Feminist epistemological and ontological positions are incompatible with neoliberal concepts of individualisation, inequality and materialism. LeBaron and Roberts (2010) link the spaces of prisons, debt and households and neoliberalism by noting 'the interplay between states, markets and households in the creation and reproduction of carceral relations' (p. 20). The link between poverty and criminalisation is abundantly evident in the Northshire women's narratives. Poverty was likely to continue or become further entrenched following criminal justice contact; women referenced struggles to financially support their children, problems with inadequate housing, and fear of debt collection agencies, for example. Furthermore, services which were supportive of women, criminalised or otherwise, were under threat at the time of the research, and continue to be dismantled or closed down at the time of writing, due to the ongoing violence of austerity (Mansfield and Cooper 2016), which will be discussed further in the final chapter.

Hannah Graham and Fergus McNeill (2018) note desistance literature has largely taken an uncritical approach to considering what 'crime' and 'offending behaviour' mean. By not questioning the particular conditions in which criminalisation, punishment and post-criminal justice contact occur, we run the risk of accepting 'offending', punishment and the CJS as value-free institutions. Through an understanding of a critical feminist, life-course perspective on social harm (Pantazis 2004), however, the wider view as to what we might want individuals, and society as a whole, to be desisting *from* may be considered. This critical conception takes into account the wider structural inequalities created under structures of patriarchal and neoliberal power.[3] Through articulating a social harms approach, desistance can be imagined, *not* as a concept which involves a move away from crime, but as one which involves a move away from harm, whether these harms emerge from interpersonal relations in the form of gendered violence, sexual abuse and trauma, or from relations with the state, in the form of inadequate mental health provision, curtailment of welfare support, or from a punitive and painful CJS. In the promotion of desistance from harm, the realities of women's lives can take centre stage, rather than their 'offences'. This reconfiguration would also challenge the stigma and shame involved in simply being a woman, particularly as imbued with the discourses of ideal womanhood.

Agency

Criminological theorists have often pondered the link (or lack of) between deviant acts or behaviour and the abstract notion of 'choice'. In particular, Cesare Beccaria and Jeremy Bentham used utilitarian principles to construct humans as rational beings and therefore criminals as calculating, arguing for certain and swift punishment to be used as general deterrence. These early theories found prominence, for example, in the work of Clarke and Cornish (1985). Later theories ranging from labelling and social constructionist theories, to critical theories including Marxist and feminist schools of thought, questioned this pervasiveness of choice. More recently, desistance theorists have elaborated on the role of choice and agency within subjective narratives of self-change (Shover 1996; Rumgay 2004). Yet, whilst critical criminology has examined the role of choice in the beginnings of offending behaviour as it relates to power structures, this has not been sufficiently examined in the context of desistance. 'Choice' is argued to be a contested value and feminist approaches can highlight its problematic usage in the discourse of desistance. Carlton and Baldry (2013: 65), for example, argue that desistance theory 'starts from the premise that an individual chooses to offend and can choose to cease offending', without acknowledgement of the structural conditions surrounding both criminalisation and desistance. Hart (2017) similarly makes the case that desistance discourse on choice can lead to responsibilisation of poor and powerless women, which disregards the structural conditions of their lived experiences.

At the same time, to suggest that women's offending behaviour is *never* the consequence of rational choice would be to misrepresent women as agents. Belinda Morrissey (2003) argues that denying women's agency in offending denies their subjectivity. Portraying women as victims only can deny their humanity and even obscure the injustices they face. Within Grace's narrative, there was a strong rational choice discourse related to the beginning of her deviant behaviour, particularly as related to growing marijuana:

> I mean I asked and everybody I spoke to … I mean "If I get caught, will she get taken away?" and things like that, and I had people telling me they'd done it before, been caught and their kids were fine (crying) … there were nothing, as far as I could see that it would have risked, otherwise I wouldn't have done it, you know if there was any chance, you know if I thought there was the slightest chance, I wouldn't have done it … It was for her [Grace's daughter] I was doing it. (Grace, age 31)

For other women the origins or continuation of offending were associated with a *lack* of choice. Paula, for example, linked her offending with her alcohol addiction:

> It wasn't pre-meditated or anything like that, it was just there at the time. (Paula, age 36)

Maruna (2001) noted that within the 'persistence scripts' of formerly imprisoned people was a view of the individual as a victim of life circumstances. These individuals appeared 'doomed to deviance' whilst a second group of formerly imprisoned people, who were also victims of the cycle of criminalisation, nonetheless, could find their way out and find an essential goodness within themselves. This desistance experience also encompassed agentic feelings which often emerged from a generative project or behaviour. Karen's narrative appeared 'doomed to deviance' and was replete with references to her offending as a personal choice. Yet it is difficult to locate within this narrative of abuse, rape, alcohol and drug addiction any moments of clarity which would have allowed for a rational choice to occur:

> And I just feel like, my path was set out at a young age and I followed it, and here I am now, you know in a train wreck. (Karen, age 36)

Whilst Karen hoped for a time that she could live the 'normal life' her mother wanted her to lead, she felt that she did not have the agency to do so, this was beyond her ability:

> My mum actually wants to see me get accommodation, live properly, go shopping, live a normal life, do things that normal women do. I don't seem to have that in me, I just feel, you know, incomplete. (Karen, age 36)

Given the conditions which surrounded Karen's offending, it is perhaps not surprising that she felt a lack of agency. Her narrative was shaped by the discourse of others, particularly criminal justice and welfare institutions. Certainly within the Women's Centre (WC) sessions there was, at times, a presupposition that crime was a rational choice for the women involved. Responsibilisation of women and the discourse of 'choice' were particularly clear in observations of the 'Thinking and Behaviour' session where offending was linked to quick and seemingly easy decisions to solve problems. At times this led to an overestimation of the choices and agency that the women had. This discourse of choice was central in staff narratives when considering a woman's propensity to desist. As Eileen noted,

> And I do really want to help people but sometimes people just don't want to be helped. You know they need to help themselves. (Eileen, group leader, Women's Centre)

Yet at other times within the WCs, and amongst the staff, there was an understanding of the complex realities of women's daily lives and the sessions were clearly largely informed by this holistic view of both offending and desistance.

Those whose narratives did not appear 'doomed' promoted a picture of themselves as essentially good people who had taken a wrong turn in life. This sense of an essentially 'good self' finds echoes within Maruna's (2001) study and Braithwaite's (1989) concept of reintegrative shame. Kelly-Marie, for example, found an agentic sense of self following her entry into the Housing for Northshire (HfN) project, finding 'someone who believed in her' in Rebecca and working in a collaborative setting with her mother to overcome drug addiction. She had generative hopes for working with women 'in a project' in the future and therefore had a strong belief that fate was on her side for the future:

> There is something else out there for me, and when the time's right it'll be there … I just take each day as it comes, I know where I'm going, I know what I want and I know what I need to get there. (Kelly-Marie, age 48)

Both Karen and Kelly-Marie experienced abuse, drug addiction and the loss of their children. Their shared beginnings were reflective of the lives of many criminalised women. For these women, the exit point of the cycle of deviance is often not illuminated. Criminalised women are likely to exit into hostile environments in an age of austerity where they experience poor employment outcomes, they are often coaxed into voluntary positions, experience a lack of secure housing and return to being sole carers or into abusive relationships (Prison Reform Trust 2014). Yet subordination and agency can exist simultaneously. Kelly-Marie's narrative indicates hope and self-efficacy.

Feminist theorists of social control have debated the centrality of 'resistance' in the lives of subjugated women (Carlen 2006). Carlen (2006) argues that this conceptualisation has become synonymous with a corrective to patriarchal assumptions about female passivity but that, in some feminist analysis, this definition can be reduced to mere expressions of agency. Weedon, however, notes that Foucauldian feminist approaches suggest resistance can begin at the individual level:

> Resistance to the dominant at the level of the individual subject is the first stage in the production of alternative forms of knowledge or where such alternatives already exist, of winning individuals over to these discourses and gradually increasing their social power. (Weedon 1999:111 in Thomas and Davies 2005: 719)

Thomas and Davies (2005) further note that post-structural feminism contends that forms of resistance can be localised and small scale, concerned with destabilising truths, challenging subjectivities and normalisations. Desistance theorists have found that often agency and resistance can be 'hidden' in complex desistance narratives (Carlsson 2016; Österman 2018). For the Northshire women, routine and micro-political forms of agency-as-resistance, as argued in Chap. 5, took the form of actively rejecting the identity of 'offender' or 'victim'. The desisting narratives provided examples of the Northshire women resisting the stigma involved with being a criminalised woman (Stone 2016). In this way, the women actively challenged meanings and discourses (Thomas and Davies 2005). Again for the criminalised Northshire women, agency and subordination often existed simultaneously.

Anti-Carceral Feminism and Abolitionism

In the current resurgence of feminist discourse, there has often been recourse to both capitalist and carceral[4] feminist approaches as solutions to patriarchal violence and harms. Capitalist feminism, which places emphasis on individual advancement, empowerment and meritocracy (Fraser 2013), does not provide a desistance-focused solution, disregarding, as it does, the clear connection between poverty and criminalisation, as well as frustrated desistance attempts (Hart 2017). Capitalist feminist discourse was often evident in the WCs when staff members spoke about 'empowering' women to make change in their own lives. Similarly, carceral feminist solutions justify the continuum of state violence which is a feature of patriarchal institutions. The carceral shadow of the prison continues to extend into the prisoner re-entry industry[5] and into carceral devolution in schools, welfare agencies and even supermarkets (Watts 2018). Balfour et al. (2018) draw distinctions between the US re-entry system which has been characterised by expansion of the panoptic, carceral state and the Canadian system where formerly imprisoned individuals exit into nothing, where their experience is characterised by the absence of state support, even that which provides a simulacrum of rehabilitation, and yet the experience of state violence is enduring in both states. In July 2018, the Conservative government published its Strategy for Female Offenders (Ministry of Justice 2018). This Strategy appeared to take the worst from both worlds of the US and Canadian systems, promoting critically underfunded (Sisters Uncut 2018) community support for women, through repackaging women's prisons as 'women's residential centres', alongside the continuation of Transforming Rehabilitation initiatives[6] to supervise the formerly imprisoned in the community a year after their release, thereby extending the carceral shadow of the prison. Charities such as INQUEST have condemned the strategy as lacking (i) clarity on funding of alternatives to custody, (ii) implementation plans and (iii) a sentencing reform strategy (Coles 2018). The strategy continues to stigmatise criminalised women, labelling them as 'offenders', and fails to address the structural inequalities which collectively provide the conditions for criminalisation. The myth of rehabilitation in the strategy has served as a useful state tool for supporting the violence of austerity, by portraying the cancelled building plans for five women's prisons as an ideological move towards rehabilitative support in the residential centres, when in fact neoliberal money saving—which also encompasses underfunding of gendered services, including refuges—is at the heart of the move (Sisters Uncut 2018). This will be discussed further in the final chapter. These kind of capitalist carceral moves, masquerading as feminism, should be a key concern of desistance theorists. This structural critique has thus far largely, with a few notable exceptions, been missing from desistance research. Even studies which consider the structural contexts of desistance (e.g., Österman 2018) have argued for reform and de-escalation, rather than a radical transformation of the current justice system.

However, elsewhere there is a growing argument that the failures of criminal justice interventions have amounted to the infliction of so much harm that the abolition of such systems must inform any fight for social justice. Criminal justice intervention, particularly in the form of prisons, but also in the carceral shadow of post-prison interventions, creates a lasting legacy of social death (Price 2015) by the destruction of social capital. Hart (2017), for example, argues for a 'critical desistance' grounded in the abolition of prisons and punishment, rather than reform of a system that serves to curtail desistance trajectories. Hart proposes a framework for a strategy of critical desistance based on the principles of social justice, emancipatory alternatives to punishment and engagement with wider social change:

> Desistance research remains inextricably bound to narratives surrounding choice, individual action and responsibility … [these have] fed into the wider narrative around the reframing of structural disadvantage into criminogenic need. (Hart 2017: 270)

She notes that crime does indeed pay for a distinct few involved in monetising the punitive state through private industry, and desistance research feeds into this system, particularly by accentuating individual responsibility and through evaluation research which emphasises individual (rather than structural) change. This mirrors the arguments of Pat Carlen (2012) against 'rehabilitation' of the law-breaking poor. What an ontological and epistemological rethinking of desistance can do, Hart (2017) offers, is work towards a social justice model which involves 'interstitial[7] strategies' to create alternatives outside the neoliberal state. She argues that there can be 'real utopias' used to open up new spaces that articulate and promote radical strategies, based on compassion, love and support, as opposed to responsibility, surveillance and prison-based interventions. Resisting carceral conceptions, engaging with wider political and social movements to resist inequality, alongside giving voice to the powerless, and highlighting injustice within the current CJS, can be a part of the desistance project. Many of these arguments reflect Carlen's (1990) seminal call for a 'woman-wise penology' which does not increase women's oppression further, nor increase the likelihood that law-breaking men will become brutalised, making them even more violently and ideologically oppressive towards women. The implications of these arguments will be explored further in the final chapter.

The Personal and the Political

'The personal is political' was a rallying slogan of second-wave feminism (Hanisch 1970) and the slogan is particularly poignant when related to the narratives of women experiencing desistance, or attempting to desist from crime. In its original conception, the slogan was a challenge towards a set of patriarchal relations which promoted family values and women's position within the domestic sphere. The feminist movement has made exponential gains since this first rallying cry. However, as with the ongoing analytical importance of patriarchy, the message here is worth repeating. Browne (2014), considering Victoria Hesford's reassessment of the slogan, notes:

> On first reading, 'the personal is political' equates to a naïve collapsing of "woman" into "experience" and "politics" but Hesford suggests it can be understood as an enigmatic and inherently unstable slogan signalling the disassembly of the modern category 'woman' and the rejection of a normative hetero sexuality. (p. 3)

For the women involved in this research, family was central to desistance. Sommers (1995: 42) noted that criminalised women tended to internalise the myth that mothers 'are endless founts of nurturance' (see also Rich 1996). When they themselves did not achieve this nurturance, particularly when they were physically absent due to incarceration, the sense of stigmatising shame was palpable. The mothers with convictions involved in this research constantly related their narratives of shame back to their apparent failures as mothers.

Romantic relationships with both men and women were often problematic for women navigating desistance because of the pervasiveness of abuse and violence within these experiences. Gendered violence occurred prior to offending, during offending, and, importantly, once criminalised women appeared to desist. When abuse was identified and heard, a woman's sense of identity could change and she was no longer alone. Therefore, within this research, violence and abuse, very personal experiences, became political within the contexts where they were discussed and shared, in a limited way with the researcher, but particularly within the Women's Centre and Housing for Northshire settings.

Mental health was an additional, seemingly personal, ubiquitous element of women's lives evident within their narratives of desistance/persistence. Fourteen of the 16 criminalised Northshire women talked about mental health issues, as did most women within the 'staff' sample. These issues ranged from anxiety and depression to suicide attempts. Most of these women who discussed mental health also discussed the medication that they were prescribed to help with these issues. Whilst the majority of these women discussed the positives of medication, most also found that discussing their problems and practical problem-solving support were the most effective methods of controlling mental health matters. Medicalisation of the marginalised was a common experience. Criminalised women connected mental health issues with their criminalisation and the social death which ensued. Many also, including staff members, related mental health issues to victimisation including domestic and childhood abuse. Finally, mental health issues were connected with feelings of hopelessness and despair, particularly where women lacked financial and social support.

As discussed in Chap. 4, work and employment are themes which social bonds theorists positively link to desistance (Sampson and Laub 1992; Farrall 2002; Horney et al. 1995; Carlsson 2012; Verbruggen et al. 2012). Employment landscapes are shaped by political will, particularly within the neoliberal context, and work had a real, personal effect on criminalised women's lives. This book has argued that criminalised women, particularly in the context of 'Help to Work' programmes, which were prevalent at the time of research, are often funnelled into voluntary, crucially unpaid, positions. It is also worth noting that many of the Northshire women were participating in non-waged care work, where they were often sole carers of children or other relatives. Employment can be viewed by both theorists and practitioners as a panacea for solving problems. Yet for many of the Northshire women, work, even where generative and meaningful, was not the answer to their difficulties. Whilst meaningful, fairly paid employment opportunities can support desistance from both crime (Maruna 2001) and harm, we should be wary of viewing work as an answer to all desistance issues, particularly when in work poverty is at an all-time high (Joseph Rowntree Foundation 2018). Safe and secure housing was a similarly important desistance-related element which was personal in its effects and political in its landscape. The implications of these findings will be discussed further in the final chapter.

For criminalised women, personal circumstances are linked to desistance experiences. Issues surrounding abuse and violence, motherhood, mental health, poverty, housing and employment often appear insurmountable. Indeed they are insurmountable alone. Desistance theory and practice can no longer be blind to the structural inequalities that women face on a daily basis, within and outside the CJS, which are formed by neoliberalism and patriarchy that views women, and working-class women in particular, as second-class citizens. What is required here is a move towards a greater equality.

Conclusion

Graham and McNeill (2018) have acknowledged that '[w]hat desistance theory and research perhaps lacks … is a well-developed archaeology. Perhaps because it begins with the assumed problems of offending and of ending offending rather than with what lies behind these problems and their construction, it lacks a well-articulated vision of the good society' (p. 449) This chapter has argued that one way to approach a vision of the good society is by considering an ontological gendered social harms

(Hillyard et al. 2004) approach which recognises these harms faced by criminalised women, created by structural inequalities, whilst also recognising the presence and absence of agency in women's actions and behaviour, and challenging the harms created by the systems which penalise them. Epistemologically, desistance theory can be compatible with intersectional feminist research where it puts control and power into the hands of women to narrate their own subjective experiences, whilst at the same time challenging the structures of the state and wider institutions.

Commentators have described a recent 'crisis' in the CJS—prisons (Jacobson 2016), access to legal aid (The Bach Commission 2017) and the partly privatised probation system (Savage 2018) have all been described as being in 'crisis'. The year 2016 saw a record high number of female deaths in prison, at 22 (INQUEST 2018). Yet, the women coming into contact with the CJS remain the same disenfranchised and marginalised group they have always been (Prison Reform Trust 2017). The newly proposed Strategy for Female Offenders (Ministry of Justice 2018) whilst noting the harms women face in prison, does not adequately challenge the structural harms which lead to criminalisation. Worse, the community-based strategy attempts to co-opt feminist arguments to provide a simulacrum of rehabilitation, which serves as a smoke screen for austerity. As has been noted above, the much lauded community services highlighted by the strategy, such as Women's Centres, are currently undergoing a funding crisis whilst domestic violence support services, refuges and mental health provision have been decimated by austerity measures (Sisters Uncut 2018). As ever, there has been a mutually reinforcing relationship between criminalisation, fractured relationships, poor mental health and limited access to employment.

Somewhat paradoxically, this 'crisis' has been paralleled by a greater focus of traditional criminology on desistance discourse. Whilst some desistance theorists have maintained that desistance can and does occur without the intervention of the CJS, the individualisation of social and structural inequalities has been a lasting legacy of desistance theory which focuses on maturation, social bonds and cognitive changes as being linked with the cessation of offending. The patriarchal and neoliberal systems which provide the backdrop to women's experiences before, during and after criminal justice contact are rarely examined by desistance theorists. Even where they are, the argument is for reform rather than radical change. Liberal approaches which add women in, (i) without reference to the structures which shape their experiences, (ii) without questioning state-based definitions of both crime and 'rehabilitation' and (iii) without considering the feminisation of social control, are incomplete. Without resistance to inequalities, women who are most negatively affected by the neoliberal, patriarchal condition will continue to be criminalised, whilst their attempts to desist (from crime) will continue to take place whilst they are facing structural harm and violence. It is worth repeating that a feminist rethinking of desistance theory should not inevitably lead to a place where women are as equal as men, or the argument that if *only* we resist and challenge *gendered* inequalities, desistance will be forthcoming. On the contrary, this rethinking enables all intersecting structural subordinations, including those based on neoliberalism, racism, heteronormative, disablist, and ageist social structures to be challenged. A critical approach will mean challenging both the systemic criminalisation of certain groups and a move towards *resistance* to the harm faced by all these groups.

The Northshire Research does not take a critical approach to desistance for the sake of it. As has been shown in the previous chapters, desistance perspectives have much to offer the theory surrounding criminalised women's experiences prior to, during and particularly following CJS contact. Nonetheless, criminalisation is largely the experience of particular groups of people. Within the female experience, it is poor women, racialised women, women with myriad experiences of childhood and adult gendered abuse and mental health problems who are systematically criminalised. As has been shown in the Northshire women's narratives, women survive and resist criminalisation and harm despite neocolonial, capitalist heteropatriarchy. This can inform 'a jurisprudence of social justice as inequality reduction' (Carlen 2012: p. 3). This resistance cannot be led by criminalised women alone; desistance theorists and practitioners clearly also have roles, as this chapter has argued. The next chapter reaches a conclusion, and, inspired by the work of Pat Carlen (1990) from almost 30 years ago, provides recommendations for the amalgamation of desistance theory and practice with feminist epistemology and jurisprudence to work towards a woman-wise community-based penology.

Notes

1. A police investigation into sexual abuse allegations, predominantly the abuse of children, against the British media personality Jimmy Savile, and subsequently others within the world of media and culture. The investigation, led by the Metropolitan Police Service, started in October 2012. It led to an increased police reporting of sexual abuse crimes and convictions of a number of high-profile men.
2. The origins of this discourse in Christian moral understandings deserve further analysis which is not possible here.
3. It is also important to note neocolonial, heteronormative and disabilist structures, to name a particular few. bell hooks speaks of 'imperialist, white supremacist, capitalist, patriarchy' (2004: 29), which is a useful concept to describe the power structures underpinning women's criminalisation and post-criminalisation experiences.
4. Relating to the prison and the wider punitive state.
5. This concept has been more recently contested by Wacquant (2018), who argues that the term can bolster the myth of rehabilitation and, using the US as an example, also argues that the industries involved serve only as a bureaucratic charade to perform a pretence of rehabilitation after custody, rather than existing as capitalist enterprises. Whether a similar argument can be made in the UK context of Transforming Rehabilitation and indeed the new Strategy for Female Offenders (2018) deserves attention, but it is something which this book does not have the capacity to explore.
6. Again in July 2018 it was announced that Community Rehabilitation Company (CRC) contracts are being cut short, with the end date being brought forward from 2022 to 2020 (House of Commons Justice Committee 2018).
7. Space between structures.

Bibliography

Balfour, G., Hannah-Moffat, K., & Turnbull, S. (2018). Planning for Precarity? Experiencing the Carceral Continuum of Imprisonment and Reentry. In A. Sarat (Ed.), *After Imprisonment Studies in Law, Politics and Society* (Vol. 77, pp. 31–48). Bingley: Emerald Publishing Limited.

Braithwaite, J. (1989). *Crime, Shame and Reintegration*. Cambridge: Cambridge University Press.
Browne, V. (2014). The Persistence of Patriarchy: Operation Yewtree and the Return to 1970s Feminism. *Radical Philosophy, 188*, 9–20.
Carlen, P. (1990). *Alternatives to Women's Imprisonment*. Milton Keynes: Open University Press.
Carlen, P. (2006). Review: Out of Order: The Political Imprisonment of Women in Northern Ireland 1972–1998. *The British Journal of Criminology, 46*(5), 951–953.
Carlen, P. (2012). *Against Rehabilitation: For Reparative Justice. Centre for Crime and Justice Studies*. Available at: https://www.crimeandjustice.org.uk/resources/against-rehabilitation-reparative-justice. Accessed 27 Dec 2018.
Carlsson, C. (2012). Processes of Intermittency in Criminal Careers: Notes from a Swedish Study on Life Courses and Crime. *International Journal of Offender Therapy and Comparative Criminology, 57*(8), 913–938.
Carlsson, C. (2016). Human Agency, Criminal Careers and Desistance. In J. Shapland, S. Farrall, & A. Bottoms (Eds.), *Global Perspectives on Desistance*. London: Routledge.
Carlton, B., & Baldry, E. (2013). In B. Carlton & M. Segrave (Eds.), *Women Exiting Prison: Critical Essays on Gender, Post-Release Support and Survival*. Abingdon: Routledge.
Clarke, B., & Chadwick, K. (2018). From 'Troubled' Women to Failing Institutions: Necessary Narrative Shifts in Decarceration of Women Post-Corston. In L. Moore, P. Scraton, & A. Wahidin (Eds.), *Women's Imprisonment and the Case for Abolition: Critical Reflections on Corston Ten Years On*. London: Routledge.
Clarke, R. V., & Cornish, D. B. (1985). Modelling Offenders' Decisions: A Framework for Research and Policy. In M. Tonry & N. Morris (Eds.), *Crime and Justice: An Annual Review of Research* (Vol. 6). Chicago: University of Chicago Press.
Coles, D. (2018). INQUEST Responds to New Ministry of Justice 'Female Offenders Strategy [Blog]'. *INQUEST* Available at: https://www.inquest.org.uk/moj-female-offenders-response. Accessed 27 Dec 2018.
Dorling, D. (2015). *Inequality and the 1%*. London: Verso.
Farrall, S. (2002). *Rethinking What Works with Offenders*. Cullompton: Willan.
Fraser, N. (2013). How Feminism Became Capitalism's Handmaiden. *The Guardian*. Available at: https://www.theguardian.com/commentisfree/2013/oct/14/feminism-capitalist-handmaiden-neoliberal. Accessed 27 Dec 2018.

Gottfredson, M., & Hirschi, T. (1990). *A General Theory of Crime*. Stanford: Stanford University Press.
Graham, H., & McNeill, F. (2018). Desistance: Envisioning Futures. In P. Carlen & L. Ayres França (Eds.), *Alternative Criminologies*. London: Routledge.
Haney, L. (2004). Introduction: Gender, Welfare, and States of Punishment. *Social Politics, 11*(3), 333–362.
Hanisch, C. (1970). The Personal Is Political. In S. Firestone & A. Koedt (Eds.), *Notes from the Second Year: Women's Liberation*. New York: Radical Feminist.
Hart, E. L. (2017). Prisoners Post-Release, The Need for a Critical Desistance. In E. L. Hart & F. J. C. Van Ginneken (Eds.), *New Perspectives on Desistance*. London: Palgrave Macmillan.
Harvey, D. (2007). *A Brief History of Neoliberalism*. Oxford: Oxford University Press.
Heidensohn, F., & Silvestri, M. (2012). Gender and Crime. In M. Maguire, R. Morgan, & R. Reiner (Eds.), *The Oxford Handbook of Criminology* (pp. 336–369).
Hillyard, P., Pantazis, C., Tombs, S., & Gordon, D. (2004). *Beyond Criminology: Taking Harm Seriously*. London: Pluto Press.
hooks, b. (2004). *The Will to Change: Men, Masculinity, and Love*. London: Atria Books.
Horney, J., Osgood, D. W., & Marshall, I. H. (1995). Criminal Careers in the Short Term: Intra Individual Variability in Crime and its Relation to Local Life Circumstances. *American Sociological Review, 60*(5), 655–673.
House of Commons Justice Committee. (2018). *Transforming Rehabilitation: Ninth Report of Session 2017–2019*. London: The Stationery Office Limited.
Inquest.org.uk. (2018). Deaths of Women in Prison. *INQUEST* [online]. Available at: http://inquest.org.uk/statistics/deaths-of-women-in-prison. Accessed 27 Dec 2018.
Jacobson, M. P. (2016). Tough Talk on Crime Has Led to a Crisis in Britain's Prisons. *The Guardian*. Available at: https://www.theguardian.com/commentisfree/2016/may/05/tough-talk-crime-crisis-britains-prisons-suicides-assaults. Accessed 5 Jan 2019.
Joseph Rowntree Foundation. (2018). *UK Poverty 2018: A Comprehensive Analysis of Poverty Trends and Figures*. London: JRF Analysis Unit.
Laub, J., & Sampson, R. (2003). *Shared Beginnings, Divergent Lives*. Harvard: Harvard University Press.
LeBaron, G., & Roberts, A. (2010). Towards a Feminist Political Economy of Capitalism and Carcerality. *Signs, 36*(1), 19–41.

Mansfield, M., & Cooper, V. (2016). The Failure to Protect Women in the Criminal Justice System. In V. Cooper & D. Whyte (Eds.), *The Violence of Austerity*. London: Pluto Press.

Maruna, S. (2001). *Making Good – How Ex-Convicts Reform and Rebuild Their Lives*. Washington, DC: American Psychological Association Books.

Matthews, R., Easton, H., Reynolds, L., Bindel, J., & Young, L. (2014). *Exiting Prostitution*. New York: Palgrave Macmillan.

McIvor, G., Murray, C., & Jamieson, J. (2011). Desistance from Crime: Is It Different for Women and Girls? In S. Maruna & R. Immarigeon (Eds.), *After Crime and Punishment: Pathways to Offender Reintegration*. Willan: Cullompton.

Ministry of Justice. (2018). *Female Offender Strategy*. London: Ministry of Justice.

Morrissey, B. (2003). *When Women Kill: Questions of Agency and Subjectivity*. London: Routledge.

Österman, L. (2018). *Penal Cultures and Female Desistance*. London: Routledge.

Pantazis, C. (2004). Gendering Harm Through a Life-Course Perspective. In P. Hillyard, C. Pantazis, S. Tombs, & D. Gordon (Eds.), *Beyond Criminology: Taking Harm Seriously*. London: Pluto Press.

Patterson, O. (1982). *Slavery and Social Death*. Cambridge, MA/London: Harvard University Press.

Pollack, S. (2013). An Imprisoning Gaze: Practices of Gendered, Racialized and Epistemic Violence. *International Review of Victimology, 19*(1), 103–114.

Price, J. M. (2015). *Prison and Social Death*. New Brunswick/London: Rutgers University Press.

Prison Reform Trust. (2014). *Transforming Lives: Reducing Women's Imprisonment*. Stockport: Soroptimist International.

Prison Reform Trust. (2017). *Why Focus on Reducing Women's Imprisonment?* London: Prison Reform Trust.

Reiner, R. (2007). Neoliberalism, Crime and Justice. In R. Roberts & W. McMahon (Eds.), *Social Justice and Criminal Justice*. London: Centre for Crime and Justice Studies.

Rich, A. (1996). *Of Woman Born – Motherhood as Experience and Institution* (3rd ed.). New York: W. W. Norton & Company.

Rodermond, E., Kruttschnitt, C., Slotboom, A. M., & Bijieveld, C. C. J. H. (2016). Female Desistance: A Review of the Literature. *European Journal of Criminology, 13*(1), 3–28.

Rumgay, J. (2004). Scripts for Safer Survival: Pathways Out of Female Crime. *The Howard Journal, 43*(4), 405–419.

Sampson, R. J., & Laub, J. H. (1992). Crime and Deviance in the Life Course. *Annual Review of Sociology, 18*, 63–84.
Savage, M. (2018). Private Probation Firms Fail to Cut Rates of Reoffending. *The Guardian*. Available at: https://www.theguardian.com/society/2018/feb/03/private-firms-fail-cut-rates-reoffending-low-medium-risk-offenders. Accessed 5 Jan 2019.
Shover, N. (1996). *Great Pretenders: Pursuits and Careers of Persistent Thieves*. Boulder: Westview.
Sisters Uncut. (2018). Women's Residential Centres – Another Dangerous Distraction [Blog]. *Sisters Uncut*. Available at: http://www.sistersuncut.org/2018/07/06/community-prisons/. Accessed 27 Dec 2018.
Sommers, E. K. (1995). *Voices From Within, Women Who Have Broken the Law*. Toronto: University of Toronto Press.
Stone, R. (2016). Desistance and Identity Repair: Redemption Narratives as Resistance to Stigma. *British Journal of Criminology, 56*(5), 956–975.
The Bach Commission. (2017). *The Right to Justice: The Final Report of the Bach Commission*. London: Fabian Society.
Thomas, R., & Davies, A. (2005). What Have the Feminists Done for Us? Feminist Theory and Organizational Resistance. *Organization, 12*(5), 711–740.
Verbruggen, J., Blokland, A. A. J., & Van Der Geest, V. R. (2012). Effects of Employment and Unemployment on Serious Offending in a High-Risk Sample of Men and Women from Ages 18 to 32 in the Netherlands. *British Journal of Criminology, 52*(5), 845–869.
Wacquant, L. (2018). Prisoner Re-entry as Myth and Ceremony. In P. Carlen & L. Ayres França (Eds.), *Alternative Criminologies*. London: Routledge.
Watts, J. (2018). No Wonder People on Benefits Live in Fear. Supermarkets Spy on Them Now. *The Guardian*. Available at: https://www.theguardian.com/commentisfree/2018/may/31/benefits-claimants-fear-supermarkets-spy-poor-disabled. Accessed 27 Dec 2018.
Weaver, B., & McNeill, F. (2010). *Changing Lives? Desistance Research and Offender Management* (3rd ed.). Glasgow: The Scottish Centre for Crime and Research.
Wilkinson, A., & Pickett, K. (2010). *The Spirit Level: Why Equality Is Better for Everyone*. London: Penguin.
Worrall, A. (1990). *Offending Women: Female Lawbreakers and the CJS*. London: Routledge.

8

Conclusion

Desisting Sisters has explored the relationship between gender and desistance by critically considering the life-course narratives of a small group of Northshire-based women. This was undertaken in response to the dearth of women's voices in the influential desistance literature, which tends to fall into maturational, social bonds or subjective theoretical perspectives. What, as previous chapters have indicated, has become clear is the absence of analysis of the social-structural conditions which support or hinder desistance attempts. Further, it has been argued that women continue to suffer under neoliberal and patriarchal social structures, whether they are desisting from crime or otherwise.

This final chapter will firstly provide a critical analysis of current (neo) liberal reform of the Criminal Justice System (CJS), in particular that which relates to women. Chapter 6 examined the penological landscape which formed the background to the Northshire women's experiences in austerity Britain, reaching the conclusion that an abolitionist, critical, desistance theory is necessary. In June 2018, the Home Office published their Female Offenders Strategy, which argued for 'earlier intervention, an emphasis on community-based solutions, and an aim to make custody effective and decent as possible for those who have to be there' (Ministry

Ú. Barr, *Desisting Sisters*, Critical Criminological Perspectives,
https://doi.org/10.1007/978-3-030-14276-6_8

of Justice 2018a: 3). Secondly, influenced by the work of Pat Carlen, almost 30 years ago (1990), this chapter will argue for a woman-wise community-based penology which is both utopian and pragmatic, and will examine what this might entail. Finally, some methodological implications and conclusions are posed.

The Female Offenders Strategy

As noted, this chapter is influenced by the pioneering work of Pat Carlen and particularly her book *Alternatives to Women's Imprisonment*. In this book, Carlen sets out trends related to the criminalisation of women and their imprisonment, explores the particular experience of women's imprisonment and post-imprisonment, and argues for a feminist jurisprudence or a 'woman-wise penology' (p. 109). In a similar fashion, *Desisting Sisters* will finish with an analysis of the implications of applying a feminist epistemology to desistance research and explore what this means in practical terms for the creation of a 'woman-wise *community-based* penology' in the current penological landscape. Taking an approach to woman-wise penology which is community based reinforces arguments of prison abolitionists such as Carlen and others set out in Chap. 6, and Carlen's justification for the continuation of 'woman-wise' probation groups, which she argued

1. … provide a space for the remedy and resistance of women's oppression.
2. … provide a forum in which women can collectively, democratically and responsibly fashion principles for the future (self) governance of their lives.
3. [… recognise] that there is no essentially 'female' cause of women's law-breaking (only historically specific economic, political and ideological conditions) [and where offence-focused groups] can slowly gain knowledge of the combinations of circumstances in which women most frequently choose to break the law and subsequently develop 'behaviour-changing' therapies which women recognize as being relevant to their needs. (1990: 117)

Carlen also argued that the 'very existence (and popularity) of probation-run women's groups in neighbourhoods bereft of most other social amenities call[ed] into question what the criminal justice system … and its agents are really for. And ensuing analysis demonstrates that far from being concerned primarily with serious lawbreakers, the CJS and its officers are more frequently providing support services for people who might not have been in trouble at all had they been in employment *and* in receipt of decent provision from the education, housing, health and welfare services' (1990: 117).

These quotes are included in full despite their relative age, having been written some 30 years ago, because of their continued and ongoing relevance to the current criminal justice context. Carlen was writing in the immediate aftermath of the publication of the 1988 Green Paper *Punishment, Custody and the Community*, just as this book is written in the immediate aftermath of the publication of the Female Offenders Strategy (Ministry of Justice 2018a). It is clear from this document that there has been some progress made in thinking about the experience of women's imprisonment. Although, as mentioned previously, the 2007 Corston Report did not immediately have an effect on the pervasive punishment and subjugation of criminalised women, there appears to have been somewhat of a long-term effect on the cultural perception of women's short-term imprisonment in England and Wales, which allowed for the 2018 Strategy to include the note that

> [t]here is a clear opportunity to take an entirely different approach to this cohort – one that addresses vulnerability, acknowledges the role of gender, treats female offenders as individuals with the potential to make a positive contribution to wider society, and ultimately breaks the cycle of reoffending with all the benefits that brings for families and society as a whole. (Ministry of Justice 2018a: 8)

Nonetheless, it would be unwise to suggest that Carlen's 1990 blueprint for the large-scale reduction, and subsequent abolition, of women's imprisonment has been achieved. Since 1990, and especially since 1993, and reflecting international trends, there has been a continued rise in the use of imprisonment for women and women have gone from representing

3.6–4.6% of the daily prison population (Ministry of Justice 2018b). On 30 June 2018 there were 3803 female prisoners in England and Wales (Ministry of Justice 2018c). The rise in the female prison population has been underpinned by the Transforming Rehabilitation (TR) policy, which, as discussed in Chap. 6, has meant that following a period of imprisonment, criminalised individuals are supervised for a period of 12 months in the community, leading to an increase in the proportion of women being recalled to prison. Importantly, these policy changes are further underpinned by the ongoing violence of austerity (Mansfield and Cooper 2016), in particular the cuts to women's services and the continued neoliberalisation of education, housing, health and welfare services. This includes the introduction of the widely critiqued Universal Credit welfare reforms despite damning research by the UN Special Rapporteur on Extreme Poverty in a visit to the UK (Alston 2018). These changes have increased the financial/economic, physical, emotional and psychological harms faced by criminalised women. Additionally, it is important to note that the rhetoric of the 1988 Green Paper *Punishment, Custody and the Community* appears to have much in common with the Female Offenders Strategy—although the latter focuses only on women—in terms of increasing the punitive nature of community sentencing, while prioritising the confidence of the public and judiciary over the safety and well-being of women. In 2018, this meant—amongst engaging with courts, improving pre-sentence reporting, increasing the use of Community Service Treatment Requirements and developing a more gender-informed probation service—the piloting of 'Residential Women's Centres' and electronic monitoring (EM), including new technologies such as location monitoring. This chapter will now highlight the problems of these latter recommendations before moving on to consider what a woman-wise community-based penology might look like.

Residential Women's Centres

Whilst at first glance, the proposal to pilot five 'Residential Women's Centres' appears as a positive step towards the reduction in women's incarceration, especially within a plan which was largely expected to announce the creation of further prison spaces, there are a number of problematic elements to it. The Centres are described as being part of 'an intensive residential support package in the community for women at risk of, or having served, short custodial sentences, supporting them to address the underlying causes of their offending behaviour' (Ministry of Justice 2018a: 21). First, the rhetoric inherent in the plan echoes previous responsibilising recommendations, including the Corston Report (2007), to enforce individualised solutions to structural inequalities experienced by marginalised populations. It should be noted that while the Residential Women's Centres in some way represent a social-structural elucidation to some of the issues faced by criminalised women around homelessness, the lack of mental health and gendered violence support, it is clear that this provision will be scant and fragmented nationwide, and will force women out of their communities, often away from children and the supportive relationships which are consistently found to be beneficial to desistance. Second, as noted by Sisters Uncut (2018) these plans would disproportionately affect those most likely to be criminalised; black and minority ethnic women, sex workers, migrants, transgender and disabled people, without challenging the reasoning behind their overcriminalisation. Third, it is unclear who will run these Residential Centres and whether contracts will be subject to a bidding process (which as shown under TR is unlikely to be beneficial for third-sector institutions). As they note:

> This move looks worryingly like a money-saving exercise masquerading as a community-centred project. For communities that are already targeted by the police, state punishment – even when dressed up as a 'community sentence' – subjects survivors to further violence and isolation from their families and communities. (Sisters Uncut 2018: blog post)

Electronic Monitoring

The Home Office makes use of research by Graham and McIvor (2015) to draw attention to the apparent link between the use of electronic monitoring (EM) and support for women in the community. The argument is made that, when used in conjunction with interventions that contain rehabilitative elements, EM is most likely to improve outcomes. What this recommendation does not note, however, is that Graham and McIvor's research concluded that the potential positive impacts of EM, and generalised effectiveness claims, 'are significantly diminished in cases where it is used without due regard for diversity and vulnerability' (2015: 10). The Northshire research highlighted some of the negative impacts of the use of electronic monitoring tags which increased stigma and produced negative mental health outcomes. Additionally, as highlighted by Carlen (1990), poor home situations are likely to make it very difficult for criminalised women to comply with curfews and monitoring requirements. As TR continues, therefore, women are more likely to be recalled to prison following failure to comply. Therefore, 'the tightening up of the non-custodial alternatives to prison is likely to result in sentencers imposing tougher alternatives regardless of the appropriateness or feasibility of the sentence and in offenders then breaching the conditions of unrealistic orders and ending up in prison anyhow' (Carlen 1990: 120). Whilst Carlen is referring to the 1988 Green Paper here, it is important to note, that almost 30 years later, under TR reforms, these problems have become even more entrenched and are unlikely to result in less women experiencing custody or custody-like institutions of pain and trauma.

Whilst many of the recommendations of the Female Offenders Strategy including diversion, trauma-informed practice and a reduction in women's incarceration are welcomed, when considering the feasibility of punishment in the community, Carlen's arguments, nearly 30 years ago, continue to ring true. Women continue to suffer the pains of unemployment, low wages and poor (or no) housing, while community facilities which would enable women to live a decent standard of public life are severely lacking throughout England and Wales.

A Woman-Wise, Community-Based Penology

What, then, would a truly woman-wise, community-based penology be comprised of? Taking into account the qualitative desistance experiences of the Northshire women, the current political and penological landscape, and the findings of previous desistance scholars that criminalised individuals are more likely to be affected by shifts in welfare provisions than penal policy (McNeill 2016; Österman 2018), a number of utopian, yet pragmatic, recommendations are outlined below. These recommendations are influenced by what Brown and Schept (2016: 12 cited in Sim 2018: 181) refer to as 'abolitionist praxis'.

Women's Centre Funding Ring-Fenced

The Female Offenders Strategy (Ministry of Justice 2018a), continuing the rhetoric of the Corston Report (2007), celebrates the role of third-sector organisations, and particularly women-only spaces such as Women's Centres, in supporting women with the pressures and challenges in their lives. The Northshire research has further revealed the importance of holistic women-only spaces in addressing harms faced by criminalised women and others. Yet, from the interviews and conversations with staff in these spaces, time is increasingly taken up with applying for funding to keep their services running. This reinforces findings from the Howard League for Penal Reform (2016), which noted that the introduction of TR has led to the 'watering down' of women's services as provided by Community Rehabilitation Companies (CRCs), who have often taken over the running of services for criminalised women. Therefore, this research supports the recommendations of the Howard League's research for ring-fenced funding for holistic, evidence-based, women-only community support.

Domestic Violence Support, Including Refuges, Funding Ring-Fenced

The link between women's experiences of gendered violence and their criminalisation has long been recognised by researchers and campaigners and has begun to gain recognition by the state (Roberts 2015a, b; Prison Reform Trust 2017; Ministry of Justice 2018a). This is less explored by the desistance literature. The Northshire women's narratives pointed to the prevalence of gendered violence and abuse in their lives prior to, during and post-criminal justice contact, even when they appeared to be desisting. However, austerity measures disproportionately affect women on an individual level and on the services they rely on for survival. As noted in the report by the UN Special Rapporteur on Extreme Poverty:

> Organisations have … highlighted the lack of specialist services available, particularly for women from ethnic minorities, disabled women and LGBT survivors … The current model for funding specialist domestic and sexual violence services has been described as not fit for purpose. (2018: 142)

Investment into Community-Based Tiered Support

Aside from Women's Centres and domestic violence refuges and support services, there are a range of community support systems which have been decimated by funding cuts over the past decade. The services are particularly those which support women in difficulties (Mansfield and Cooper 2016; Alston 2018). The Northshire research has highlighted the centrality of tiered support around mental and physical health, childcare, alcohol and drug addiction and positive links with schools, to be central to criminalised women's desistance experiences. Arguably, if the support was in place initially, as Carlen (1990) noted, there would be a lot less criminalised women.

In-Work Poverty Abolished

Desistance literature makes much of the links between employment and desistance (Farrall 2002; Maruna 2001; Österman 2018). Yet, the Joseph Rowntree Foundation (2018) has found that in-work poverty is currently growing faster than employment rates, driven by increasing poverty amongst working parents. In addition, the Northshire research highlighted the prominence of patriarchal discourses in the promotion of criminalised women's desire to taken on hyper-moral (Matthews et al.

2014) unpaid voluntary roles. This further entrenches the feminisation of poverty, as has been described by the UN Report on extreme poverty (Alston 2018). The importance of meaningful, and often, generative employment experiences to desistance where appropriate is not questioned by this research; however, the meaning and the rewards of work requires a re-evaluation and a drastic change from their current neoliberal form.

Abolishing Universal Credit

Although the Northshire research was carried out just as Universal Credit was being trialled, and had not yet been introduced in Northshire, Katie, Ruth[1] and Heather had been criminalised as a result of transgressions related to welfare receipt. As discussed in previous chapters, this was the first experience of criminalisation for all three. Research on the introduction of Universal Credit suggests it is an unsuitable scheme which will disproportionately harm former prisoners and women in particular. Firstly, former prisoners face a five-week delay upon release to receive their first payments of Universal Credit (Day 2018). This means they are released with £46 only, a discharge grant which has not changed in 15 years. With the combined pressure of TR measures meaning 12-month supervision periods following release, it is hardly surprising that people are being recalled to prison at increasing rates. Additionally, it has been found that women are resorting to sex work as they become less well-off under Universal Credit measures and as first payments are delayed (Field 2018). The harms faced by sex workers, including criminalisation, violence, drug use, disease, discrimination and exploitation, have been well documented in feminist research (Sanders and Platt 2017). Finally, a joint report by the Women's Budget Group, Surviving Economic Abuse and the End Violence Against Women Coalition (2018) has warned that by introducing Universal Credit, the state is facilitating gendered violence by putting single payments into the bank and other accounts of partners, which risks financial abuse. Women may feel unable to leave an abusive relationship and the measures could result in carers (usually mothers) losing child maintenance payments.

Affordable Social Housing

As discussed in Chap. 4, the lack of provision of secure and stable housing was a key factor in the criminalisation and the frustrated desistance attempts in the lives of the Northshire women. In the first quarter of 2018, 26,400 households made a homelessness application at their local authority. Of this, 13,740 were accepted as statutory homeless (MHCLG 2018). The Homelessness Reduction Act 2017 requires local authorities to intervene at earlier stages to prevent homelessness and requires local authorities to provide new homelessness services to all those affected, including criminalised individuals. Public authorities are further required to notify local authorities of service users they think may be at risk of homelessness. The issues around housing are pervasive in desistance and gender-based research, as recognised by Carlen (1990). Whilst the problems with Residential Women's Centres, and particularly their scant provision throughout England and Wales, are noted above, as found by the Northshire research, the requirement that homelessness in all its forms be addressed at the local level is key to promoting desistance from both crime and harm more widely.

A Continuation of Supportive Staff-Service User Relationships

One of the important findings in Chap. 6 was the centrality of relationships in supporting women's desistance, to include relationships between staff in probation, the Women's Centres and the Housing for Northshire projects. With the introduction of the Transforming Rehabilitation Agenda, and the part privatisation of probation, there was concern that relationships with staff would generally be compromised (Burke 2013); this has been found to be true (User Voice 2016), particularly in the failure to have continuity of relationships. Many of the Northshire women described poor relationships with staff, which were characterised by a lack of respect and consideration for the realities of their lives. Nonetheless, the relationships particularly evident, for example, in Bridget's, Shelly's, Michaela's and Kelly-Marie's narratives were found to be central in supporting their desistance from both crime and harm.

Sentencing Reform and Decarceration

Although, as noted previously, welfare provision is more likely to affect desistance than penal policy (McNeill 2016; Österman 2018), the Northshire research makes clear that the criminal (in)justice system itself is a key player in the harm-causing institutions in the lives of criminalised women. One of the most effective supports to criminalised women would be to divert them entirely from the system in the first place. Importantly, the Female Offenders Strategy (2018) notes the place of out-of-court disposals (OOCDs) in diverting women if they come into contact with the police, but points out that often these stand only as a warning not to reoffend rather than dealing with the underlying issues surrounding their criminalisation. The decimation of public and third-sector support organisations as a result of austerity measures has not helped this issue. Whilst this research does not support the Strategy's suggestion of attaching conditions to OOCDs (which will inevitably lead in many cases to breach and (re)criminalisation, including imprisonment), it is important that women are offered unconditional support from a range of services at this point.

The Strategy refers to a case study in Greater Manchester where there has been a focus on women by the devolved authorities, which includes a coalition of Women's Centres supporting women, criminalised or otherwise, police triage and a problem-solving court. This problem-solving approach means that imprisonment is resisted, the outcomes are women-centred and holistic. The court is different in appearance to regular courts: women are not in a dock and the magistrates have received training in trauma-informed practice, and are arguably, therefore, more interested in positive outcomes for the women. This is particularly important as Lightowler's (2018) research shows that the pervasiveness of patriarchal assumptions of the 'good woman' are prevalent in the courts, where women are twice as likely to receive harsher sentences than men for violent offences when intoxication is a contributing factor. As noted by the Female Offenders Strategy (Ministry of Justice 2018a) the Greater Manchester approach has resulted in a number of benefits including an overall reduction of 40% in the number of adult women sentenced to immediate custody (as compared to 3% overall in England and Wales), a reduction in arrests, a greater access rate to support services, and a reduction in reoffending. Whilst this approach is imperfect, particularly in the surrounding context of austerity, neoliberalism and patriarchal discourse elsewhere, the Northshire research suggests that there is much that can be gained from a rollout of OOCDs and problem-solving courts for women in all areas across England and Wales.

Closure of Women's Prisons

The final, but most important, factor in the creation of a women-wise community-based penology is the abolition of women's imprisonment. The feminist theoretical grounding for this argument was explained in the preceding chapter, whilst Chap. 6 explored the empirical evidence in the current research for the harms and 'social death' (Price 2015) inflicted by imprisonment on criminalised women, their communities, friends and families. Carlen (1990) effectively considers critiques of this arguably utopian proposal, concluding that only a very small proportion of women in prison pose a danger to the public, and even these women's needs are not best served by the current system. Along with closing women's prisons, the eight measures listed above would go some way to ensuring that both less women are imprisoned and less women will reoffend.

It is worth noting that these women-wise, community-based recommendations are proposed in a time where, in the year 2017–2018, there were four self-inflicted deaths in women's prisons (Ministry of Justice 2018d). In the same period, there were 119 deaths of women serving sentences in the community, with self-inflicted deaths accounting for 25% of this figure; 80% of these women who died (either of 'natural', unrecorded or self-inflicted causes) were aged under 50 (Ministry of Justice 2018e). Safety and death are significant indicators of the health of the criminal (in)justice system because they represent the thick end of the wedge in the experience of harm and violence. It is clear therefore that liberal reform alone will not significantly support women likely to be criminalised. Instead, radical strategies, based on compassion, love and support, as opposed to responsibility, surveillance, punishment and prison-based interventions (Hart 2017) in combination with a *real* end to austerity, are necessary to make a real difference to the experience of desistance from harm in women's lives.

Methodological Implications

The Northshire research has contended that it is important to learn from criminalised women what works best for them in terms of desistance-promotion. Desistance literature has emphasised maturity, relationships, work, shame, hope, self-efficacy and identity transformation. These themes are also prevalent in women's narratives about their desistance journeys. Yet when we allow space for women to voice their own personal experiences, the make-up, shape and intricacies of desistance pathways become clear, including the structural contexts which enable (or otherwise) them to desist from harm. Criminalised women's narratives reflect the experiences of women in general marginalised as a result of the intersections of class, 'race' and sexuality. Desistance from harm can therefore be a collective feminist social project which challenges the structures of the neoliberal and patriarchal state.

In order to challenge inequality, it is important that an awareness be brought to desistance discourse. 'Female offenders' individualises and responsibilises women whilst 'criminalised women' locates the structural inequalities inherent in criminalisation and desistance. As has been clear throughout the Northshire research, those who come into contact with the CJS are a particular group of marginalised and subjugated women. Prisons and probation services are not full of wealthy, white, heterosexual women. Criminalised women are those who are materially deprived and have come from contexts of abuse and neglect from the state. These contexts do not often disappear when women embark on desistance, although they may be hidden. Resistance to interlinking oppressions of neoliberalism and patriarchy start with the very language used to explore and support desistance and allow these inequalities to come to the fore. Similarly, the current research contends that desistance theorists and practitioners should avoid the lauding of redemption stories as proof of the success of responsibilising individuals to make changes in their own lives. Whilst *Desisting Sisters* concurs with Maruna's (2001) support of the redemption ritual and the productive power of the narrative, the particular redemption narratives used productively by the state (to support punitive measures and the myth of individual rehabilitation) tend to overemphasise the individual strength and determination required to change and underemphasise the role of material circumstances and social solidarity.

Conclusion

A brief glance at desistance literature shows that, much like wider criminological research in the past, it has paid scant attention to 'the woman question' (Gelsthorpe and Morris 1988). The normative view in criminological research on desistance appeared to be that gender had no significant implication. Yet this research has found gender to be *central* in desistance experiences or otherwise. Men's desistance theory and practice can learn much from women's narratives. The Northshire research has enabled a view of desistance as a complicated journey, replete with stops and starts and reactions to structural (often gendered) inequalities.

As Fergus McNeill (2017) has noted, what individuals are desisting *into* must form the basis of research. Criminalised women lead complicated lives. Desistance for these women required hope and self-efficacy, as well as recognising and challenging the harms they faced, whether these were harms related to relationships, housing, poverty, abuse, mental and physical health, or an amalgamation of them all. In spite of the harms many of the women faced, some still managed to desist from crime. Desistance was not, for the Northshire women, something which occurred naturally, but occurred, or indeed did not occur, within the complicated social structures of their daily lives. As argued by Carlen in 2012:

> Today, re-integration, re-settlement or re-entry are often used instead of re-habilitation. Yet all these terms, with their English prefix 're-', imply that the lawbreakers or ex-prisoners, who are to be 're-habilitated'/'re-integrated'/'re-settled' or 're-stored', previously occupied a social state or status to which it is desirable they should be returned. Not so. The majority of criminal prisoners worldwide have, prior to their imprisonment, usually

> been so economically and/or socially disadvantaged that they have nothing to which they can be advantageously rehabilitated. Sure, they are returned to their place in society, but from that disadvantaged place they are, too frequently, returned to prison again, and again and again. (p. 3)

The social-structural harms facing criminalised women, it has been found, require addressing before any promotion of cognitive and identity changes. Cognitive changes are particularly difficult in a society which sees women lawbreakers as 'doubly deviant' and simultaneously penalises women financially for being women, through greater austerity measures. The Northshire women's narratives have shown that women can make important contributions to what is known about desistance. The fact that they are travelling these journeys at all can be commended and celebrated, whilst avoiding the assumption that this is due to any (neo)liberal reform which individualises women's struggles as resilience only.

Ultimately, and perhaps strangely, the goal of critical, abolitionist, harm-based desistance research and practice is to eliminate the need for the theory at all. In challenging the unequal structures faced by criminalised women, this will pave the way for the elimination of criminalisation, both by challenging the structures which criminalise and by moving towards a utopian equal society based on solidarity. Nonetheless, the fact remains that, in the short term, many women have been criminalised. Yet, importantly, (some) women are desisting by resisting criminalisation, and therefore resisting the structural conditions of their contact with the CJS. At the same time, it is important to note both where this is not occurring *and* where this is occurring within harmful contexts. Desistance from harm is both an individual and a social-structural endeavour.

Note

1. Despite Ruth's only transgression being her inability to pay back housing benefit overpayment. It is worth noting, as discussed in previous chapters, that both Heather and Katie denied culpability in their accused wrongdoing, although both had been advised to 'go guilty'.

Bibliography

Alston, P. (2018). *Statement on Visit to the United Kingdom, By Professor Philip Alston, United Nations Special Rapporteur on Extreme Poverty and Human Rights.* Available at: https://www.ohchr.org/EN/NewsEvents/Pages/DisplayNews.aspx?NewsID=23881&LangID=E. Accessed 27 Dec 2018.

Burke, L. (2013). Grayling's Hubris. *Probation Journal, 60*, 377–382.

Carlen, P. (1990). *Alternatives to Women's Imprisonment.* Milton Keynes: Open University Press.

Corston, J. (2007). *The Corston Report: A Report by Baroness Jean Corston of a Review of Women with Particular Vulnerabilities in the Criminal Justice System.* London: Home Office.

Day, A. (2018). Universal Credit: Prisoners 'Lured Back Into Crime' By Benefit Delays. *Huffington Post.* Available at: https://www.huffingtonpost.co.uk/entry/universal-credit-prisoners-being-set-up-to-fail-and-lured-back-into-crime-by-benefit-delays_uk_5be595aae4b0dbe871aa26f2. Accessed 27 Dec 2018.

Farrall, S. (2002). *Rethinking What Works with Offenders.* Cullompton: Willan.

Field, F. (2018). The Climbdown on Universal Credit Is Painfully Inadequate. *The Guardian.* Available at: https://www.theguardian.com/commentisfree/2018/oct/16/climbdown-universal-credit-benefit-claimants-poverty. Accessed 27 Dec 2018.

Gelsthorpe, L., & Morris, A. (1988). Feminism and Criminology in Britain. *British Journal of Criminology, 28*(2), 93–110.

Graham, H., & McIvor, G. (2015). *Scottish and International Review of the Use of Electronic Monitoring* (Report No. 8). Scottish Centre for Crime and Justice Research.

Hart, E. L. (2017). Prisoners Post-Release, The Need for a Critical Desistance. In E. L. Hart & F. J. C. Van Ginneken (Eds.), *New Perspectives on Desistance.* London: Palgrave Macmillan.

Homelessness Reduction Act. (2017). Available at: http://www.legislation.gov.uk/ukpga/2017/13/contents/enacted. Accessed 12 Mar 2019.

Joseph Rowntree Foundation. (2018). *UK Poverty 2018: A Comprehensive Analysis of Poverty Trends and Figures.* London: JRF Analysis Unit.

Lightowler, C. (2018). Drunk Women Convicted of Assault Treated Harsher in Sentencing Than Drunk Men [Blog]. *The Conversation.* Available at: https://theconversation.com/drunk-women-convicted-of-assault-treated-harsher-in-sentencing-than-drunk-men-103631. Accessed 27 Dec 2018.

Mansfield, M., & Cooper, V. (2016). The Failure to Protect Women in the Criminal Justice System. In V. Cooper & D. Whyte (Eds.), *The Violence of Austerity*. London: Pluto Press.

Maruna, S. (2001). *Making Good – How Ex-Convicts Reform and Rebuild Their Lives*. Washington, DC: American Psychological Association Books.

Matthews, R., Easton, H., Reynolds, L., Bindel, J., & Young, L. (2014). *Exiting Prostitution*. New York: Palgrave Macmillan.

McNeill, F. (2016). The Fuel in the Tank or the Hole in the Boat? Can Sanctions Support Desistance. In J. Shapland, S. Farrall, & A. Bottoms (Eds.), *Global Perspectives on Desistance: Rethinking What We Know and Looking to the Future* (pp. 265–281). Routledge: Oxford.

McNeill, F. (2017). Post-script: Guide, Guard and Glue – Electronic Monitoring and Penal Supervision. *European Journal of Probation, 9*(1), 103–107.

Ministry of Housing, Communities & Local Government. (2018). *Statutory Homelessness and Prevention and Relief, January to March (Q1) 2018: England*. London: Ministry of Housing, Communities and Local Government.

Ministry of Justice. (2018a). *Female Offender Strategy*. London: Ministry of Justice.

Ministry of Justice. (2018b). *Offender Management Statistics Bulletin, England and Wales*. London: Ministry of Justice.

Ministry of Justice. (2018c). *Women and the Criminal Justice System 2017 Statistics*. London: Ministry of Justice.

Ministry of Justice. (2018d). *Safety in Custody Quarterly: Update to June 2018*. London: Ministry of Justice.

Ministry of Justice. (2018e). *Deaths of Offenders in the Community*. London: Ministry of Justice.

Österman, L. (2018). *Penal Cultures and Female Desistance*. London: Routledge.

Price, J. M. (2015). *Prison and Social Death*. New Brunswick/London: Rutgers University Press.

Prison Reform Trust. (2017). *Why Focus on Reducing Women's Imprisonment?* London: Prison Reform Trust.

Roberts, J. (2015a). *'It Was Do or Die' – How a Woman's Experience of Domestic Abuse Can Influence Her Involvement in Crime: A Qualitative Investigation of the Experiences of Community-Based Female Offenders*. Doctoral Thesis, University of Leicester, Leicester.

Roberts, R. (2015b). Is Lady Justice Blind or Just Blinkered. In H. Mills, R. Roberts, & L. Townhead (Eds.), *Empower, Resist, Transform: A Collection of Essays* (pp. 9–11). London: Centre for Crime and Justice Studies.

Sanders, T., & Platt, L. (2017). Is Sex Work Still the Most Dangerous Profession? The Data Suggests So [Blog]. *The Conversation*. Available at: https://theconversation.com/is-sex-work-still-the-most-dangerous-profession-the-data-suggests-so-81854. Accessed 27 Dec 2018.
Sim, J. (2018). We Are All (Neo-)Liberals Now: Reform and the Prison Crisis in England and Wales Justice. *Power and Resistance, 1*, 165–188.
Sisters Uncut. (2018). Women's Residential Centres – Another Dangerous Distraction [Blog]. *Sisters Uncut*. Available at: http://www.sistersuncut.org/2018/07/06/community-prisons/. Accessed 27 Dec 2018.
The Howard League. (2016). *Is This the End of Women's Centres?* London: All Party Parliamentary Group for Women.
User Voice. (2016). *"Transforming Rehabilitation": The Operational Model from the Service User's Perspective*. London: National Audit Office.
Women's Budget Group, Surviving Economic Abuse & the End Violence Against Women Coalition. (2018). *Universal Credit Risks Increasing Women's Vulnerability to Abuse*. Available at: https://wbg.org.uk/wp-content/uploads/2018/09/Universal-Credit-2018.09.12-event-press-release-sea-wbg-FINAL.pdf. Accessed 27 Dec 2018.

Appendix: Methodology

> Women are rarely credited with having any real knowledge, even knowledge of themselves. People in conflict with the law are rarely granted credibility. On these two counts, female lawbreakers have been silenced. (Sommers 1995: 3)

The Northshire research is based on observations conducted from Spring 2014 to Spring 2015 at five Women's Centres (WCs) located across Northshire as well as 23 semi-structured interviews with women with recent convictions (n = 16) and staff members (n = 6). The criminalised women either were part of the Housing for Northshire (HfN) Project or were completing/had recently completed Specified Activity Orders at Northshire WCs. Initial contact with gatekeepers was made through the University of Central Lancashire, which had links with the Probation Trust who eventually put me in contact with Northshire WCs. Over the next year I attended 17 observations of group sessions in Easton and Southton as well as Central Town, Northton and Weston and interviewed 12 WC-attending women. I also had contact with Rebecca, Project Manager at the Housing for Northshire Project, via Twitter. Before carrying out any interviews, Rebecca allowed me to interview her in a pilot interview. This interview took place at Easton WC. I went to Rebecca's

Ú. Barr, *Desisting Sisters*, Critical Criminological Perspectives,
https://doi.org/10.1007/978-3-030-14276-6

Easton office for the first time in winter 2014. On my first visit I interviewed Shelly and Michaela at a nearby café. On my second visit I interviewed Kelly-Marie, as well as Josie, a project volunteer and Rebecca herself, this time as a formal interview. Around this time I also interviewed WC staff. All those whom I interviewed gave up their time voluntarily to do this.

Methodological Approach and Justification

> Research, which has so far been an instrument of dominance and legitimation of power elites, must be brought to serve the interests of dominated, exploited and oppressed groups, particularly women. (Mies 1983: 123)

The association between feminist and qualitative research is not new. Researchers such as Oakley (1981) have claimed that research methods such as qualitative interviewing help women's voices be heard. Sommers notes that the rhetoric of objectivity within quantitative research 'has concealed the fact that, until very recently, most research has been male centred … women's experiences have been interpreted through a masculine filter, which has been concealed by the rhetoric of objectivity' (1995: 8). Yet the dichotomous quantitative/qualitative divide in feminist research has since been called into question (Westmarland 2001). What is of more interest to feminist researchers is the concept of power. For example, Jones (1996) noted that a feminist methodology must involve a levelling of any potential (not only gendered) power imbalance between the researched and researcher. One way to pursue this is through the use of narrative interviewing styles which enable the researched to give voice to their own experiences and stories, using their own language and with their own emphases and omissions.

The Role of the Researcher

During the course of the Northshire research, the levelling of power balances was not always possible. As a middle-class student with no direct experience of the Criminal Justice System (CJS) and minimal local connections, I was acutely aware of my status as 'outsider' throughout both interviews and observations. Nonetheless, there were many 'everyday' connections, which somewhat negated this problem, not limited to my gender but also my relational identity as an auntie and my national (Irish) identity, where common connections were made. These power differentials within identity features are important when conducting feminist research. Erin Saunders, although employing a feminist methodology in her research on sex workers, noted that there was still a power differential in her research. 'I am not sure that it is ever possible to overcome the power imbalance in the research relationship, especially when I, as a "White" "Western" woman, research an "Other". From an ethical perspective, it seems to me that the research relationship fosters an exploitative relationship in a number of ways, and I will have to seriously consider how (or if) I can avoid this in future' (quoted in Bryman 2012: 397). This issue was something I faced throughout my research journey, not least when Rebecca noted,

> And obviously what's happening, like with any other private sector, is that they're bringing in sort of ... women shall we say... Right I'm going to say it, white, middle-class women, who actually look down about, 'what these poor people need.' And I find that actually, not even insulting, I find it an utter travesty. (Rebecca, age 46)

These features of my identity are something that I could not change. Like Saunders, however, the recognition of this power differential was something which I noted throughout my research and did not restrict me from employing a feminist methodology throughout the fieldwork and analysis. For example, women would ask for advice on their relationship with their housing agency; I was very clear that I was not in a position to offer advice and, whilst directing women to agencies which could help, was clear that I hoped this did not prevent them from becoming involved in the research process.

Qualitative methods have informed this research with particular homage paid to feminist and narrative styles. Semi-structured, qualitative interviewing has informed the bulk of the research whilst observation has also been employed as a method, in addition to providing a useful introductory route into the research.

Observation Research

When conducting observation research, there are multiple levels of subjective interpretation between the researched and the researcher. Nonetheless, observation can have many advantages to the researcher and indeed those who are being researched. Overt consensual observation formed the initial method of data collection. I attended group sessions for women who had been sentenced with a Specified Activity Requirement or referred by their offender managers. Group sessions were constructed around eight different themes as constructed by the probation service in conjunction with Northshire WC: substance misuse awareness, health and well-being, housing and money management, community and citizenship, employment training and education, thinking and behaviour, victim awareness and family and relationships. I attended at least one of each of these sessions. Service users also attended introductory and conclusion one-to-one sessions although I did not sit in on these sessions on Mary's (Criminal Justice Project Manager). The aims of the observation sessions included scene setting, observing relationships and various activities and discussions as well as providing an introductory platform to the research and particularly to recruit for phase two of the research. Mental notes and jotted notes (both on paper and on my smartphone 'notes' section) were gathered during the observations and elaborated upon on the train ride home. Once home/at university, field notes were typed up with full information about events, people and conversations, as well as initial understandings about interpretation, impressions and feelings. Throughout the observations, only 2 of 37 service users chose to opt out. There were as little as one and as many as six service users in each group. Often WC volunteers and trainee group leaders were also in attendance alongside employed group leaders. Staff members also gave their informed consent during these sessions.

Reinharz (1992) saw feminist ethnography as significant as a representation of women's lives and activities once seen as subsidiary to men's, as a way of understanding women through their own perspective (through mitigation of power differentials) and as an understanding of women in context. The use of observation/ethnographic fieldwork avoids divorcing individuals from their social and historical circumstances. The women involved in this research had an opportunity to get to know the researcher and the research project to a certain extent even before observation began. Waiting areas of the WCs provided an opportunity to engage with the potential participants. Women often knew each other from previous weeks and mostly there were good relationships clearly evident between them. Most weeks however saw a new face so I was often not the only new person to the group. Connections were particularly formed in the discussion of children and Irish backgrounds.

One of the potential strengths of observation research is non-interference. The focus of observation research is on the natural behaviour of the subjects; behaviour is not modified by the researcher in the way that, for example, structured interviews only focus on subjects chosen by the researcher (Adler and Adler 1994). Nonetheless it was recognised that my presence in the meetings was not without influence on behaviour and speech, on the part of both the staff and service users. An additional strength of observations is that there are no constraints placed upon those who are being studied. Service users and staff did not have to give up their time to fill in a questionnaire or take part in an interview; for example, they simply carried on with their weekly session, and those who did not want to take part in the second phase of the research project could still be a part of the research (or not as they choose). Furthermore, observation research meant that the researcher was also located within the context being investigated, which can lead to enlightening incidents or meaningful encounters. For example, the observation research revealed that many of the women involved had been victims of domestic violence, something which was not directly questioned in the interviews. Additionally the observation research highlighted many of the issues the women had with their offender managers, something which tended to be discussed at length with group leaders.

As I was not relying on second-hand accounts of behaviour, data were not subject to the sources of error which interviews or questionnaire surveys, and so on, are, including the unconscious motivations of respondents to tell the interviewer what they think the interviewer wants to hear or memory effects. Nonetheless this was somewhat constricted by the necessity of informed consent; without doubt there were modifications to behaviour because of my presence, with group leaders joking with service users; 'Make sure you say you enjoy it now in front of Una' (Claudia, Group Leader, Rose Centre). On the other hand, observation data can benefit from the advantages of the use of research styles which Glaser and Strauss believe empower researchers to reclaim their craft from the 'great men' (Weber, Durkheim, Marx, etc.) who, it was once believed, 'had generated a sufficient number of outstanding theories on enough areas of social life to last for a long while' (1967: 10). Research in this case was conducted without preconceptions in an organic manner.

However, I found it difficult to observe everything that was occurring around me. In fact, it was impossible to do so (Adler and Adler 1994). It was often remarked at the end of a session that I must have sore hands from writing so much. This meant that anything which was observed was done so selectively. Lapses in concentration and distractions certainly have negatively affected the reliability of my observation. I was often drawn into group discussion or asked to take part in role plays. Whyte (1979) argued that observations should be constructed in a collaborative manner. My participation in group activities was part of this collaboration and enabled trust to build. Nonetheless this interrupted the note-taking process. More importantly, my research was an intrusion into the lives of the staff and the Northshire women and the relationships formed (for this reason recording devices were not used). This intrusion was controlled by the researcher (and to an extent the staff) and, as Stacey (1998) noted, the researcher also has control over when to leave. Skeggs (1994) conversely suggested that this viewpoint constructs women as victims and overstates the power of the researcher. Skeggs argued that women are able to resist exploitation and 'the feminism of the research has provided a framework which they use to explain that their individual problems are part of a wider structure and not their personal fault' (1994: 88). The women enjoyed the research and frequently remarked on this, found it cathartic and illuminating, and hoped it would give voice to their experiences as well as improve the lives of others. Although the former two benefits were resigned to the interview research, certainly the latter point was a motivation for many women taking part in the observation research, and enabled them to do so in a less intrusive setting.

Selectivity was also affected by physical barriers such as the availability of seats and space. We always observe for an eventual audience, in the case of the Northshire research, the PhD examiners and supervisors, reviewers and readers of the book, whilst at the same time attempting to 'give voice' to the experiences of criminalised women. Jack Sanger noted that 'the process of planning, selecting, ordering and eventually recording events may determine what we see in the first place' (1996: 4). Although attempting to reclaim from the 'great men', my research was informed by what I already 'knew' from the great men (and women) of desistance theory. For example a woman's declaration of attempts to 'give up drugs' may have nothing to do with the process of desistance, but because this was the area I was conducting research into, I would naturally view it as so. It was difficult to know what I was looking for at the beginning, especially on my first visit to the WC, where I tried (and failed) to observe everything. However, as my research became more focused, so too did my data collection which became more structured. Nonetheless, my observation research was inductive; I did not use systematic coding sheets to record observations. I made notes according to what I found important on the day and built upon themes which began to emerge in my notes as well as the wider reading. This inductive method also fed into construction of the interview schedule.

Goulding (2000) noted the problem of the degree of chance occurrences in comparison with real behaviour. Perhaps when I observed a woman complaining about her probation officer, this had been the result of a wider problem, for example, in her relationships or financial situation. I was furthermore constrained by time and practicality issues; for example, my own inability to drive and being reliant on public transport. I went some way to eliminate these weaknesses by the use of multiple observations across various conditions (Goulding 2000). I did this by attending each of the centres more than once and observing the same sessions led by different group leaders at different times and places. Finally, there was a gap of interpretation as what I perceive behaviour to be may not actually be correct. Service users were additionally being observed by the staff and so, for example, the stating of their intentions to 'go straight' may be viewed in this light. The inclusion of semi-structured narrative interviews arguably enabled me to overcome this barrier.

Semi-Structured Interviews

Semi-structured interviews were the central research method used. At the end of observation sessions, I would explain to the women the second stage of the research project. I would ask women who were interested to provide me with contact details (a phone number or email address) to arrange an interview at a time and place convenient for them. I explained that there were no monetary incentives but I offered to buy the women lunch or a coffee/tea as a thank you for their participation. About 57% (n = 21) of the WC service users agreed to interviews and 57% of these (n = 12) actually took place. Four WC staff members also agreed to be interviewed. The staff interview schedule was very similar to the schedule used to interview the criminalised women, with some additional questions on the end, specifically regarding their work. As previously noted, I used a snowballing technique following a recruitment process on Twitter to make connections with Rebecca and the HfN Project where I interviewed three service users and two staff members. Again the same interview schedule was used for the HfN cohort. The total number of women interviewed was 21, with two follow-up interviews (at least six months following the first interview; time constraints meant this could not be completed with many participants), meaning the total number of interviews was 23. Much like in the work of Evelyn Sommers (1995) I found that some were concerned with what benefit they would receive through participation, but were satisfied when I said I hoped they would come to a better understanding of themselves. Others agreed to be interviewed to 'help others going through similar things'. Kelly-Marie's and Katie's feedback following the interviews was typical:

Una: Have you talked about your life like that before?

Kelly-Marie: Not really, no. Because you get your psychiatrists and whatnot and they go about it a totally different way and things like that. I have looked at me life and done a map of my life, do you know what I mean? Done it on programmes and things. But to actually sit down and go from A to B to end up at C and finish at D, no I haven't.

Una: How did you find it?

> Kelly-Marie: Like I say, I found closure on some things and some things are still a bit raw. But nevermind. (Kelly-Marie, age 48)

> I'm glad I've helped, I'm really glad I've helped. And I hope it helps somebody else, I really do … thank you very much for letting me speak about it, it does help, you know talking to somebody about it and I'm just glad I've helped you. (Katie, age 60, second interview)

Additionally, it was apparent that some of the women did not have friends to talk to or found the experience cathartic:

> It was fine; it was like talking to a friend, it was lovely … You know, I mean Rover's [Julie's dog] lovely but he doesn't answer back, well he doesn't answer (laughs). (Julie, age 59, first interview)

> I knew it had to be talked about … well I think I probably needed to offload it anyway. (Karen, age 36)

Interviews took place between August 2014 and April 2015 in the various Northshire WCs, the HfN offices, women's homes including in Karen's communal 'Housing for Ex-Offenders' accommodation and local and chain cafes. I met family members, friends and pets, went on walks and admired gardens. I laughed and cried with the women. Without exception, the women involved in this research were welcoming and generous with their time. Often busy cafes created problems and interviews needed to be replayed several times whilst transcribing due to background noise. Pets also were problematic here. Staff interviews were interrupted by colleagues but content was not compromised. Interviews took, on average, 50 minutes and were recorded following consent and transcribed verbatim and coded using N-Vivo software. Following transcription, interviews (alongside observation notes) were coded and analysed for patterns in tone, theme, plot, roles, value structure, coherence and complexity (Maruna 2001). 'Nodes' (themes) were constructed using reference to the wider literature as well as to the themes which were salient throughout the women's narratives and during the observation stage. Following analysis, it was clear that many of the findings reflected the themes of traditional desistance research. There was a deliberate choice to follow the theories through the analysis. The reason for this was that traditional desistance literature has neglected the female voice. In addition themes were constructed with reference to feminist research.

The interviews were based on 'life-course narratives'. A life-course perspective provides 'the most compelling framework [by which to study the process of desistance] and it can be used to identify institutional sources of desistance and the dynamic social processes inherent in stopping crime' (Laub and Sampson 2001: 1). Topics that interviews covered included youth, education, offending, experience of probation and the CJS, identity, substance misuse, accommodation, finance, lifestyle, relationships with family, friends and partners, neighbourhood, community and society, emotional well-being, values and beliefs, health, victimisation and aspirations for the future. These topics were influenced by the research of McIvor et al. (2011). McAdam's (1995) life story interviewing template was also used for reference in terms of structure and content of the schedule.

In his exploration of doping narratives within the world of sport, Majid Yar (2014) notes that Clifford Shaw's 'The Jackroller: A Delinquent Boy's Own Story' is often cited as the first significant landmark criminological work to use an offender's self-narrative as a source of data. The accounts of why the individual acted as he did are taken here at face value and placed on a par with other criminological methods to understand the how and why of crime. This narrative approach spread throughout the discipline, and emerged particularly as a tradition within desistance with Maruna's (2001) publication of *Making Good*. Within these approaches, Denzin notes, 'the storyteller should be considered both the expert and authority on his or her own life' (1998, 59, quoted in Yar 2014: 13). The narrative methodology nonetheless presents the researcher with a number of issues, not the least of these being that human beings are likely to misattribute causes and contexts of desistance (in this example). Certain actions, events or life changes may be seen as having a larger effect than they actually did or, similarly, true causes or contexts are skimmed over. As Hunter (2009) notes, as narratives are subjective, this means they do not provide the kind of objectivity central to positivist research. Yet this subjectivity also makes them valuable. Sommers argues,

> If we are to uncover real knowledge of women in conflict with the law, we must cut through both the irrelevant templates constructed by experts and the prejudices held by society … There is a tradition in social research of emulating the methods of natural science. In practice, this has produced uncomfortable unions between notions of rigour adopted from the natural sciences and the complex and highly contextual nature of objects under investigation in the social sciences. One fundamental notion of the natural sciences, objectivity, is particularly problematic. The notion of objectivity implies … that the observer is somehow removed from his or her historical context and able to make observations that are independent of his or her bias or subjective interpretation. (1995: 8)

The subjective texts which result from this form of interviewing are sources of sociological data as they offer insight into the processes and events which inform (or otherwise) desistance. I was not therefore interested in whether the women were bending the truth or 'not remembering correctly'; what I was interested in was what was important to them, experiencing or otherwise desistance. As Yar (2014: 13) contended, 'I do not wish to offer assessments as to their "truthfulness" in the sense of corroborating evidence … Instead, my interest lies with how these claims (about what happened, why the individual acted as they did, how they felt about it, the consequences they experienced and so on) form a part of a narrative strategy that the story-teller uses.' Chesney-Lind and Morash (2013) made the case that feminist researchers believe that research subjects can contribute intrinsic information on their experiences, that their truths are important and must be understood in the context of patriarchy. Narrative methods sit well within the feminist tradition as they offer individuals the opportunity to tell their stories, in their own words and from their own subjective perspective; narrative methods give voice to those who are often voiceless, particularly within the patriarchal, neoliberal, criminal (in)justice system.

Yet narrative research can be problematic. As Sommers (1995) has noted, the position of the researcher is also subjective and situated within power hierarchies. Even the attempt to level the playing field by an elaboration of my research, for example, may have resulted in research participants 'telling me what I want to hear'. Moreover, how one responds to questions about desistance is completely subjective on a number of factors: not only who is asking but what has happened that day, week, month; where they are being asked; and so on. When participants were faced with questions like 'Where do you see yourself in five years' time?' or 'Describe your current significant relationships', these questions are highly subjective. This did not render them invalid however, provided they are treated precisely as subjective and situated forms of sense making (Yar 2014). Furthermore, although I reiterated throughout that I did not have connections to either project nor the wider CJS, women may still have self-censored particularly relating to past and present criminal activity; 'techniques of neutralisation' (Matza and Sykes 1957) or a 'denial of the deviant self' (Yar 2014) may be employed. Additionally, staff may have been reluctant to critique their working practices for fear that this may reach their colleagues or bosses. There was little remedy for these issues within qualitative research excepting repeated studies. I did not, for example, check official records to corroborate women's narratives. Indeed, this kind of 'verification' would have contradicted the feminist, narrative method principles which guided this research. These methodological dilemmas must be viewed in the light of feminist objectives of giving voice to the powerless. My aim was not, as I have noted, to reach some objective form of 'truth', but to understand desistance from those actually desisting, attempting to desist, or attempting to promote desistance.

Limitations

In addition to the above weaknesses of observation and narrative techniques, there are general limitations of the methodology. The most obvious limitation of the Northshire research was the relatively small sample. As well as the personal limitations of time and money for travel during a self-funded PhD, women make up only a small percentage of the CJS. On top of this, the shame which can be prevalent in women's experiences of the CJS and the ramifications of the 'double deviance' thesis meant that women were unlikely to self-identify as 'good' candidates for study. When asked about the second stage of research, women were often heard to say, 'I would have nothing to say' or 'I'm not really a criminal.' The self-selecting nature of the study obviously therefore had implications for the generalisability of the research. Additionally, it can be questioned whether the women observed and interviewed were representative of criminalised women generally. The women had limited ranges in their offending backgrounds—a very limited number of the women encountered throughout had been sentenced for violent crimes, for example. There were a similar (small) number who had white-collar crime convictions. Additionally, the women shared many of the same socio-economic background or ethnic background features. For example, all the interviewees, reflecting the makeup of the female CJS population within Northshire, and a majority of those observed, were white.

Furthermore, this research did not have any guidelines for measuring desistance quantitatively. It was for this reason that for the majority of women, follow-up interviews were unnecessary. It was not the aim of the Northshire research to plot an exact map of desistance from crime, with a starting point indicated. All the women involved (staff and service users alike) described desistance-like processes, whether these were subjective changes, social-structural influences or simply maturational processes. However, this must be questioned: are these progressions described prevalent as a result of the filtering process, which means that those interviewed are more likely to be successful desisters? After all, women were contacted through agencies (the Women's Centres and the HfN Project) whose aims included desistance encouragement. Women in these agencies were confronted with their moves towards desistance (or lack thereof) directly in these institutions. For this reason, were those who volunteered for interviews and observations more likely to be those who have successfully negotiated or begun to travel desistance journeys? Again, this is certainly a valid critique of the generalisability of this research.

The above issues are important because they raise questions about who is involved in this research and what effect this may have on the outcomes. Many of the questions raised, however, can be answered by the stipulation that this is a qualitative piece of research into the subjective experience of desistance and gendered harm, rather than a quantitative exercise into *who* is likely to desist or persist. Although it is difficult to argue for generalisability with small-scale samples, this argument should not be used to undermine their importance. There is no claim that the Northshire women interviewed speak for *all* criminalised women, yet their experiences draw attention to the gaps, and the overlaps, in the literature.

Ethical Considerations

Throughout the Northshire research, ethical implications were kept at the forefront. As noted above, before the interviews commenced with the WC participants, we had been introduced. Again before the HfN interviews took place, an introductory meeting was held where full disclosure about the research aims was provided. It was important to stress throughout that the research was separate from any CJS intervention and completely voluntary, to ensure informed consent with no possibility of coercion. Before interviews took place there was a signed agreement by the interviewer and interviewee to give the right to withdraw at any point. All participants were also provided with an information sheet which helped to answer questions and concerns as well as provided my contact information, and the right to withdraw. These issues were also confirmed verbally and any additional problems or concerns addressed.

Calverley (2013) has noted the non-neutral position of the interviewer. As noted above, as a white, middle-class student interviewer with no criminal career, I may have been viewed as an 'outsider'. Nonetheless, feminist research strives to be empowering and inclusive. Certainly in-depth, narrative interview techniques allowed for subjective, emotional issues to come to the fore, breaking the barriers of the public/private divide. On a practical level, steps such as making the participant feel comfortable and not under obligation to participate or divulge any information that they were not comfortable with also helped achieve this aim. Additionally it was the decision of the women who were interviewed where the interview should take place: whilst many chose relatively 'neutral' places like local cafes or the WCs, others chose their own homes, perhaps closing the power-relationship gap slightly. Staff interviews all took place at the places of work of the staff. Importantly, I was aware of the organisations that could offer help and advice if the respondent became upset through the process. Due to the narrative style of the interview, this was often the case; interviews were full of emotion and often brought up troubled pasts as well as hopeful and not so hopeful futures. I provided the contact details of Northshire WCs to all participants, on the advice of staff there. I also provided my contact details should the women want to contact me to withdraw at any time or simply to chat. It is true to say I became friends with many of the staff and criminalised women I interviewed.

Protecting the anonymity of the participants was of paramount importance throughout the process, particularly due to the sensitive nature of the research topic and the narrative interview style. As noted above, participants were assured that they would not be pressed for information on past offences and it would be their prerogative to divulge information. The centrality of this ethical consideration became apparent particularly during Julie's second interview. During this interview, Julie spoke about a previous conviction for arson which she had not raised in our first interview. This revelation also indicated that Julie was becoming more comfortable with our relationship and the trust between us had grown. Julie's story also indicated the importance of multiple meetings. Potential sample lists and interview transcripts were encrypted with passwords and any hard copies locked away. All participants and places mentioned in this book have been given pseudonyms.

Throughout this research I was acutely aware of the problems of 'speaking for' the women I was researching. I often questioned myself—'What right do I have to speak for these women?'—cutting and moulding their narratives to fit into the themes raised both by previous research and my own deductions. As noted above, I do not share all their experiences; thankfully, I have not experienced the CJS first-hand, nor have I experienced domestic violence or abuse. Yet as Hart (2014) noted, I share an important feature with them: my gender. Other overlaps in identity surrounding age, nationality and day-to-day experiences were also important in this research but the fact that as a (relatively) powerful woman I could share the experiences of other women effectively justifies the voicing of their experiences. Even if we do not accept this argument that shared characteristics allow us to 'speak for' certain groups, an alternative justification can be considered. Letherby (2001) notes that white middle-class feminists often consider the problematic notion of speaking for an 'other'. Yet, by the very fact of aiming to speak for an 'other' we are reinforcing this 'otherness'. Nonetheless, speaking *only* 'for' ourselves enables and forgives the marginalisation of these less powerful voices. This is something which this book therefore seeks to redress.

Bibliography

Adler, P. A., & Adler, P. (1994). Observational Techniques. In N. K. Denzin & Y. S. Lincoln (Eds.), *Handbook of Qualitative Research*. Thousand Oaks: Sage Publications.

Alston, P. (2018). *Statement on Visit to the United Kingdom, By Professor Philip Alston, United Nations Special Rapporteur on Extreme Poverty and Human Rights.* Available at: https://www.ohchr.org/EN/NewsEvents/Pages/DisplayNews.aspx?NewsID=23881&LangID=E. Accessed 27 Dec 2018.

Annison, J., & Brayford, J. (2015). Context; Transforming Rehabilitation: Implications for Women. In J. Annison, J. Brayford, & J. Deering (Eds.), *Women and Criminal Justice: From the Corston Report to Transforming Rehabilitation*. Bristol: Policy Press.

Aresti, A., Eatough, V., & Brooks-Gordan, B. (2010). Doing Time After Time: An Interpretative Phenomenological Analysis of Reformed Ex-Prisoners' Experiences of Self-change, Identity and Career Opportunities. *Psychology Crime and Law, 16*(3), 169–190.

Asquith, S., & Samuel, E. (1994). *Criminal Justice and Related Services for Young Adult Offenders: A Review*. Edinburgh: HMSO.

Balfour, G., Hannah-Moffat, K., & Turnbull, S. (2018). Planning for Precarity? Experiencing the Carceral Continuum of Imprisonment and Reentry. In A. Sarat (Ed.), *After Imprisonment Studies in Law, Politics and Society* (Vol. 77, pp. 31–48). Bingley: Emerald Publishing Limited.

Ú. Barr, *Desisting Sisters*, Critical Criminological Perspectives,
https://doi.org/10.1007/978-3-030-14276-6

Bandura, A. (1989). Human Agency in Social Cognitive Theory. *American Psychologist, 44*, 1175–1184.

Barr, U. (2018). Gendered Assisted Desistance: A Decade from Corston. *Safer Communities, 17*(2), 81–93.

Barry, M. (2006). *Youth Offending in Transition: The Search for Social Recognition.* London: Routledge.

Barry, M., & McIvor, G. (2008). *Chaotic Lives: A Profile of Women Offenders in the CJS in Lothian and Borders.* Peebles: Lothian and Borders Justice Authority.

Becker, H. (1963). *Outsiders.* New York: Free Press.

Bersani, B. E., Laub, J. H., & Nieuwbeerta, P. (2009). Marriage and Desistance from Crime in the Netherlands: Do Gender and Socio-Historical Context Matter? *Journal of Quantitative Criminology, 25*, 3–24.

Bindel, J., & Wistrich, H. (2003). *The Map of My Life: The Story of Emma Humphreys.* London: Astraia Press.

Bottoms, A., & Shapland, J. (2010). Steps Towards Desistance Among Young Adult Recidivists. In S. Farrall, R. Sparks, S. Maruna, & M. Hough (Eds.), *Escape Routes.* London: Routledge.

Bottoms, A., & Shapland, J. (2011). Steps Toward Desistance Among Male Young Adult Recidivists. In S. Farrall, M. Hough, S. Maruna, & R. Sparks (Eds.), *Escape Routes: Contemporary Perspectives on Life After Punishment.* London: Routledge.

Bottoms, A., Shapland, J., Costello, A., Holmes, D., & Muir, G. (2004). Towards Desistance: Theoretical Underpinnings for an Empirical Study. *The Howard Journal, 43*(4), 368–389.

Braithwaite, J. (1989). *Crime, Shame and Reintegration.* Cambridge: Cambridge University Press.

Broad, R., & Spencer, J. (2015). Understanding the Marketisation of the Probation Service Through an Interpretative Policy Framework. In M. Wasik & S. Santatzoglou (Eds.), *The Management of Change in Criminal Justice: Who Knows Best?* Basingstoke: Palgrave Macmillan.

Browne, V. (2014). The Persistence of Patriarchy: Operation Yewtree and the Return to 1970s Feminism. *Radical Philosophy, 188*, 9–20.

Bryman, A. (2012). *Social Research Methods* (4th ed.). Oxford: Oxford University Press.

Burke, L. (2013). Grayling's Hubris. *Probation Journal, 60*, 377–382.

Burnett, R. (1992). *The Dynamics of Recidivism.* Oxford: Centre for Criminological Research, University of Oxford, Research Report for the Home Office.

Burnett, R., & Maruna, S. (2004). So Prison Works, Does It? The Criminal Careers of 130 Men Released from Prison under Home Secretary, Michael Howard. *Howard Journal of Criminal Justice, 43*, 390–404.

Burnett, R., & McNeill, F. (2005). The Place of the Officer–Offender Relationship in Assisting Offenders to Desist from Crime. *Probation Journal, 52*(3), 247–268.

Bushway, S. D., Piquero, A. R., Broidy, L. M., Cauffman, E. E., & Mazerolle, P. (2001). An Empirical Framework for Studying Desistance as a Process. *Criminology, 39*(2), 491–516.

Calverley, A. (2013). *Cultures of Desistance: Rehabilitation, Reintegration and Ethnic Minorities*. London: Routledge.

Carlen, P. (1988). *Women, Crime and Poverty*. Milton Keynes: Open University Press.

Carlen, P. (1990). *Alternatives to Women's Imprisonment*. Milton Keynes: Open University Press.

Carlen, P. (2006). Review: Out of Order: The Political Imprisonment of Women in Northern Ireland 1972–1998. *The British Journal of Criminology, 46*(5), 951–953.

Carlen, P. (2012). *Against Rehabilitation: For Reparative Justice. Centre for Crime and Justice Studies*. Available at: https://www.crimeandjustice.org.uk/resources/against-rehabilitation-reparative-justice. Accessed 27 Dec 2018.

Carlsson, C. (2011). Using "Turning Points" to Understand Processes of Change in Offending. *British Journal of Criminology, 52*, 1–16.

Carlsson, C. (2012). Processes of Intermittency in Criminal Careers: Notes from a Swedish Study on Life Courses and Crime. *International Journal of Offender Therapy and Comparative Criminology, 57*(8), 913–938.

Carlsson, C. (2016). Human Agency, Criminal Careers and Desistance. In J. Shapland, S. Farrall, & A. Bottoms (Eds.), *Global Perspectives on Desistance*. London: Routledge.

Carlton, B., & Baldry, E. (2013). In B. Carlton & M. Segrave (Eds.), *Women Exiting Prison: Critical Essays on Gender, Post-Release Support and Survival*. Abingdon: Routledge.

Carlton, B., & Seagrave, M. (2011). Women's Survival Post-Imprisonment: Connecting Imprisonment with Pains Past and Present. *Punishment & Society, 13*(5), 551–570.

Carr, N. T., & Stovall Hanks, R. (2012). If "60 Is the New 40," Is 35 the New 15? Late Onset Crime and Delinquency. *Deviant Behaviour, 33*, 393–411.

Cederstrom, C., & Spicer, A. (2015). *The Wellness Syndrome*. Cambridge: Polity.

Chadwick, K., & Little, C. (1987). The Criminalisation of Women. In P. Scraton (Ed.), *Law, Order and the Authoritarian State*. Milton Keynes: Open University Press.

Chesney-Lind, M., & Morash, M. (2013). Transformative Feminist Criminology: A Critical Re-Thinking of a Discipline. *Critical Criminology, 21*, 287–304.

Christie, N. (1986). The Ideal Victim. In E. Fattah (Ed.), *From Crime Policy to Victim Policy*. Basingstoke: Macmillan.

Christie, N. (2004). *A Suitable Amount of Crime*. Abingdon: Psychology Press.

Clarke, B., & Chadwick, K. (2018). From 'Troubled' Women to Failing Institutions: Necessary Narrative Shifts in Decarceration of Women Post-Corston. In L. Moore, P. Scraton, & A. Wahidin (Eds.), *Women's Imprisonment and the Case for Abolition: Critical Reflections on Corston Ten Years On*. London: Routledge.

Clarke, R. V., & Cornish, D. B. (1985). Modelling Offenders' Decisions: A Framework for Research and Policy. In M. Tonry & N. Morris (Eds.), *Crime and Justice: An Annual Review of Research* (Vol. 6). Chicago: University of Chicago Press.

Clinks. (2013). *Introducing Desistance: A Guide for Voluntary, Community and Social Enterprise Sector Organisations*. London: Do It Justice.

Codd, H. (2013). *In the Shadow of Prison: Families, Imprisonment and Criminal Justice*. Cullompton: Willan.

Coles, D. (2018). INQUEST Responds to New Ministry of Justice 'Female Offenders Strategy [Blog]'. *INQUEST* Available at: https://www.inquest.org.uk/moj-female-offenders-response. Accessed 27 Dec 2018.

Corston, J. (2007). *The Corston Report: A Report by Baroness Jean Corston of a Review of Women with Particular Vulnerabilities in the Criminal Justice System*. London: Home Office.

Cullen, J. T., Jonson, C. L., & Nagin, D. S. (2011). Prisons Do Not Reduce Recidivism. *The Prison Journal, 48*, 485–655.

Davies, P. (2011). *Gender, Crime and Victimisation*. London: Sage Publications.

Day, A. (2018). Universal Credit: Prisoners 'Lured Back Into Crime' By Benefit Delays. *Huffington Post*. Available at: https://www.huffingtonpost.co.uk/entry/universal-credit-prisoners-being-set-up-to-fail-and-lured-back-into-crime-by-benefit-delays_uk_5be595aae4b0dbe871aa26f2. Accessed 27 Dec 2018.

Dorling, D. (2015). *Inequality and the 1%*. London: Verso.

Drake, D. (2012). *Prisons, Punishment and the Pursuit of Security*. Basingstoke: Palgrave Macmillan.

Drake, D., & Scott, D. (2017). Build Communities Not Prisons [Blog]. *Centre for Crime and Justice Studies*. Available at: https://www.crimeandjustice.org.uk/resources/build-communities-not-prisons-0. Accessed 27 Dec 2018.

Drake, D., Havard, C., & Muncie, J. (2018). The Dubious 'Science' of Risk Prediction in Criminal Justice. [Blog] Centre for Crime and Justice Studies. Available at: https://www.crimeandjustice.org.uk/resources/dubious-science-risk-prediction-criminal-justice. Accessed 27 Dec 2018.

Edgar, K., Jacobson, J., & Biggar, K. (2011). *Time Well Spent: A Practical Guide to Active Citizenship and Volunteering in Prison*. London: Prison Reform Trust.

Ellison, M., Fox, C., Gains, A., & Pollock, G. (2013). An Evaluation of the Effect of Housing Provision on Re-Offending. *Safer Communities, 12*(1), 27–37.

Faith, K. (2011). *Unruly Women: The Politics of Confinement and Resistance*. New York: Seven Stories Press.

Farrall, S. (2002). *Rethinking What Works with Offenders*. Cullompton: Willan.

Farrall, S. (2014). Citizenship Values and Desistance from Crime: Exploring Change Over Time. In S. Farrall, B. Hunter, G. Sharpe, & A. Calverley (Eds.), *Criminal Careers in Transition*. Oxford: Oxford University Press.

Farrall, S., & Bowling, B. (1999). Structuration, Human Development and Desistance from Crime. *British Journal of Criminology, 39*(2), 253–268.

Farrall, S., & Calverley, A. (2006). *Understanding Desistance from Crime* (Crime and Justice Series). London: Open University Press.

Farrall, S., Sharpe, G., Hunter, B., & Calverley, C. (2011). Theorising Structural and Individual-Level Processes in Desistance and Persistence: Outlining an Integrated Perspective. *Australian and New Zealand Journal of Criminology, 44*(2), 218–234.

Farrall, S., Hunter, B., Sharpe, G., & Calverley, A. (2014). *Criminal Careers in Transition: The Social Context of Desistance from Crime*. Oxford: Oxford University Press.

Farrington, D. P., & West, D. J. (1995). Effects of Marriage, Separation, and Children on Offending by Adult Males. In Z. Blau Smith & J. Hagan (Eds.), *Current Perspectives on Aging and the Life Cycle* (4th ed.). Greenwich: JAI Press.

Ferraro, K. (2006). *Neither Angels nor Demons: Women, Crime, and Victimization*. Boston: Northeastern University Press.

Field, F. (2018). The Climbdown on Universal Credit Is Painfully Inadequate. *The Guardian*. Available at: https://www.theguardian.com/commentisfree/2018/oct/16/climbdown-universal-credit-benefit-claimants-poverty. Accessed 27 Dec 2018.

Foucault, M. (1976/2009) Alternatives to the Prison: Dissemination or Decline of Social Control? Theory, Culture and Society, 26(6), pp. 12–24.

Fraser, N. (2013). How Feminism Became Capitalism's Handmaiden. *The Guardian*. Available at: https://www.theguardian.com/commentisfree/2013/oct/14/feminism-capitalist-handmaiden-neoliberal. Accessed 27 Dec 2018.

Gartner, R., & Piliavin, I. (1988). The Aging Offender and the Aged Offender. In P. B. Baltes, D. L. Featherman, & R. M. Lerner (Eds.), *Life-Span Development and Behaviour* (9th ed.). Hillsdale: Lawrence Erlbaum Associates.

Gelsthorpe, L., & Morris, A. (1988). Feminism and Criminology in Britain. *British Journal of Criminology, 28*(2), 93–110.

Gelsthorpe, L., & Morris, A. (2002). Women's Imprisonment in England and Wales: A Penal Paradox. *Criminology and Criminal Justice, 2*(3), 277–301.

Gilligan. (1982). *In a Different Voice: Psychological Theory and Women's Development*. Harvard: Harvard University Press.

Giordano, P. C., Cernokovich, S. A., & Rudolph, J. L. (2002). Gender, Crime and Desistance: Toward a Theory of Cognitive Transformation. *American Journal of Sociology, 107*, 990–1064.

Giordano, P. C., Longmore, M. A., Schroeder, R. D., & Seffrin, P. M. (2008). A Life Course Perspective on Spirituality and Desistence from Crime. *Criminology, 46*, 99–131.

Glaser, D. (1964). *Effectiveness of a Prison and Parole System*. Indianapolis: Bobbs-Merrill.

Glaser, B. G., & Strauss, A. L. (1967). *The Discovery of Grounded Theory: Strategies for Qualitative Research* (11th ed.). New York: Aldine Atherton.

Glueck, S., & Glueck, E. (1950). *Unravelling Juvenile Delinquency*. New York: Harvard University Press.

Goffman, E. (1968). *Stigma: Notes on the Management of Spoiled Identity*. Harmondsworth: Pelican Books.

Gomm, R. (2016). *Women Making Meaning of Their Desistance from Offending: An Interpretative Phenomenological Analysis*. Doctoral Thesis, Durham University, Durham.

Gottfredson, M., & Hirschi, T. (1990). *A General Theory of Crime*. Stanford: Stanford University Press.

Goulding, C. (2000). The Museum Environment and the Visitor Experience. *European Journal of Marketing, 34*(3/4), 261–278.

GOV.UK. (2018). *HM Prison Service*. [online] Available at: https://www.gov.uk/government/organisations/hm-prison-service. Accessed 27 Dec 2018.

Gove, W. (1985). The Effect of Age and Gender on Deviant Behaviour: A Biopsychosocial Perspective. In A. Rossi (Ed.), *Gender and the Life Course*. New York: Aldine.

Graham, J., & Bowling, B. (1995). *Young People and Crime* (Research Study No. 145). London: HMRSO.

Graham, H., & McIvor, G. (2015). *Scottish and International Review of the Use of Electronic Monitoring* (Report No. 8). Scottish Centre for Crime and Justice Research.

Graham, H., & McNeill, F. (2018). Desistance: Envisioning Futures. In P. Carlen & L. Ayres França (Eds.), *Alternative Criminologies*. London: Routledge.

Grover, C. (2010). Social Security Policy and Vindictiveness. *Sociological Research Online, 15*(2), 8.

Haney, L. (2004). Introduction: Gender, Welfare, and States of Punishment. *Social Politics, 11*(3), 333–362.

Hart, E. L. (2014). Power, Pregnancy and Prison: The Impact of a Researchers Pregnancy on Qualitative Interviews with Women Prisoners. In K. Lumsden & A. Winter (Eds.), *Reflexivity in Criminological Research: Experiences with the Powerful and the Powerless*. Basingstoke: Palgrave Macmillan.

Hart, E. L. (2017). Prisoners Post-Release, The Need for a Critical Desistance. In E. L. Hart & F. J. C. Van Ginneken (Eds.), *New Perspectives on Desistance*. London: Palgrave Macmillan.

Hart, E. L., & Van Ginnekin, E. F. J. C. (2017). Introduction. In E. L. Hart & F. J. C. Van Ginneken (Eds.), *New Perspectives on Desistance*. London: Palgrave Macmillan.

Harvey, D. (2007). *A Brief History of Neoliberalism*. Oxford: Oxford University Press.

Hattery, A. J., & Smith, E. (2010). *Prisoner Re-entry & Social Capital*. Maryland: Lexington Books.

Healy, D. (2012). *The Dynamics of Desistance* (2nd ed.). New York: Routledge.

Healy, D., & O'Donnell, I. (2006). Criminal Thinking on Probation: A Perspective from Ireland. *Criminal Justice and Behaviour, 33*, 782–802.

Heidensohn, F. (1985). *Women and Crime: The Life of a Female Offender*. New York: New York University Press.

Heidensohn, F. (2004). Gender and Crime. In M. Maguire, R. Morgan, & R. Reiner (Eds.), *The Oxford Handbook of Criminology*. Oxford: Oxford University Press.

Heidensohn, F., & Silvestri, M. (2012). Gender and Crime. In M. Maguire, R. Morgan, & R. Reiner (Eds.), *The Oxford Handbook of Criminology* (pp. 336–369).

Hillyard, P., Pantazis, C., Tombs, S., & Gordon, D. (2004). *Beyond Criminology: Taking Harm Seriously*. London: Pluto Press.

HMIP. (2016). *Desistance and Young People*. Manchester: Her Majesty's Inspectorate of Probation.

Hogarth, L. (2017). *Trapped in the Justice Loop? Past, Present and Future of the Woman-Centred Services at the Heart of the Systems-Change Called for in the Corston Report* (Briefing 18). London: Centre for Crime and Justice Studies.

Homelessness Reduction Act. (2017). Available at: http://www.legislation.gov.uk/ukpga/2017/13/contents/enacted. Accessed 12 Mar 2019.

hooks, b. (2004). *The Will to Change: Men, Masculinity, and Love*. London: Atria Books.

Horney, J., Osgood, D. W., & Marshall, I. H. (1995). Criminal Careers in the Short Term: Intra Individual Variability in Crime and its Relation to Local Life Circumstances. *American Sociological Review, 60*(5), 655–673.

House of Commons Justice Committee. (2013). *Women Offenders After the Corston Report: Second Report of Session 2013–2014*. London: The Stationery Office Limited.

House of Commons Justice Committee. (2018). *Transforming Rehabilitation: Ninth Report of Session 2017–2019*. London: The Stationery Office Limited.

Hudson, B. (2006). Beyond White Man's Justice: Race, Gender and Justice in Late Modernity. *Theoretical Criminology, 10*(1), 29–47.

Hunter, B. (2009). White-Collar Offenders After the Fall from Grace: Stigma, Blocked Paths and Resettlement. In R. Lippens & D. Crewe (Eds.), *Existentialist Criminology*. Routledge-Cavendish: Abingdon.

Inquest.org.uk. (2018). Deaths of Women in Prison. *INQUEST* [online]. Available at: http://inquest.org.uk/statistics/deaths-of-women-in-prison. Accessed 27 Dec 2018.

Jacobson, M. P. (2016). Tough Talk on Crime Has Led to a Crisis in Britain's Prisons. *The Guardian*. Available at: https://www.theguardian.com/commentisfree/2016/may/05/tough-talk-crime-crisis-britains-prisons-suicides-assaults. Accessed 5 Jan 2019.

Jamieson, J., McIvor, G., & Murray, C. (1999). *Understanding Offending Amongst Young People*. Edinburgh: The Scottish Executive.

Johnson, M. P. (2006). Conflict and Control: Gender Symmetry and Asymmetry in Domestic Violence. *Violence Against Women, 12*(11), 1003–1018.

Jones. (1996). Men and Feminist Research. In J. Pilcher & A. Coffey (Eds.), *Gender and Qualitative Research* (Cardiff Papers in Qualitative Research). Aldershot: Avebury.

Jordan, J. (2004). Beyond Belief? Police, Rape and Women's Credibility. *Criminology and Criminal Justice, 4*(1), 29–59.

Joseph Rowntree Foundation. (2016). *UK Poverty 2016: A Comprehensive Analysis of Poverty Trends and Figures*. London: JRF Analysis Unit.

Joseph Rowntree Foundation. (2018). *UK Poverty 2018: A Comprehensive Analysis of Poverty Trends and Figures*. London: JRF Analysis Unit.

Katz, J. (1988). *Seductions of Crime: Moral and Sensual Attractions in Doing Evil*. New York: Basic Books.

Katz, R. (2000). Explaining Girl's and Women's Crime and Desistance in the Context of their Victimization Experiences. *Violence Against Women, 6*, 633–660.

Kennedy, H. (1993). *Eve Was Framed: Women and British Justice*. London: Vintage.

King, S. (2013). *Desistance Transitions and the Impact of Probation*. Abingdon: Routledge.

King, R. D., Massoglia, M., & Macmillan, R. (2007). The Context of Marriage and Crime: Gender, the Propensity to Marry, and Offending in Early Adulthood. *Criminology, 45*(1), 33–65.

Knight, B. J., Osborn, S. G., & West, D. J. (1977). Early Marriage and Criminal Tendency in Males British Journal of Criminology. *British Journal of Criminology, 17*, 348–360.

Laub, J. H., & Sampson, R. J. (2001). Understanding Desistance from Crime. *Crime and Justice, 28*, 1–69.

Laub, J., & Sampson, R. (2003). *Shared Beginnings, Divergent Lives*. Harvard: Harvard University Press.

Laub, J. H., Nagin, D. S., & Sampson, R. J. (1998). Trajectories of Change in Criminal Offending: Good Marriages and the Desistance Process. *American Sociological Review, 63*, 225–238.

LeBaron, G., & Roberts, A. (2010). Towards a Feminist Political Economy of Capitalism and Carcerality. *Signs, 36*(1), 19–41.

LeBel, T. P., Burnett, R., Maruna, S., & Bushway, S. (2008). The "Chicken and Egg" of Subjective and Social Factors in Desistance from Crime. *European Journal of Criminology, 5*(11), 131–159.

Leibrich, J. (1993). *Straight to the Point: Angles on Giving Up Crime*. Otago: University of Otago Press.

Letherby, G. (2001). *Feminist Research in Theory and Practice*. Buckingham: Open University Press.

Leverentz, A. (2006). The Love of a Good Man? Romantic Relationships as a Source of Support or Hindrance for Female Ex-Offenders. *Journal of Research in Crime and Delinquency, 43*(4), 459–488.

Leverentz, A. (2014). *The Ex-Prisoner's Dilemma: How Women Negotiate Competing Narratives of Re-entry and Desistance*. New Brunswick: Rutgers University Press.

Levi-Strauss, C. (1962). *The Savage Mind*. Oxford: Oxford University Press.

Lightowler, C. (2018). Drunk Women Convicted of Assault Treated Harsher in Sentencing Than Drunk Men [Blog]. *The Conversation*. Available at: https://theconversation.com/drunk-women-convicted-of-assault-treated-harsher-in-sentencing-than-drunk-men-103631. Accessed 27 Dec 2018.

Lloyd, A. (1995). *Doubly Deviant, Doubly Damned: Society's Treatment of Violent Women*. London: Penguin Social Sciences.

Mansfield, M., & Cooper, V. (2016). The Failure to Protect Women in the Criminal Justice System. In V. Cooper & D. Whyte (Eds.), *The Violence of Austerity*. London: Pluto Press.

Maruna, S. (1999). Desistance and Development: The Psychosocial Process of "Going Straight". *The British Criminology Conferences: Selected Proceedings, 2*, 1–19.

Maruna, S. (2001). *Making Good – How Ex-Convicts Reform and Rebuild Their Lives*. Washington, DC: American Psychological Association Books.

Maruna, S., & Farrall, S. (2004). Desistance from Crime: A Theoretical Reformulation. *Kölner Zeitschrift für Soziologie und Sozialpsychologie, 43*, 171–194.

Maruna, S., & LeBel, T. P. (2003). Welcome Home? Examining the "Re-entry Court" Concept from a Strength Based Perspective. *Western Criminology Review, 4*, 91–107.

Maruna, S., LeBel, T. P., Mitchell, N., & Naples, M. (2004). Pygmalion in the Reintegration Process: Desistance from Crime through the Looking Glass. *Psychology Crime and Law, 10*(3), 271–281.

Maruna, S., LeBel, T. S., Naples, M., & Mitchell, N. (2009). Looking-glass Identity Transformation: Pygmalion and Golem in the Rehabilitation Process. In B. Veysey, J. Christian, & D. J. Martinez (Eds.), *How Offenders Transform Their Lives*. Willan: Devon.

Matsueda, R. L., & Heimer, K. (1997). 'A Symbolic Interactionist Theory of Role Transitions', Role Commitments. In T. P. Thonberry (Ed.), *Advances in*

Criminological Theory, Vol. 7, Developmental Theories of Crime and Delinquency. New Brunswick: Transaction.

Matthews, R., Easton, H., Reynolds, L., Bindel, J., & Young, L. (2014). *Exiting Prostitution.* New York: Palgrave Macmillan.

Matza, D. (1964). *Delinquency and Drift.* New York: Wiley.

Matza, D., & Sykes, G. M. (1957). Techniques of Neutralization: A Theory of Delinquency. *American Sociological Review, 22*(6), 664–670.

McAdams, D. P. (1995). *The Life Story Interview.* Available at: https://www.sesp.northwestern.edu/docs/Interviewrevised95.pdf. 7 June 2016.

McDermott, S. (2012). *Moving Forward: Empowering Women to Desist from Offending.* London: The Griffins Society.

McIvor, C., Murray, C., & Jamieson, J. (2004). Is Desistance from Crime Different for Women and Girls? In R. Immarigeon & S. Maruna (Eds.), *After Crime and Punishment: Ex-offender Reintegration and Desistance from Crime.* Willan: Cullompton.

McIvor, G., Trotter, C., & Sheehan, C. (2009). Women, Resettlement and Desistance. *Probation Journal, 56*(4), 347–361.

McIvor, G., Murray, C., & Jamieson, J. (2011). Desistance from Crime: Is It Different for Women and Girls? In S. Maruna & R. Immarigeon (Eds.), *After Crime and Punishment: Pathways to Offender Reintegration.* Willan: Cullompton.

McNaughton, C., & Sanders, T. (2007). Housing and Transitional Phases Out of 'Disordered' Lives: The Case of Leaving Homelessness and Street Sex Work. *Housing Studies, 22*(6), 885–900.

McNeill, F. (2003). Desistance-Focused Probation Practice. In W.-H. Chui & M. Nellis (Eds.), *Moving Probation Forward: Evidence, Arguments and Practice* (pp. 146–162). Harlow: Pearson Longman.

McNeill, F. (2012). Four Forms of Offender Rehabilitation: Towards an Integrated Perspective. *Legal and Criminological Psychology, 17*(1), 18–36.

McNeill, F. (2016). The Fuel in the Tank or the Hole in the Boat? Can Sanctions Support Desistance. In J. Shapland, S. Farrall, & A. Bottoms (Eds.), *Global Perspectives on Desistance: Rethinking What We Know and Looking to the Future* (pp. 265–281). Routledge: Oxford.

McNeill, F. (2017). Post-script: Guide, Guard and Glue – Electronic Monitoring and Penal Supervision. *European Journal of Probation, 9*(1), 103–107.

Mead, G. H. (1934). *Mind, Self, and Society from the Standpoint of a Social Behaviourist.* Chicago: University of Chicago Press.

Meisenhelder, T. (1977). An Exploratory Study of Exiting from Criminal Careers. *Criminology, 15*(3), 319–334.

Merton, R. K. (1957). *Social Theory and Social Structure*. New York: Free Press.

Mies, M. (1983). Towards a Methodology for Feminist Research. In G. Bowles & R. Duelli Klien (Eds.), *Theories of Women's Studies* (pp. 64–82). London: Routledge.

Mills, H. (2015). Addressing Violence Against Women Beyond Criminal Justice. In H. Mills, R. Roberts, & L. Townhead (Eds.), *Empower, Resist, Transform: A Collection of Essays* (pp. 7–9). London: Centre for Crime and Justice Studies.

Ministry of Housing, Communities & Local Government. (2018). *Statutory Homelessness and Prevention and Relief, January to March (Q1) 2018: England*. London: Ministry of Housing, Communities and Local Government.

Ministry of Justice. (2011). *Adult Re-convictions: Results from the 2009 Cohort*. London: Ministry of Justice.

Ministry of Justice. (2012). *Swift and Sure Justice: The Governments Plans for Reform of the CJS* (CM 8388). London: Ministry of Justice.

Ministry of Justice. (2013). *Analysis of the Impact of Employment on Re-offending following Release from Custody, Using Propensity Score Matching*. London: Ministry of Justice.

Ministry of Justice. (2016). *Statistics on Women and the Criminal Justice System 2015*. London: Ministry of Justice.

Ministry of Justice. (2018a). *Female Offender Strategy*. London: Ministry of Justice.

Ministry of Justice. (2018b). *Offender Management Statistics Bulletin, England and Wales*. London: Ministry of Justice.

Ministry of Justice. (2018c). *Women and the Criminal Justice System 2017 Statistics*. London: Ministry of Justice.

Ministry of Justice. (2018d). *Safety in Custody Quarterly: Update to June 2018*. London: Ministry of Justice.

Ministry of Justice. (2018e). *Deaths of Offenders in the Community*. London: Ministry of Justice.

Moffitt, T. (1993). Adolescent-Limited and Life-Course-Persistent Antisocial Behaviour: A Developmental Taxonomy. *Psychological Review, 100*, 674–701.

Moore, L., & Wahadin, A. (2018). The Post-Corston Women's Penal 'Crisis' in England and Wales: Exploring the Failure of Reform. In L. Moore, P. Scraton, & A. Wahidin (Eds.), *Women's Imprisonment and the Case for Abolition: Critical Reflections on Corston Ten Years On*. London: Routledge.

Moore, L., Scraton, P., & Wahidin, A. (Eds.). (2018). *Women's Imprisonment and the Case for Abolition: Critical Reflections on Corston Ten Years On*. London: Routledge.

Morrissey, B. (2003). *When Women Kill: Questions of Agency and Subjectivity*. London: Routledge.

Northshire.gov.uk. (2018). *Mid-Year Population Estimates*. [Online] Available at: https://www.Northshire.gov.uk/Northshire-insight/population-and-households/population/mid-year-population-estimates/. Accessed 26 Dec 2018.

Oakley, A. (1981). Interviewing Women: A Contradiction in Terms. In H. Roberts (Ed.), *Doing Feminist Research* (pp. 30–62). London: Routledge & Kegan Paul.

Office for National Statistics. (2012). *2011 Census*. London: Office for National Statistics.

Office for National Statistics. (2015). *English Indices of Deprivation 2015*. London: Office for National Statistics.

O'Neill, D. (2017). *Film as a Radical Pedagogic Tool*. New York/London: Routledge.

Österman, L. (2018). *Penal Cultures and Female Desistance*. London: Routledge.

Pantazis, C. (2004). Gendering Harm Through a Life-Course Perspective. In P. Hillyard, C. Pantazis, S. Tombs, & D. Gordon (Eds.), *Beyond Criminology: Taking Harm Seriously*. London: Pluto Press.

Patterson, O. (1982). *Slavery and Social Death*. Cambridge, MA/London: Harvard University Press.

Perry, E. (2013). 'She's Alpha Male': Transgressive Gender Performances in the Probation 'Classroom'. *Gender and Education, 25*(4), 396–412.

Petersilia, J. (2003). *When Prisoners Come Home: Parole and Prisoner Re-entry*. New York: Oxford University Press.

Pickett, K., & Wilkinson, R. (2009). *The Spirit Level: Why Equality Is Better for Everyone*. London: Penguin.

Player, E. (2014). Women in the CJS: The Triumph of Inertia. *Criminology and Criminal Justice, 14*(3), 276–297.

Pollack, S. (2013). An Imprisoning Gaze: Practices of Gendered, Racialized and Epistemic Violence. *International Review of Victimology, 19*(1), 103–114.

Price, J. M. (2015). *Prison and Social Death*. New Brunswick/London: Rutgers University Press.

Prison Reform Trust. (2014). *Transforming Lives: Reducing Women's Imprisonment*. Stockport: Soroptimist International.

Prison Reform Trust. (2017). *Why Focus on Reducing Women's Imprisonment?* London: Prison Reform Trust.

Prison Reform Trust. (2018). *Broken Trust: The Rising Numbers of Women Recalled to Prison*. London: Prison Reform Trust.

Probyn, E. (2005). *Blush: Faces of Shame*. Minneapolis: University of Minnesota Press.

Public Health England. (2014). *Northshire Prospectus*. London: Public Health England.

Radcliffe, P., & Hunter, G. (2013). *The Development and Impact of Community Services for Women Offenders: An Evaluation*. London: The Institute for Criminal Policy Research, School of Law, Birkbeck College.

Reiner, R. (2007). Neoliberalism, Crime and Justice. In R. Roberts & W. McMahon (Eds.), *Social Justice and Criminal Justice*. London: Centre for Crime and Justice Studies.

Reinharz, S. (1992). *Feminist Methods in Social Research*. Oxford: Oxford University Press.

Rex, S. (1999). Desistance from Offending: Experiences of Probation. *The Howard Journal, 38*(4), 366–383.

Rich, A. (1996). *Of Woman Born – Motherhood as Experience and Institution* (3rd ed.). New York: W. W. Norton & Company.

Richards, G. (2018). What It's Like Growing Up as a Working-class Girl in the UK. *The Conversation*. Available at: https://theconversation.com/what-its-like-growing-up-as-a-working-class-girl-in-the-uk-93403. Accessed 27 Dec 2018.

Roberts, J. (2015a). *'It Was Do or Die' – How a Woman's Experience of Domestic Abuse Can Influence Her Involvement in Crime: A Qualitative Investigation of the Experiences of Community-Based Female Offenders*. Doctoral Thesis, University of Leicester, Leicester.

Roberts, R. (2015b). Is Lady Justice Blind or Just Blinkered. In H. Mills, R. Roberts, & L. Townhead (Eds.), *Empower, Resist, Transform: A Collection of Essays* (pp. 9–11). London: Centre for Crime and Justice Studies.

Rodermond, E., Kruttschnitt, C., Slotboom, A. M., & Bijieveld, C. C. J. H. (2016). Female Desistance: A Review of the Literature. *European Journal of Criminology, 13*(1), 3–28.

Rumgay, J. (2004). Scripts for Safer Survival: Pathways Out of Female Crime. *The Howard Journal, 43*(4), 405–419.

Rutter, M., Giller, H., & Hagell, A. (1998). *Antisocial Behaviour by Young People*. New York: Cambridge University Press.

Sampson, R. J., & Laub, J. H. (1992). Crime and Deviance in the Life Course. *Annual Review of Sociology, 18*, 63–84.

Sampson, R. J., & Laub, J. H. (1993). *Crime in the Making: Pathways and Turning Points Through Life*. London: Harvard University Press.

Sampson, R. J., & Laub, J. H. (2005). A Life-Course View of the Development of Crime. *Annals of the American Academy of Political and Social Science, 602*, 12–45.

Sampson, R. J., Laub, J. H., & Wimer, C. (2006). Does Marriage Reduce Crime? A Counterfactual Approach to Within-Individual Causal Effects. *Criminology, 44*(3), 465–508.

Sanders, T., & Platt, L. (2017). Is Sex Work Still the Most Dangerous Profession? The Data Suggests So [Blog]. *The Conversation*. Available at: https://theconversation.com/is-sex-work-still-the-most-dangerous-profession-the-data-suggests-so-81854. Accessed 27 Dec 2018.

Sanger, J. (1996). *The Compleat Observer? A Field Research Guide to Observation*. London: The Palmer Press.

Sapouna, M., Bisset, C., & Conlong, A. (2011). *What Works to Reduce Reoffending: A Summary of the Evidence*. Justice Analytical Services. Edinburgh: Scottish Government.

Savage, M. (2018). Private Probation Firms Fail to Cut Rates of Reoffending. *The Guardian*. Available at: https://www.theguardian.com/society/2018/feb/03/private-firms-fail-cut-rates-reoffending-low-medium-risk-offenders. Accessed 5 Jan 2019.

Scott, D., & Codd, H. (2010). *Controversial Issues in Prisons*. Maidenhead: Open University Press.

Scraton, P. (1990). Scientific Knowledge or Masculine Discourses? Challenging Patriarchy in Criminology. In L. Gelsthorpe & A. Morris (Eds.), *Feminist Perspectives in Criminology*. Milton Keynes: Open University Press.

Sheehan, R., McIvor, G., & Trotter, C. (2007). *What Works with Women Offenders*. Cullomtpon: Willan.

Shover, N. (1996). *Great Pretenders: Pursuits and Careers of Persistent Thieves*. Boulder: Westview.

Sim, J. (2010). Punishing the Poor: The Neoliberal Government of Social Insecurity. *British Journal of Criminology, 50*, 589–593

Sim, J. (2018). We Are All (Neo-)Liberals Now: Reform and the Prison Crisis in England and Wales Justice. *Power and Resistance, 1*, 165–188.

Sisters Uncut. (2018). Women's Residential Centres – Another Dangerous Distraction [Blog]. *Sisters Uncut*. Available at: http://www.sistersuncut.org/2018/07/06/community-prisons/. Accessed 27 Dec 2018.

Skeggs, B. (1994). Situating the Production of Feminist Ethnography. In M. Maynard & J. Purvis (Eds.), *Researching Women's Lives from a Feminist Perspective* (pp. 72–93). Basingstoke: Taylor and Francis.

Skeggs, B. (1997). *Formations of Class and Gender: Becoming Respectable*. London: Sage Publications.

Smart, C. (1977). *Women, Crime and Criminology: A Feminist Critique*. London: Routledge.

Smart, C. (1995). The Woman of Legal Discourse. In *Law, Crime and Sexuality: Essays in Feminism* (pp. 186–202). London: Sage Publications.
Smart, C. (2016). In J. Sim & H. Monk (Eds.), *Women, Crime and Criminology: A Celebration*. Bristol: EG Press.
Sommers, E. K. (1995). *Voices From Within, Women Who Have Broken the Law*. Toronto: University of Toronto Press.
Sommers, I., & Baskin, D. R. (1994). Factors Related to Female Adolescent Initiation into Violent Street Crime. *Youth Society, 25*, 468–489.
Soothill, K., & Francis, B. J. (2009). When Do Ex-Offenders Become Like Non-Offenders? *The Howard Journal, 48*(8), 373–387.
Stacey, J. (1998). *Brave New Families: Stories of Domestic Upheaval in Late 20th Century America* (2nd ed.). Berkeley: University of California Press.
Stanko, E. A. (1998). Making the Invisible Visible in Criminology: A Personal Journey. In S. Holdaway & P. Rock (Eds.), *Thinking About Criminology*. London: UCL Press.
Steffensmeier, D., Zhong, H., & Liu, Y. (2017). Age and Its Relation to Crime in Taiwan and United States: Invariant, or Does Cultural Context Matter? *Criminology, 55*, 377–404.
Stone, R. (2016). Desistance and Identity Repair: Redemption Narratives as Resistance to Stigma. *British Journal of Criminology, 56*(5), 956–975.
Stubbs, J., & Tolmie, J. (2008). Battered Women Charged with Homicide: Advancing the Interests of Indigenous Women. *Australian & New Zealand Journal of Criminology, 41*, 131–161.
The Bach Commission. (2017). *The Right to Justice: The Final Report of the Bach Commission*. London: Fabian Society.
The Howard League. (2016). *Is This the End of Women's Centres?* London: All Party Parliamentary Group for Women.
The Offender Rehabilitation Act. (2014). Available at: http://www.legislation.gov.uk/ukpga/2014/11/contents/enacted. Last Accessed 12 Mar 2019.
The Pilgrim Trust. (2015). *Working It Out: Employment for Women Offenders*. London: Prison Reform Trust.
Thomas, R., & Davies, A. (2005). What Have the Feminists Done for Us? Feminist Theory and Organizational Resistance. *Organization, 12*(5), 711–740.
Uggen, C. (2000). Work as a Turning Point in the Life Course of Criminals: A Duration Model of Age, Employment, and Recidivism. *American Sociological Review, 67*, 529–546.
Uggen, C., & Kruttschnitt, C. (1998). Crime in the Breaking: Gender Differences in Desistance. *Law and Society Review, 32*, 339–366.

Uggen, C., Manza, J., & Behrens, A. (2004). Less Than the Average Citizen: Stigma, Role Transition and the Civic Reintegration of Convicted Felons. In S. Maruna & R. Immarigeon (Eds.), *After Crime and Punishment: Pathways to Offender Reintegration* (pp. 261–294). Cullompton: Willan Publishing.

Umberson, D., Anderson, K. L., Glick, J., & Shapiro, A. (1998). Domestic Violence, Personal Control and Gender. *Journal of Marriage and Family, 60*(2), 442.

User Voice. (2016). *"Transforming Rehabilitation": The Operational Model from the Service User's Perspective*. London: National Audit Office.

Vaughan, B. (2007). The Internal Narrative of Desistance. *The British Journal of Criminology, 47*(3), 390–404.

Verbruggen, J., Blokland, A. A. J., & Van Der Geest, V. R. (2012). Effects of Employment and Unemployment on Serious Offending in a High-Risk Sample of Men and Women from Ages 18 to 32 in the Netherlands. *British Journal of Criminology, 52*(5), 845–869.

Wacquant, L. (2018). Prisoner Re-entry as Myth and Ceremony. In P. Carlen & L. Ayres França (Eds.), *Alternative Criminologies*. London: Routledge.

Waddell, G., & Burton, K. (2006). *Is Working Good for Your Health and Well-Being?* London: Department for Work and Pensions.

Walklate, S. (2007). *Handbook of Victims and Victimology*. London: Routledge.

Warr, M. (1998). Life–Course Transitions and Desistance from Crime. *Criminology, 36*, 183–216.

Warr, M. (2002). *Companions in Crime*. Cambridge, UK: Cambridge University Press.

Watts, J. (2018). No Wonder People on Benefits Live in Fear. Supermarkets Spy on Them Now. *The Guardian*. Available at: https://www.theguardian.com/commentisfree/2018/may/31/benefits-claimants-fear-supermarkets-spy-poor-disabled. Accessed 27 Dec 2018.

Weaver, B., & McNeill, F. (2010). *Changing Lives? Desistance Research and Offender Management* (3rd ed.). Glasgow: The Scottish Centre for Crime and Research.

Weaver, B., & McNeill, F. (2014). Lifelines: Desistance, Social Relations, and Reciprocity. *Criminal Justice and Behaviour, 42*(1), 95–107.

Westmarland, N. (2001). The Quantitative/Qualitative Debate and Feminist Research: A Subjective View of Objectivity. *Forum: Qualitative Research, 2*(1), 13.

Whyte, W. F. (1979). On Making the Most of Participant Observation. *The American Sociologist, 14*, 56–66.

Wilkinson, A., & Pickett, K. (2010). *The Spirit Level: Why Equality Is Better for Everyone*. London: Penguin.

Women in Prison. (2017). *Key Facts*. Available at: http://www.womeninprison.org.uk/research/key-facts.php. Accessed 25 Sept 2017.

Women's Budget Group. (2016). *Rethinking Austerity Is Overdue: It Has Hit Women and Ethnic Minorities Hardest*. Available at: https://wbg.org.uk/media/rethinking-austerity-overdue-hit-women-ethnic-minorities-hardest/. Accessed 27 Dec 2018.

Women's Budget Group, Surviving Economic Abuse & the End Violence Against Women Coalition. (2018). *Universal Credit Risks Increasing Women's Vulnerability to Abuse*. Available at: https://wbg.org.uk/wp-content/uploads/2018/09/Universal-Credit-2018.09.12-event-press-release-sea-wbg-FINAL.pdf. Accessed 27 Dec 2018.

Worrall, A. (1990). *Offending Women: Female Lawbreakers and the CJS*. London: Routledge.

Wright Mills, C. (1940). Situated Actions and Vocabularies of Motive. *American Sociological Review, V*, 904–913.

Yar, M. (2014). *Crime, Deviance and Doping*. Basingstoke: Palgrave Macmillan.

Young, J. (1991). Left Realism and the Priorities of Crime Control. In K. Stenson & D. Cowell (Eds.), *The Politics of Crime Control*. London: Sage.

Index[1]

[1] Note: Page numbers followed by 'n' refer to notes.

Ú. Barr, *Desisting Sisters*, Critical Criminological Perspectives,
https://doi.org/10.1007/978-3-030-14276-6